AF409836

THE IKA STORY

THE IKA STORY

James F. McCloud

MOTORLIBROS

MotorLibros is an imprint of Lenguaje claro Editora
Portugal 2951, (B1606EFA) Carapachay, provincia de Buenos
Aires, Argentina
www.lenguajeclaro.com
info@lenguajeclaro.com

Layout: Diana González
Cover: Miur Nagur, based on the original edition

McCloud, James
  The IKA Story / James McCloud. - 2a ed. - Carapachay: MotorLibros,
2020.
  254 p. ; 23 x 15 cm.

  ISBN 978-987-47650-2-4

  1. Empresas Industriales. 2. Automóviles Clásicos. 3. Memoria
Autobiográfica. I. Título.
  CDD 388.3409

Se terminó de imprimir en el mes de noviembre de 2020.

TABLE OF CONTENTS

Introduction

This is the story of the early beginnings of a company that aspired to be something more than just a profitable commercial operation. We wanted to prove, and did, that the capabilities of the manufacturing sector of Argentina could cope not only with the integral production of vehicles but with their development as well. Building the infrastructure of human capabilities that was the backbone of our company probably inspired us more than any other single element. Each new venture was a challenge that taxed the limits of our resources and required innovative ideas and decisions to bring it to a satisfactory conclusion. When mistakes were made we would insist they be recognized so that we could do something about them. The prime requisite for any discussion in my office was, "put it all on top of the table," and with the resiliency we had we always managed to recuperate and land back on our feet.

I don't have any reason for writing this book other than the enjoyment of recalling the milestones that occurred during IKA's formative stages and the subsequent years that I had the privilege of participating in its management. I would suspect, moreover, that there are a lot of my former colleagues who will find some of the reminiscences amusing, and my sons will get an insight into the reason Dad was away from home so much.

My years in Argentina were the most fruitful and enjoyable of any I have experienced in my professional life. IKA was a continuous expansion program and one that never lacked for surprises that would blow in from the least suspected quarter. As Henry Kaiser said, "Problems are opportunities in work clothes." Using this criterion, I can assure you we had our share of challenges.

JAMES F. MCCLOUD
Est. Huinca-Lu
Traful, Neuquen
Argentina

Chapter I | Pre-Incorporation —
Most of 1954

In the early 1950s, Kaiser-Frazer went through a major restructuring. Willys Motors, Inc. was acquired, the Willow-Run plant was sold to General Motors and the new company that had emerged, Kaiser Motors Corporation, made its headquarters in Toledo, Ohio, the location of Willys' main plant and principal offices. The restructuring also involved the withdrawal from passenger car production and concentration on the Jeep Four Wheel Drive utility vehicle line. At this point in time, the major facilities owned and operated by Kaiser Motors consisted of the main assembly, machining and press plants in Toledo, the Detroit Engine Division, the Dowagiac, Michigan, foundry and the Shadyside, Ohio, press plant. The latter three facilities were suppliers for Willow-Run vehicle assembly and, with the decision taken to produce the Jeep line only, would eventually become redundant.

The Detroit Engine Division not only manufactured automotive engines for the Kaiser and Frazer automobiles but was also engaged, during the Korean War, in the manufacture of the R-1300 Aircraft engine under license to the Wright Aeronautical Corporation. As the Korean conflict drew to a close, aircraft engine contracts, which had been very profitable, would be completed and the Engine Division, which also included the Dowagiac foundry, would be faced with a shut-down. This was foreseeable in 1953, and various studies were undertaken to find products that would fit the Division's managerial and manufacturing capabilities.

Not the least of the problems, and probably the paramount consideration, would be the development of a flexible enough labor agreement with Local 280 of the UAW-CIO to permit the diversity of product that would be required. As General Manager of the Division, it became apparent to me that, for various reasons

— the specialized equipment and tooling we had, the inflexibility of our labor contracts, plant location, lack of specialized marketing capabilities and the like — it was highly improbable a new product venture would prove feasible. We had studied everything from manufacturing pin-setting machines for bowling alleys to agricultural equipment. The Engine Division did have some diversification during this period, working as a sub-contractor to General Motors, and manufacturing components for its Hydramatic transmission. GM lost its Livonia, Michigan, transmission plant in a major fire and had to gear up several component manufacturers in order to keep its lines going. In fact, it was this fire that caused GM's acquisition of the Willow-Run facility from Kaiser Motors.

Another project that the Engine Division took on was the design and operation of a production line for the manufacture and assembly of a miniaturized Sonobuoy, the underwater expendable sonar device used by the Navy for submarine detection. The code name for the project was "Operation Tinkertoy." After the design and process engineering was completed at the Engine Division, Kenny Flood, Gordon Woods and Jules Lussier set up the plant in Arlington, Virginia. The operation was a success and the process was in the vanguard of then existing technology. The chips that were printed with electronic circuitry were of ceramic and about one inch square and one sixteenth of an inch thick. These were stacked up in modules and assembled into the sonobuoys using automated assembly and transfer lines that we had designed. Nothing to compare to today's microchips — but in the early fifties, a real breakthrough in mechanized electronics component manufacture.

This was about the time I became acquainted with Hickman Price. He was a nephew of Joseph Frazer and, during the K-F days, had worked in the export division. Hickman left K-F and joined Willys Motors prior to its acquisition by the Kaiser interests. As Manager of Export for Willys, Hickman had organized a fine overseas distribution network. In Brazil, in particular, the dealer organization there had built, and was operating, an assembly plant in Sao Paulo for Willys FWD vehicles. Due to the ever-present foreign exchange shortage, the pressure was on for the assembly plants to start manufacturing components locally and reduce the hard currency requirement per vehicle.

The common policy followed by automobile manufacturers at that time in South America was to set up an assembly plant in a given country, sized in accordance with the market potential, and ship CKD (Completely Knocked Down) vehicles to it. For a given allocation of foreign exchange by the Central Bank of the country involved, a greater number of vehicles could be produced. Perhaps the biggest saving was in freight costs which were reduced substantially and this system also made possible the local procurement of "easy buy items" such as tires, upholstery materials, paint, batteries, flat glass, etc. The hard core of the CKD package consisted of manufactured parts peculiar to a given model that were designed and manufactured by the automobile company itself or by vendors using designs and tooling supplied by the company. These were the tough parts — engines, transmissions, differentials, brake assemblies, stampings, steering gear, axle forgings, frames, instruments, etc.

The investment required for an assembly plant and its associated assembly jigs, welding fixtures and painting equipment was minimal compared to machining, gear making, stamping, forging and foundry. The import dollars replaced by each dollar of assembly plant investment were substantially greater than the replacement dollars involved with machine and tooling investment. Coupling this problem with periodic model changes which primarily affected the "tough parts," it is easy to understand the reluctance of the prime manufacturer to break through the assembly barrier and produce these parts locally.

Hickman Price's idea was to invest the Detroit Engine Division's machines and tooling in Brazil, build an engine plant and, together with the existing assembly plant and dealer body, form a company that would be the first integrated automobile plant in South America. He showed up one day in Detroit with Vauvau Aranha, who was the head of the Brazilian dealer association. Vauvau was a great personality, spoke excellent English and was the son of a former finance minister. Euclydes, his brother, later became one of the prime movers in Willys Overland do Brasil. In the tour of the Engine Division facilities I'll never forget Hickman, who was quite dramatic and, at times, somewhat flamboyant, standing in the middle of six acres of concentrated machine lines saying to Vauvau, "This is all yours! Say the word and it will be on the next boat." I thought Hickman was a bit premature but it was still a good idea. The trouble was that someone else, completely independently and at the same time, had the same brainstorm. The difference was, that person had the ear of Mr. Henry J. Kaiser.

DeLesseps "Chep" Morrison, then mayor of New Orleans, worked very closely with the Kaiser interests in the early days of the Kaiser Aluminum and Chemical Corporation's activities in Louisiana. Mayor Morrison had also organized an entity called International House that served as a meeting place and sounding board for South American public and private sector contacts. International House was directed by Mario Bermudez, a Colombian by birth. Mario had excellent relationships with various heads of state in South America. Chep and Mario proposed that Mr. Kaiser tour South America and investigate investment possibilities for the surplus manufacturing facilities we had.

Although somewhat reluctant to entertain investing in South America, for reasons that will be brought to light later in this story, Mr. Kaiser considered the Morrison advice very seriously and asked his son Edgar and Gene Trefethen to develop the Morrison idea into an action plan. Edgar, who was spending most of his time in Toledo in those days, swung into action and had Hickman Price put his plans on the back burner until the results of Henry Kaiser's projected tour of South America unfolded. This decision is the reason that Argentina became the first Latin American country in integrated vehicle manufacture even though Brazil's infrastructure and population should have given it priority. But I'm getting ahead of the story.

Shortly after the foregoing I was called to Oakland by Mr. E. E. Trefethen. In those days, with Edgar Kaiser involved primarily in the automobile business with offices in Toledo, Mr. Kaiser, in Oakland, depended principally on Gene Trefethen to administer all of the other operating companies — quite a task when one considers the size and complexities of the companies involved.

We met in Mr. Henry J. Kaiser's office on July 15, 1954. This meeting marked the beginning of Kaiser's Latin American ventures that would encompass major developments in the automotive, aluminum, mining and heavy construction industries for the next two decades. It also marked the first overseas venture by any Kaiser company since the Cuban highway job in the twenties. Present at the meeting — in addition to Mr. Kaiser, Gene Trefethen and myself — were Bob Elliott, Mr. Kaiser's special assistant who wrote most of Kaiser's speeches, Mario Bermudez, George Havas, General Manager of Kaiser Engineers, and some others whose names I can't recall.

We reviewed a report written by E. O. Jewell, then World Trade Development Director for International House, that described priorities and conditions in various countries, potential financing sources and the shortages in the vehicle population that they all had. The report concentrated on four countries: Argentina, Brazil, Colombia and Venezuela, the only ones, according to the Jewell report, that had the potential to support an automotive manufacturing scheme. Mr. Kaiser concluded our discussions and requested that we develop a plan of action concentrating on these four, even though his itinerary would take him to other countries as well. Descriptive brochures and proposals were to be prepared that he would present to the authorities involved.

I was assigned the task of developing, with my organization in Detroit, a listing and description of all the surplus equipment that Kaiser Motors would be able to make available for investment in South America. This entailed not only my plants — the Engine Division and the Dowagiac Foundry — but in addition, the Shadyside, Ohio, press plant, the tools and dies for the Kaiser Passenger car, which were located in several different places, and the company-owned special tooling that was in vendor plants. Most important was the description of what this equipment could do in reducing the imported content of the vehicles to be manufactured. I was originally slated to go with the Kaiser party but at the last minute Mr. Kaiser decided that he didn't need any engineers along — preferring a more generalized approach on the first contact. The trouble was that while Mr. Kaiser didn't want any engineers around, he was still going to be exposed to some pretty penetrating technical questions which no one in the Kaiser entourage could answer. And that is exactly what happened.

Much has been written about Henry Kaiser, and by writers more prolific than I. However, I was fortunate to be close to Mr. Kaiser and his sons Edgar and Henry Jr. on many occasions, starting with my work in the Kaiser Shipyards during World War II. As superintendent of the outfitting dock at Kaiser Yard 3 in Richmond, California, I would see Mr. Kaiser from time to time when he visited the Yard. Yard 3 is where we built the C4 Troopships, the largest vessels constructed in any of the seven Kaiser operated yards. These ships were designed to transport 4000 troops and provide all the necessities on voyages of long duration.

Whenever Mr. Kaiser had an important visitor in the Oakland office he customarily showed him the Richmond shipyards. This was, of course, during the war years. The Kaiser group managed four shipyards in Richmond, California, and three in the Portland, Oregon, and Vancouver, Washington area. If one of the C4s was about ready for delivery when Mr. Kaiser was visiting Yard 3 with one of his guests, he would board the ship and I usually was elected to show the party around. Some of the visitors I remember were Vyacheslav Molotov, Foreign Minister of the U.S.S.R. under Stalin, Lord Halifax of the British Purchasing Commission in the U.S., Admirals Land and Vickery, the heads of the U.S. Maritime Commission and others of like stature. Few questions from Mr. Kaiser, but penetrating ones. Usually my immediate superiors, Clay Bedford, Einar Larson and Kenny Flood were in the visiting party, but since the outfitting and final completion of the C4s were my direct responsibilities, comments and questions were usually directed to me. This was a pretty august group and, for a 25-year-old engineer, quite a heady experience.

Mr. Kaiser knew what he wanted and when he chose his entourage for the South American junket he was less concerned about technical aspects than he was with the personalities and political climates he would be involved with. It should be noted that a paramount Kaiser principle was "no payoffs." The Kaisers, Henry, Edgar and Henry, Jr., had high business ethics and woe befall anyone in the organization if he was caught trying to buy someone off. This would be Mr. Kaiser's first trip to Latin America since the Kaiser Paving Company's highway job in Cuba. There, according to stories I had heard, everyone had their "hand out" and Mr. Kaiser made it absolutely clear to everyone on the team that anything we did concerning the South American auto venture would have to bear his scrutiny.

I vividly remember my disappointment when Gene Trefethen told me I was not included in the roster for the trip. But Gene also said, "Don't worry, the Boss will come back with something," and he sure did.

In addition to Mr. and Mrs. Henry Kaiser, the group included Mayor and Mrs. Morrison, Mario Bermudez, Mr. and Mrs. Bob Elliot and Mr. and Mrs. William Weintraub. Bill Weintraub was the Senior Partner of Norman, Craig and Kummell, the advertising agency used by Kaiser-Frazer. Mr. Kaiser placed a high value on Bill Weintraub's perceptions and opinions. A New Yorker of discriminating taste, a famous art collector, Bill became a great friend and supporter of our work in the Argentine.

With the creative help of Kaiser Engineers' proposal department, brochures were prepared for each of the countries to be visited and contained a proposed automotive integration scheme that gradually, over a five year period, arrived at practically 100% local content exclusive of certain raw materials that had to be imported. This would vary from country to country but, in general, raw materials included cold rolled steel sheets for body panels, pig iron for castings, steel billets for forgings, copper wire for wiring harnesses, aluminum and zinc for die castings, etc. The proposals were very preliminary and generalized. In essence, they stated the Kaiser Group's readiness to invest tools and equipment into joint venture companies that would be formed with either government or private entities, or a combination of both. No stipulations were made as to control. Kaiser was willing to accept a minority position, and public ownership of stock in the proposed corporations was encouraged. Certain assumptions were made relative to vendor capabilities in the various countries, the volume of vehicles to be produced and sold, the amount of capital that could be raised in the public and private sectors; and it was the criteria formulated by these assumptions that caused the Kaiser entourage its initial difficulties. With some advance technical research and "on site" investigations it would have been clear that the only two South American countries that could even come close to qualifying were Argentina and Brazil. Mind — we are talking of South America, not Latin America. For some unknown reason Mexico was not included at the outset, even though it was the second largest country, in terms of population. I wondered why Mexico was not included but undoubtedly the influence of Mario Bermudez and International House in laying out the itinerary caused the concentration on South America. Mexico, at the time, had a fairly good foreign exchange position and seemed to have no trouble in affording the importation of built-up vehicles and CKDs to satisfy its internal market.

The tour started in August 1954. During the two weeks or so that the trip lasted I received reports from Oakland, from time to time, on progress. In Brazil and Colombia Mr. Kaiser was very well received. Bermudez's contacts coupled with Mr. Kaiser's prestige gained access to the top people in these governments. After the usual courtesy calls on the Head of State, the pertinent Ministers of Government met with the group, reviewed the proposals and discussed Kaiser's plan for vehicle manufacture. As discussions progressed it became apparent that we should have done a lot more "homework" in anticipating the many technical criticisms of the plan that came out during the meetings. As a result, Kaiser began to get somewhat frustrated and, in typical H.J. style, became critical of the engineers who had put these proposals together. And I was at the top of the list. Luckily, Argentina was the next stop.

When Kaiser landed at the Ezeiza International airport that serves Buenos Aires, there was a welcoming party displaying a large banner that proclaimed, "President Peron welcomes Mr. Henry J. Kaiser." Brigadier General Juan San Martin, Secretary of Air, was the senior official representing President Peron. The reason for the presence of the Secretary of the Argentine Air Force became apparent later when it was learned that the Air Force, in an entity it had organized in Córdoba, Industrias Aeronáuticas y Mecánicas del Estado (IAME), was manufacturing, on a unitized hand-made basis, a vehicle called the Justicialista.

IAME was also involved in air frame fabrication and assembly. Although there was a definite lack of process engineering and specialized tooling that is needed in repetitive precision machining of components, it was the skills of the work force that were really impressive. I would later see there the production of what I believe was the world's only wooden jet airplane — the Pulque — which was truly an impressive piece of work. Because of the Air Force's position in manufacturing, it had been designated as the coordinator of Mr. Kaiser's visit. Following a courtesy call on President Peron, detailed discussions started with Brigadier San Martin. Mr. Kaiser's willingness to assume management responsibility, invest capital equipment, enter into licensing agreements and form a public corporation in partnership with the Air Force made a favorable impression on San Martin and the President. At the conclusion of these discussions Mr. Kaiser was asked to prepare and present a definitive proposal. Kaiser was elated and the wires started burning between Buenos Aires and Oakland as he passed on instructions for the definitive proposal, and at the same time wanted to know, in his own inimitable fashion, why the proposals he had with him didn't answer all the questions. Oakland was instructed to have everything ready for his second visit to Argentina in October when he would present the final proposal.

With the important meetings concluded, the Kaisers and others in the group were shown around Buenos Aires, hosted at some dinner parties, one of which was at Olivos, the Presidential residence. There, President Peron showed Mr. and Mrs. Kaiser around the grounds which are indeed beautiful. During the walk Mrs. Kaiser admired one of the latest Mercedes 190s parked in one of the garages. The President, who was really a gracious host said "Madam, please accept this car as a gift from the Argentine people in appreciation for the work your husband's company is doing for them." Mrs. Kaiser was overwhelmed and Henry immediately reciprocated by ordering that a new Kaiser Manhattan be sent to the President. It was on the next boat. The Kaiser group was also taken to Córdoba for a tour of IAME. There they were hosted by Brigadier Ferro Sessarego who was in charge and whose confidence in Argentina's human capabilities was certain to inspire an already exuberant Kaiser.

The party continued on to Chile and Peru but there was nothing of importance that came out of the meetings in those two countries. There was also a stop in Caracas, Venezuela, if my memory is correct, but by this time Kaiser was weary of receptions and calls on government officials and wanted to get home. He had finished his job and, as far as he was concerned, Argentina was an accomplished fact. As Trefethen had prophesied, "the Boss would come home with something."

With the highest authority in Argentina receptive, it was now up to the "troops" to develop a definitive proposal that not only met the feasibility test but was beneficial for both Kaiser and Argentina. We had to keep in mind also that this was not merely the disposal of surplus capacity, but that the Kaiser organization would be responsible for the implementation of whatever plan was finally approved. This was not a sale that one could walk away from. We were in for the duration.

In late August I was again called to Oakland to be part of the working group that would develop a firm and definitive proposal for presentation to President Peron and the Argentine authorities in October. This gave us less than two months to create a plan that others like GM, Ford and Chrysler had been studying inconclusively for years.

The leader of our team was George Havas, General Manager of Kaiser Engineers, Inc., a division of the Henry J. Kaiser Company. This was a year before Kaiser Industries Corp. was organized and in those days there were no presidents of Kaiser Subsidiaries who did not have the name Kaiser. By all that was holy, George Havas was the real President of Engineers. George was born in Hungary, educated in Germany, emigrated to Cuba and in the Twenties was working as an engineer in a sugar refinery when he was hired by the Kaiser Paving Company during the course of its highway job outside Havana. A "complete" engineer, Havas had supervised Kaiser Engineer's efforts in the design and construction of dams, auto plants, shipyards, steel mills, aluminum smelters ... you name it. George was fluent in Spanish as well as quite a few other languages and his technical background coupled with his European origins enabled him to understand and cope with, much better than any of us, the vagaries of the Argentine scene. Others in the team were Lloyd N. Cutler — at that time a partner in the Oscar Cox law firm, Kaiser's Washington, DC counsel, and who later formed his own firm, Wilmer, Cutler and Pickering — T.A. "Tim" Bedford, one of my first bosses in the shipyards, John V. Banks then finishing up at Willow-Run, Jack Hughes, Paul Havas, Bruno Franceschi and other Kaiser Engineers personnel from time to time.

It soon became apparent to Havas and the rest of us that we knew nothing at all about the support structure one could expect to encounter in Argentina. What was the status of the vendor industry? Was floor plan and retail financing available? Since our plan called for public participation in the ownership of the new company, who would underwrite the stock issue? What raw materials were available from SOMISA, the only integrated Argentine steel mill? How skilled was Argentine labor? What was a typical labor contract like — pay rates, fringe benefits, job classifications, etc.? These and a host of other questions had to be answered before we could intelligently propose a manufacturing scheme that would, over a period of five years, allow the production of vehicles with practically zero imported content, exclusive of raw materials. We were at an impasse and, as a result, John Banks and I were selected to go to Argentina immediately and were given two weeks to come up with the answers.

I had known John for a long time and worked with him very well. What I didn't know, at that time, was that in addition to his work on the survey, Banks had been asked to consider taking on the general manager's job in the new company if and when it came to pass. Apparently John didn't think an Argentine career was "his cup of tea" and, lucky for me — as it later proved out —, declined the offer.

Banks and I took off from Detroit on August 31. The original plan was to fly from Lima, Peru, to Córdoba for a meeting with

Brig. San Martin but when we arrived in Lima we were late for the connecting flight and had to continue on to Buenos Aires. In the days of propeller-driven DC6s, the elapsed time from Detroit to Buenos Aires was about 30 hours, so Banks and I had plenty of time to brief ourselves and plan our strategy. Neither of us spoke Spanish and we didn't have the foggiest idea of what we might be encountering. We had been informed, before departure, that we would be assisted by the Tiphaine organization, the Willys and K-F distributor for Argentina. We sent Daniel Tiphaine a telegram from Lima telling him of our change in plans.

We finally arrived at the Ezeiza airport and took a taxi to the Plaza Hotel. Shortly after arrival, Tiphaine called from the lobby and we got together in our room to discuss a plan of action. Daniel Tiphaine was a very personable fellow and spoke excellent English. He told us that the Air Minister had arranged for one of the Air Force planes to fly us to Córdoba the next day and that he was assigning a Bruno Ossowski to help us during our stay. Ossowski, a Pole, had been able to flee Poland before the German invasion and had joined the Polish Brigade in England, fighting with the Royal Air Force. He served as a maintenance technician during the war and with his excellent mechanical background was ideally suited to help us analyze the industrial potential of the Argentine vendors. Without his help, Banks and I would not have been very effective. When IKA was organized, Bruno was one of the first to join and became Service Manager, with Daniel Tiphaine's approval, I might add. The first time I met Bruno, however, our relationship was strained a bit when he bawled me out for slamming the door on his old Jaguar. Autos were so precious in Argentina that you treated them with respect.

Bruno called for us the next morning and took us to the military airport at Aeroparque. After waiting some time for the weather to clear we took off for Córdoba in an Air Force AT11 Beechcraft. About midway we had to land because Córdoba was closed in. We put down at a small town named Marcos Juarez to wait out the storm. We were driven into town in an old Oakland sedan — about a 1929 model — and had lunch at the hotel. After lunch we finally took off and in about an hour landed at IAME's airstrip. There we were met by Brigadier Ferro Sessarego, the Commanding Officer.

I took an immediate liking to Sessarego. He was open and communicative and personally showed us around the facilities. IAME tried to do everything. Cars, aircraft engine maintenance, small automotive engines, plastics, testing facilities. To me, IAME represented a colossal experiment in a government subsidized industrialization program. But skills were being developed, albeit there was no production processing. Two automobiles, the Justicialista coupe and the Rastrojero pickup, a motorbike called La Puma and the La Pampa tractor were all being built in various parts of the plant with no apparent area boundaries from one product to the other. In one building you would see airplanes being repaired, a general purpose machine shop and automobile frame assembly. All the operators I watched were good. They knew what they were doing, made their own setups, kept their work places meticulously clean and seemed to have a good attitude towards their work. Sessarego also showed us a lot of idle machines that he indicated would probably be available for investment in the new company.

Banks and I were scheduled to return to Buenos Aires on Saturday, September 4, but we received word that Edgar Kaiser and George Havas were coming to Córdoba and wanted us to be on hand. Edgar had told us before we left the States that he was contemplating a visit to follow up on Henry J.'s meetings and to meet the government people he had talked to. Edgar and George got in about 5 pm with the Air Minister and Brigadier Santiago Diaz-Bialet, an IAME director who worked closely with San Martin and seemed to handle all administrative details. We then toured some of the IAME facilities again. On Sunday we had a nice drive through the Sierras de Córdoba followed by lunch at the Air Minister's home. We flew back to Buenos Aires in the Air Minister's DC 3 and Edgar and George returned to the States.

Back in Buenos Aires our calendar started to fill up and since our time was limited, John and I decided to split up. Bruno Ossowski arranged for another car and driver and we started our survey of potential supplier plants. We covered a lot of territory in two weeks, visiting parts manufacturers, foundries, forge shops and also the General Motors and Ford assembly plants. Walt de Schryver of GM and Joe Roda of Ford were helpful with suggestions for suppliers. Meetings with several automobile dealers brought out the fact that even with the severe shortage of cars, selling wasn't easy because of the lack of available retail financing. But price was the big factor. Due to a build-up of customs duties freight and the high cost of locally furnished items such as tires, batteries, etc., cars were priced at two to three times their value in their country of origin. The scarcity of product itself brought about a tremendous over-pricing that also put a damper on turnover.

John and I would get back to the Plaza Hotel about 8 pm and rehash what we had learned that day over a bottle of Argentine champagne, which was excellent and cheap — our budget couldn't handle the Plaza prices for imported Scotch whiskey.

As we neared the end of our survey, it became apparent that it was very questionable that the parts industry, such as it was, could support our proposed production and integration program. In the plants we visited there was a noteworthy absence of production tooling, the reason being that the parts manufacturers were only concentrating on the "after market" — the term used in the industry for the replacement parts market — and long production runs of a given part were not common if they existed at all. The Argentine companies were accustomed to short run "job shop" production on multiple use equipment. There was a positive aspect, though: the fact was that the production operators were, as a general rule, more skilled than those employed in typical high-production shops in the U.S. I saw operators performing multiple tasks that, in a typical UAW-CIO plant, would require several different classifications of labor. I had the impression that the Argentine operator was not only accustomed to performing multi-classification tasks but enjoyed having the over-all responsibility for the operation. If one thing of real value came out of our trip, it was this factor which became one of the basic precepts of our labor agreements. We were able to reduce the number of job classifications in the production, maintenance and skilled trades to a common-sense breakdown and definition of classification responsibility, as compared to the redundancies contained in the typical UAW labor contract.

We had a real problem, however. There was no way, constituted as it was, that Argentine industry would be able to satisfy our requirements for the parts we normally would be procuring from outside sources. There were, of course, exceptions: electrical components — starters, generators, regulators, etc. — brake shoes, clutches, wiring harnesses, glass and a few other miscellaneous parts were being manufactured by vendors who would have the potential to graduate from small runs to production quantities. The big stuff we usually bought, such as major forgings and castings, transmissions, differentials, universal joints, transfer cases, carburetors, not to mention tools and dies, just wasn't there. It became apparent to me, on this first visit, that we would have to do far more vertical integration of our inhouse capabilities than we had planned in Oakland, in order to carry out our five-year import deletion program.

Most of the companies we visited were very cooperative but reluctant to let us into the working areas. As an example, we were told that the only real forge shop that existed was the one owned and operated by Becciu. When we visited, Señor Becciu very courteously met with us and discussed our program but would not let us into his shop. He later became a very good friend and I never failed to remind him of not letting me see his forging hammers. After discussion and looking at some of the parts he produced, it was apparent that, with the equipment he had, it would have been impossible for him to produce production quantities of crankshafts, camshafts, connecting rods and other major forgings. Becciu later became a principal supplier of miscellaneous small forgings. But there never was a question of Argentina's technical capabilities — capacity was the problem.

On our visits to the GM and Ford assembly plants, which were not operating at the time, we learned that the Central Bank, for some time, had not been issuing import permits for the number of CKD units required to maintain even minimum production runs. This also applied to Chrysler, which assembled its units in a plant owned by Fevre y Basset, the Chrysler distributor. We were advised to require, in our contract, a Government-backed commitment for the entire five years of the integration program that would guarantee the availability of foreign exchange for the imports necessary.

The only automotive company receiving regular import permits was Mercedes Benz. It was not only able to maintain production in its truck and bus assembly plant but was also importing built-up units, mainly taxis but some private passenger cars as well. The principal owner and operator of the Mercedes Benz plant, Señor Jorge Antonio, had the connections to get his imports prioritized, supposedly because they were for public sector transport and haulage. But rumors abounded as to how the Mercedes products were retailed — exorbitant mark-ups, under-the-table payments and the like — because of the scarcity, but Banks and I figured that politics and intrigue were something we didn't have time for.

One experience, even though it was humorous, brought home very sharply one aspect of living in Argentina under the Peron regime. One day for lunch we wandered into one of the better restaurants located on a side street just off Calle Florida, a principal Buenos Aires shopping street. Buenos Aires has excellent restaurants, on a par with any in the world. We had been eating a lot and really didn't need lunch. I said to John, "Wouldn't it be great if we could just have a small luncheon, something like a typical business lunch in the U.S." Looking over the menu I noticed, in a corner section blocked out by a heavy dark line, the title *Menú Económico,* and it seemed to me that this was probably a special light lunch for people on the go. It listed a very reduced selection and was amazingly cheap. So I said to John, "This looks like what we've been looking for, let's order it!"

When the waiter came and we placed our order, he gave us a withering look and proceeded to remove the tablecloth, napkins and most of the silverware. We couldn't figure out what he was mad about and when we ordered a bottle of the best wine on the list, he looked at us as if we were crazy. Well, we ate the meal, such as it was, paid our bill, left a good tip and departed. On the way out I looked back over my shoulder and the waiter was standing by the table watching us leave and shaking his head as if he couldn't believe what had happened. We told Ossowski about this and he couldn't stop laughing. Bruno explained that the serving of the Menú Económico was a mandatory requirement imposed by the Government on all restaurants so that any destitute person could walk into any place serving meals, even the Plaza Hotel, and get a full meal for a ridiculously low price. Bruno also said that the average Argentine was so proud that he would go hungry rather than order the *Menú Económico.* We now understood why the waiter reacted the way he did and I can assure you we never went back.

During the course of our Buenos Aires survey I was asked by San Martin to return to Córdoba and spend a day or so to help develop a preliminary list of the machines that I thought would be best suited to our purposes. I flew to Córdoba in an Aerolíneas Argentinas commercial flight and met again with Sessarego and his team. After a closer review of the equipment that had been indicated as available for investment I selected a few machines that could be tooled up for production but, most important, I selected a list of tool room equipment including three-dimensional milling, boring, jig bore and other like type machines that would prove invaluable for the body and engine tooling that we were going to have to make for the CJ5 Jeep production. It was interesting to note that most all of the new equipment I saw was Czechoslovakian with a few British machines. Sessarego was well versed on the Kaiser preliminary proposal and had done his homework getting ready for my return visit. We finished our work early in the afternoon and the Brigadier invited me to my first Argentine barbecue. The Argentine *asado* has no equal and from this point on I was sold!

I returned to Buenos Aires and Banks and I wrapped up our survey. Our time was running out and we would have to get back to Oakland and work on the definitive proposal. We had gathered a lot of basic information that would be of importance in developing a coherent proposal. Argentina had greatly impressed me. I liked the country and its people and was not concerned about the political undertones that surfaced from time to time. It seemed to me that if we were able to organize the company with enough financial strength to give ourselves a fighting chance, we would find a way to comply with the commitments we would be giving.

Banks and I left for the States on Thursday, September 16. We had used Panagra, which flew the West Coast, coming down so we decided to return on Pan American via the East Coast of South America. Panam used Boeing Stratocruisers in those days and this was a real comfortable airplane. We worked all the way up, getting our notes and personal observations organized and, by the time we reached San Francisco, we were tired but ready with a comprehensive report that would guide the development of the definitive proposal which was due to be presented by Mr. Kaiser in October.

Mr. Kaiser was delighted that John and I had completed our work a little ahead of schedule so he started putting the pressure on to get the proposal finished ahead of schedule with the net result that John and I, Paul Havas, Tim Bedford, and quite a few others worked for about a week, averaging 14 to 18 hours a day, to wrap it up. The two leaders of our effort were George Havas and Lloyd Cutler. The rest of us supplied technical input.

George and Lloyd really put on a performance. They would sit down with Della Weigand, George's secretary, and dictate whole chapters at a sitting, leaving blank spaces for tabulations and other data that the technical group would fill in. We were in constant communication with Toledo and the Detroit Engine Division, where they were also burning the midnight oil, finalizing the asset listings. Toledo and Detroit also put a lot of effort into developing preliminary plant layouts of the machining, assembly, paint and trim lines, the press plant, upholstery shop, maintenance and other facilities. When the layouts were completed we drew a line around them and thereby defined the configurations of the various buildings. The support group in the East was headed up by Carl Olson in Product Engineering, Bill Heard handled the Works Engineering aspects and Pete Mapes in Procurement made all the vendor contacts. Homer Kelley in Toledo handled the listings for most of the Kaiser car body tooling. The biggest concentration of tooling was still located at the Willow-Run plant and we had to make sure that none of it would be scrapped out since the word had already gone out that the Kaiser Manhattan was to be discontinued. In some instances we had a tough job getting the cooperation we needed out of the ex Kaiser-Frazer tool engineering division that was now located in Toledo and it was like pulling teeth to get comprehensive listings, valuations, process sheets and all the other data we would need in order to put the Kaiser back into production.

As far as some in Toledo were concerned, the Argentine project was just another "will o' the wisp" that Oakland was chasing. I remember visiting with Max Pearce, at his plant in Shadyside, Ohio, to determine what tooling was located there and get the list of the Shadyside presses that had been earmarked for Argentina. Max wasn't about to release any of the Shadyside equipment stating that there wasn't a "chance of a snowball in hell" of the Argentine project going ahead. He really didn't want to talk to me about it at all. The humorous sequel was that Max later went to Brazil with Hickman Price when that project got going and took the presses remaining in Shadyside that didn't go to Argentina.

One key decision we took at the time which was also a potentially disastrous assumption had to do with the power plants that we planned for the different vehicles that we would be producing. The basic engine produced in Detroit for the Kaiser and Frazer automobiles was the Continental-designed six-cylinder, in-line, L- head engine. This engine had a displacement of 226 cubic inches (3.6 liters) and developed about 125 horsepower. While ideal for the Kaiser passenger car and the Jeep pickup, panel delivery and station wagon, it was too big for the CJ5 military Jeep. The CJ5s built in Toledo used a Willys 4-cylinder engine and to manufacture this in Argentina would require a completely separate machine line which would not be economically feasible.

Olson and I had discussed this problem when the Argentine project first started taking shape and the idea of designing a 4-cylinder version of the basic Continental Six emerged. Carl had Paul Bastien, our Chief Engine Designer, go to work on the problem and he produced enough design information to allow the tool engineers to come up with preliminary process and cost estimates to tool up the proposed 4-cylinder engine. By chopping off two cylinders from the six block and having the foundry replace them with a slave skeleton, we could, through minor alterations to the Cylinder Block machine line, process both the four and the six blocks. The same applied to the cylinder head. The 4-cylinder cam, crankshaft and manifolds were essentially the only parts that required a separate tool-up. Connecting rods, flywheel, flywheel housing, oil pump, water pump, studs and other connecting parts remained the same. While all this sounds pretty simple and straightforward, no one in his right mind would design a new engine, such as we were proposing to do, and go directly into production without an extensive testing and field development program. Although a couple of prototype fours were built in the States, I can't recall any vehicle testing being done until we had started plant construction in Córdoba. The financial constraints overrode engineering conservatism and we had to "bite the bullet" and include the Engine Division 4-cylinder version of the Continental Six in the product lineup that was in the definitive proposal.

Another critical item that had to be cranked into the proposal had to do with the organization that would be required to start up and operate the new entity. I developed an organization chart that required some 100 expatriates in various managerial and supervisory positions. This was a big cost item, estimated at over one million dollars, to move one hundred families. This was one area where Havas and I greatly differed. George knew a lot about the country, its universities and its human resources and thought I should cut back substantially on my requirements. But with the time constraints imposed I just couldn't agree that one could build a plant and put it into operation in the short time allowed with a green organization hired off the street and one that had absolutely no concept of Detroit production methods or the products we would be producing. It wasn't easy but I stood my ground with George. After the plant started up and the North Americans trained their counterparts, there could be, and was, a rapid exodus of expatriate personnel.

We finished the proposal in about ten days, in line with H.J.'s schedule for the October presentation he had promised Peron. I was instructed, this time by Edgar Kaiser, to be prepared to join the group that would be leaving on September 29. Since this was the following Wednesday, I was able to return to Detroit and see Gus and the boys, Kim, Kelly and Mark. I had been gone about a month and I sure missed them. There were also a lot of details to catch up with at the Engine Division plus the need to bring my organization up to date on what might be in store for them.

I thought the final version of the definitive proposal was an excellent job. The Havas-Cutler authorship, with the help of the technical group, produced a document that clearly set out the benchmarks of the Kaiser Plan. It has been a constant source of amazement to me over the years how the basic tenets we incorporated in this document held up throughout the subsequent negotiations and the first five years of the new company's life.

The proposal provided that Kaiser Motors Corporation would join with IAME in establishing an Automotive Manufacturing Company. The suggested name for the new company was Industrias Kaiser de Argentina (IKA). The "de" was later dropped.

The new company would manufacture the Kaiser passenger car, the CJ5 Jeep and the Jeep utility vehicle line consisting of a pickup, station wagon and panel delivery. The capacity of the plant would be 40,000 units per year on a single shift basis. The first vehicle would contain a substantial proportion of components manufactured in the U.S., but when the plant reached maximum production, 40 months after go-ahead, essentially 90% of the required components would be manufactured in the country. We further stated in the proposal that the facilities of the new company would enable it to manufacture the same components of the finished vehicle that Kaiser then was manufacturing in its own operations in the U.S. The company would buy from subcontractors and vendors in Argentina essentially the same components which Kaiser purchased in the U.S. It was recognized in the proposal that the new company would have to conduct an intensive vendor assistance program in Argentina. This program would not only enable IKA to work along the same lines as we did in the States but would also create a vendor body that would manufacture for other Argentine auto producers that would enter the market eventually.

The production schedule proposed that the first Jeep would be produced in the fourteenth month after go-ahead, or February 1956. Actually, the first Jeep left the assembly line in Córdoba in April, 1956, about two months behind schedule but with good reason — we were a bit delayed by a revolution and an interdiction, both of which we'll talk about later. We stated that the Argentine content would start out at 57.5% in the first Jeep and 77% in the first Kaiser passenger car, with all vehicles at or near 100% forty months after go-ahead. We exceeded the initial content goals but we never attained 100% although we came mighty close. It was never economically feasible to consider such items as spark plugs, certain special bearings, some carburetor parts, etc. All in all, though, we achieved a greater Argentine content integration, by far, than that required in later government regulations and, I am sure, than any terminal plant in Argentina today.

Three plant locations were proposed for consideration: Rosario, Córdoba and Buenos Aires, in that order, because we were aware that government policy favored industry decentralization away from Buenos Aires.

The proposal included our estimate of the initial capital that would be required to build and start up the new facility, put it into operation and achieve a positive cash flow.

The initial capital would consist of:

A. Machinery, equipment, tools, dies, jigs and fixtures furnished by Kaiser and IAME.
B. Peso financing in Argentina raised by sale of stock and a development loan to be extended by the Industrial Bank.
C. Profit on sale in Argentina of 1000 passenger cars to be purchased from Kaiser Motors.

The following was the estimate of the capital in pesos that would be required, using a peso/dollar (m$n-U$S) exchange rate of 14:1.

Item		m$n
Machinery and equipment		138,706,000
Buildings and installation		135,924,000
Tools, dies, jigs and fixtures		156,253,000
	sub-total	430,883,000
Working capital		160,000,000
	sub-total	590,883,000
Less anticipated profit from sale of 1000 Kaiser automobiles		111,000,000
	Total capital required at 14:1	479,883,000 U$S 34,277,357

Given the above estimate of total capital required, we proposed that it emanate from the following sources:

CAPITAL TO BE FURNISHED BY KAISER

The capital to be furnished by Kaiser, partly as an investment and partly as a sale for dollars, had an estimated value of U$S 15,121,500 and is itemized as follows:

Item		U$S
Machinery and equipment		4,814,100
Tools, dies, jigs and fixtures		8,362,400
100 Kaiser cars		1,945,000
	Total	15,121,500

It was proposed that of this U$S 15,121,500 worth of assets to be furnished by Kaiser, U$S 10,121,500 be a capital investment and U$S 5,000,000 worth be sold for dollars to the new company. This would be accomplished as follows:

Capital Investments	U$S	m$n
Tools, dies, jigs and fixtures	8,362,400 or	117,074,000
Machinery and equipment	1,759,100 or	24,627,000
Total	10,121,500 or	141,701,000
Sale for Dollars		
Machinery and equipment	3,055,000 or	42,770,000
1000 Kaiser cars	1,945,000 or	27,230,000
Total	5,000,000 or	70,000,000

CAPITAL TO BE FURNISHED BY IAME

It was proposed that IAME furnish machinery and equipment then owned or on order, that had an estimated value of U$S 3,120,000 or m$n 43,683,000. IAME might also make a further capital investment as described in the following paragraph:

REMAINING CAPITAL REQUIREMENT

The capital investments of Kaiser (m$n 141,701,000) and IAME (m$n 43,683,000), total m$n 185,384,000. An additional amount of m$n 294,499,000 would have to be provided to equate to the total required of m$n 479,883,000, with practically all of this additional amount in cash which would be used for working capital, construction and pre-production outlays. The additional capital required could be obtained by any one or a combination of the following means:

A. Contribution of additional facilities or tools, dies, jigs and fixtures by IAME, either in physical form or as a cash investment,
B. Sale of share capital to private investors in Argentina, or
C. Loans from Argentine lending institutions.

RESULTING CAPITAL STRUCTURE

A feasible capital structure could be as follows:

A. Assumptions	m$n
1.Kaiser investment	141,701,000
2.IAME invests facilities having a value of m$n 43,683,000, and so that its share ownership be as originally contemplated, it invests additional facilities or cash to bring its total investment to	80,000,000
3.Common or preferred stock sold to private Argentine investors for a total amount of	150,000,000
Sub-Total Capital	371,701,000
4. Argentine lending institutions extend loans to the new company of	108,182,000
Total	479,883,000

B. Resulting ownership	
Kaiser	38.2%
IAME	21.6%
Private	40.2%

In addition to the financial structure of the new company as described above, the proposal also provided for other eventualities that could cause serious delays if not provided for in the final agreement. The most important features that we wanted incorporated in the final contract are detailed below:

A. Method to be used in the valuation of equipment to be invested.
We could foresee a problem relating to the valuation of used equipment, particularly the set of Kaiser passenger car tooling that would be the prime investment of Kaiser, and felt it necessary to come into agreement on a procedure as part of the October accord.

B. Patent licensing, engineering and technical assistance.
Kaiser would license the new company to use all existing patents and trademarks under its control which were required to produce the vehicles included in the proposal. Royalties would be computed in dollars on the following basis:

1. U$S per vehicle produced in any year
   40 per vehicle on first 10,000
   25 per vehicle on second 10,000
   20 per vehicle on third 10,000
   15 per vehicle on fourth 10,000
2. One half of this royalty would be payable to Kaiser in pesos and the remaining one half of this royalty would be paid in dollars at the official free market rate of exchange established by the Argentine Central Bank.
3. The above royalty would be reduced with respect to any vehicle, engine or spare part by the same percentage as the percentage of the total cost of said vehicle, engine or spare part represented by components obtained from United States sources.
4. Engineering services and technical assistance from Kaiser was provided for at cost and in the currency used, i.e., for U.S. personnel living in Argentina, only a portion of their salary was paid in dollars. The purpose of this article was to set forth the estimated dollar exchange requirements of the new company for the first few years of operation.

C. Management.
The agreement would provide that Kaiser would have sole responsibility for the management of the company, subject to general policies prescribed by the Board of Directors and stockholders. Representation on the board would in general conform to the respective stock interests of Kaiser, IAME and private investors.

D. Other commitments by Kaiser.
Kaiser would unconditionally guarantee that the machinery and equipment to be furnished, whether by sale or investment, would be in good operating condition, and that the facilities of the new company would be engineered, installed and operated in an efficient manner in accordance with practices prevailing in the United States automotive industry, with such adaptations as were required to meet local conditions in Argentina.

E. Required actions of the Argentine government.
The proposal required that the Argentine government take the necessary steps in the form of appropriate decrees or equivalent binding governmental action to:

1. Approve the Kaiser investment as qualified under law 14,222 with right of capital repatriation after ten years in five equal annual installments.
2. Customs duties exemption on the physical goods forming the Kaiser investment.
3. Reduce the applicable duty on the new company's imports of components, raw materials, spare parts and finished or semi-knocked down vehicles for a period of five years.
4. Authorize the purchase, by the new company, of U$S 5,000,000 of foreign exchange at a rate no higher than the official free market rate to cover the initial dollar purchases of machinery and vehicles from Kaiser as set forth in the proposed capitalization of the new company.
5. Agree in principle to authorize the purchase of foreign exchange required for the first few years of operation.

I believe I have related the most important parts of the definitive proposals that we completed in Oakland in time for H. J. Kaiser's second trip to Argentina. They were printed in English and Spanish.

The West Coast contingent — consisting of Henry and Edgar and their wives, George Havas and Tim Bedford — went from San Francisco to Miami where Lloyd Cutler, Mario Bermudez and I met them. We all left Miami on a Panagra flight the evening of Wednesday, September 29. We didn't have any group discussions that evening since it was late and after dinner we all went to bed. In those days Panagra had berths on the DC6s.

The next morning after taking off from Lima, Edgar called us together in the lounge to discuss our program.

Edgar began by stating that we should settle Argentina one way or another before we did anything else in Latin America. Kaiser Motors' cash position at the time was not good and he felt it was of utmost importance to close the Argentine deal or go back home and start disposing of some assets to provide cash. Henry, on the other hand, wanted to get us started on the Argentine negotiations and go to Colombia and get things rolling there. We finally convinced Mr. Kaiser that he would have to spend some time in the Argentine and keep Colombia in the wings. We had a lot of discussion on how we might complete the Argentine negotiations rapidly and reviewed the various conditions set out in the proposal. While Edgar felt that the Argentine authorities, particularly Dr. Gomez Morales, the Secretary of Economic Affairs, would accept the capitalization figures we were submitting and wouldn't try to negotiate us down, Cutler felt otherwise. He cautioned that we were proposing a corporate capitalization of over 370 million pesos, which would make the new company one of the biggest in Argentina. At that time there were only about ten corporations in the country capitalized in excess of 100 million pesos. This led to a review of the possible ways of reducing the total peso requirements; some of them we talked about were:

- Reduce production volume.
- Reduce the variety of product in the early stages.
- Rent the Chrysler assembly plant in the San Justo suburb of Buenos Aires and put the engine and press plant in the Pampa tractor plant that might become available in Córdoba.
- Cut the price on the Kaiser equipment that we had pegged at 3 million dollars to allow, within the 5 million dollars cash to Kaiser, a greater number of imported cars and an increase of peso income.

These ideas and many others were tossed back and forth during what I look back on as a memorable plane ride. We finally concluded that the proposal should stay as is and the alternatives we had identified should serve as back-up positions if the need arose in the negotiations. As far as I was concerned, the most important question posed during the whole trip was when Edgar asked Tim Bedford and me if we were ready to move to Argentina. I was but Tim wasn't.

We finally landed in Ezeiza in the afternoon and were whisked through customs and driven to the Plaza Hotel in a fleet of Mercedes limousines that had been sent by the President's office.

The next morning, Friday, October 1, 1954, we were received by President Peron who had with him Brigadier General San Martin, Brigadier Santiago Diaz-Bialet, Dr. Gomez Morales and Dr. Miguel Revestido, Secretary of Finance, among others. I could sense, in the enthusiasm of the President, that he was impressed with the fact that Mr. Kaiser, who had committed just a little more than a month previous to return with a definitive proposal in October, had lived up to his reputation as a doer.

The formal presentation of the proposal was made by Mr. Kaiser to the President, and English and Spanish copies were distributed. A meeting of the Kaiser group and Dr. Gomez Morales' team was scheduled for that afternoon in Morales' office.

In this first meeting with Morales and his associates, we spent the whole afternoon explaining and clarifying points contained in the proposal. This was a long meeting with everything having to be translated, but when we finished, practically all of the major conditions had been agreed upon. All of this was somewhat boring for Mr. Kaiser who usually shunned long meetings and a lot of detail. I always carried a few cigars in those days and even though Henry's doctors had told him not to smoke, he motioned to me for a cigar. After he lit up he calmed down and we got on with the business.

A surprise attendee at the meeting was Señor Jorge Antonio. In introducing him, Dr. Morales explained that the President had requested Antonio's appraisal of our scheme since he was, unquestionably, the most important automobile executive in the country. It seemed odd to us, though, that a potential competitor would be brought into our negotiations. This was the only meeting that he attended and, although he voiced no comments at the time, he must have thought our project a viable one, as later events proved. When the meeting broke up, Antonio invited everyone to an *asado* the next day, Saturday, at his estancia in the suburbs of Buenos Aires.

We were picked up about noon and driven to Antonio's estancia, which took about an hour's drive. There was a large group of people at the *asado,* and, probably as a courtesy to the Kaisers, most everyone spoke English. One of the guests was Cesar Rubin, Jorge Antonio's brother-in-law, an engineer who worked in the Mercedes Benz organization. I would be seeing a lot of Rubin in the next few months when he worked as a member of the Evaluation commission that reviewed the equipment values we had proposed — but more about that later in the story.

The arrangements for the *asado* were impeccable. The food, wines and service were excellent in all respects. We toured the stables and the grounds and I was really impressed. After the *asado* I noticed Mr. Kaiser sitting on a garden lounge settee talking to Jorge Antonio with George Havas sitting in a chair facing them and doing the translating. I took a photo of the three of them and when I look at it now, over 30 years later, it brings back some vivid memories because it was there and then that Antonio informed Mr. Kaiser that he, Antonio, would have to play a role in the Kaiser project in order for it to succeed.

George Havas later told us that, in his opinion, what Señor Antonio really wanted was distribution rights for our future production. After we returned to the hotel, Mr. Kaiser, with Havas filling in the details, discussed the Antonio demand with Edgar, Lloyd Cutler and Juan Martin Allende.

Dr. Juan Martin Allende had recently joined our task force. Juan Martin was an associate in the law firm of his uncle, Dr. Victor Goytia. The Goytia firm had been selected by Cutler to handle all legal aspects of our proposal that related to Argentine law. A graduate of the University of Buenos Aires Law Faculty, Juan Martin had also studied at New York University. I've worked with a lot of lawyers. Some pontificate and tell you why something can't be done. Allende, on the other hand, would come up with suggestions and ideas that would lead to solutions, not problems. In the years that we worked together in IKA there was never an important decision taken without Juan Martin's advice. He was much more than just our outside counsel, and IKA's success was due as much to him as any single person. A year or so after IKA was up and running, Juan Martin and Dr. Teodosio C. Brea organized their own firm, Estudio Allende y Brea, and IKA became one of its first clients.

Returning to the Antonio question, Mr. Kaiser instructed Edgar to inform the President that if the Kaiser organization had to depend on Señor Antonio's influence in order to succeed in its venture in Argentina, it would return to the U.S. The next morning Edgar, George Havas and Juan Martin Allende met with Dr. Gomez Morales and, as it was later related to me by Juan Martin, Edgar informed Gomez Morales of the discussion between Señor Antonio and his father and asked him if the Government's position was the same as that of Señor Antonio. Dr. Gomez Morales excused himself and when he returned he told Edgar, "The Boss says you're free to do what you want." There were words to the effect that the President believed that a Kaiser-Antonio joint arrangement would be a successful one but in no way was it mandatory.

Following the Antonio incident, meetings continued in rapid succession with Dr. Gomez Morales' team and on the evening of October 4, 1954, a Letter Agreement was signed by Brigadier Juan I. San Martin, representing IAME, Henry J. Kaiser as Chairman of Kaiser Motors Corporation, Edgar F. Kaiser as President of Willys Motors, Inc., Dr. Alfredo Gomez Morales as Secretary of Economic Affairs and Dr. Miguel Revestido as Minister of Finance. The latter two signatories were parties to the agreement in order to express official governmental approval of certain provisions to the extent that such provisions exceeded the authority of IAME.

The Letter Agreement, or "Agreement in Principle" as it was commonly known, closely followed the Kaiser Definitive Proposal. The principal conditions contained in the October 4th agreement were as follows:

1. IAME and Kaiser agreed to subscribe and pay in, jointly, not less than 51% of the initial share capital to be issued by the new company.
2. Kaiser estimated the value of its contribution of capital as m$n 140,000,000, the equivalent of U$S 10,000,000 and IAME estimated that its contribution would have a value of m$n 80,000,000. The definitive value of the machinery, equipment and other assets to be invested by Kaiser and IAME, and the

values of the items to be sold by Kaiser to the new company, would be established by IAME and Kaiser taking into consideration the opinion of a Mixed Valuation Commission to be appointed jointly by the two entities. This Commission was to value the items under consideration by using as a basis their replacement value in their country of origin, less wear and tear due to use and pursuant to the instructions that IAME and Kaiser jointly would hand over to it within five days. The report of the Commission was to be submitted within thirty days unless an extension was mutually agreed to by both parties.

3. The new company would purchase from Kaiser one thousand Kaiser passenger cars at Kaiser's current export price for semi-knocked down automobiles. The distribution and sale of the one thousand automobiles would be made in accordance with procedures and prices to be established with the pertinent authorities.

4. The foreign exchange requirements of the new company were listed in the document, and provisions were made for their issuance on terms no less favorable than those granted to the various sectors of Argentine industry.

5. The five year production and import deletion schedules detailed in the Definitive Proposal were quoted practically verbatim in the Agreement.

6. The additional cash required by the company to carry it through the pre-production period and until it became profitable, would be secured through the sale of stock to the public and loans that would be arranged by the Central Bank through the Industrial Bank.

7. Matters such as Board representation, technical direction, management, patents, royalties, guarantees of equipment condition and other miscellaneous conditions and obligations assumed by the parties remained as stated in the Definitive Proposal.

8. There were several other conditions that the signatories and the Government obligated themselves to fulfilling before a final agreement could be signed. A period of sixty days was set within which all conditions would be satisfied and the company organized.

There was a lot of work that remained to be done in the next sixty days, most of which would be in valuations.

The day after we signed the agreement, Cutler, Allende, Havas and I met with Brigadier Santiago Diaz-Bialet to develop the instructions that would be given the Mixed Valuation Commission once it was appointed. In essence, the methodology we developed in the Instructions based the valuation of new machinery and equipment on the purchase price in the country of origin. All valuations were to be made in dollars and a table of exchange rates for various currencies was included for conversion purposes. For all used equipment, valuations were to be made based on replacement value less wear and tear due to use. To simplify the work of the Commission, the Instructions provided that items whose replacement value was less than U$S 6000 would be valued by lots. The Commission was required to carry out a sufficient number of individual analyses to establish their value. To the values thus established, the estimated or actual cost of packing and transportation to the port of embarkation was to be added but any dismantling expense was expressly excluded. This latter expense was one that Kaiser and IAME agreed to absorb and applied mainly to presses at Shadyside and Córdoba that would have to be dismantled prior to moving, but it was a substantial sum of money.

Edgar Kaiser appointed George Burpee, the managing partner of the firm of Coverdale and Colpitts, a leading engineering consultant that specialized in valuation work, as senior representative of Kaiser on the Mixed Valuation Commission, with James Drumm, a financial consultant and former head of the National City Bank in Argentina, and myself as the second and third members. The three members appointed to represent IAME's and the Government's interests were:

- Ing. (Engineer) Jaime Barcezat, Chief Inspector, IAME.
- Ing. Ernesto Gaudioso, Industrial Bank, proposed to represent the Ministries of Finance and Industry.
- Ing. Cesar Rubin, Mercedes Benz, proposed to represent the future private investors in the new company.

The first meeting of the Commission was scheduled for Monday, October 11th, in the Air Minister's office. Since we had a few days, we left Cutler in Buenos Aires to finish up the Valuation Instructions with Diaz-Bialet along with some other loose ends, and Havas, Bedford, Allende and I took the night train to Córdoba for a meeting with IAME to get final definition on the listing of machines and equipment it would be investing.

We got into Córdoba Thursday morning, October 7, checked into the Hotel Crillon and then went to IAME's offices. Arrangements had been made for us to see the FIAT plants on the south side of the city. There were two major plants, a railroad diesel engine plant and a tractor plant, both of which had been recently completed. This gave us a good opportunity to get current construction cost data to compare to the estimates contained in our proposal. The Córdoba trip also gave George Havas an opportunity to see a brother who had emigrated to Argentina when he went to Cuba. He hadn't seen him in years and it was quite a reunion. George's sister was married to a Señor Csaky, also a Hungarian immigrant, who owned and operated a steel fabricating plant in Córdoba. Csaky gave us a lot of steel fabricating cost data, which caused us to revise our preliminary construction design concepts and substitute reinforced concrete wherever possible due to the high cost of steel.

The next couple of days were spent finalizing the lists with Brigadier Sessarego, Comandante Montfort and others, culminating in a meeting with San Martin on Sunday. We concluded that the proposed investment by IAME of m$n 80,000,000, which roughly amounted to U$S 5,700,000, would consist of U$S 1,700,000 of machines on hand, about U$S 1,300,000 of new machines that would be purchased in either East Germany or Czechoslovakia in accordance with specifications to be developed by the new company, and the remainder, approximately U$S 2,000,000, would be in tooling that IAME would build in its shops with designs to be furnished by us. The tooling referred to was for the Jeep and consisted of body and frame dies and machine shop tooling and fixtures for the new 4L-151 engine that we were developing in the Detroit Engine Division. All in all, a very productive four days in Córdoba. We now had the IAME investment pinned down and when I returned to the States I would get the Kaiser list finished.

Juan Martin Allende was from Córdoba and his parents and three of his brothers lived there. After our meeting with San Martin on Sunday we had the pleasure of having lunch at his parents' home and then flew back to Buenos Aires with the Air Minister in an Air Force DC3.

While we were in Córdoba, Edgar Kaiser and his wife Sue had gone to Brazil, had returned and were waiting for us at the Plaza Hotel. Also on hand were George Burpee and James Drumm, who had come from the States to attend the first meeting of the Commission that was scheduled for the next morning. After dinner that evening, whatever doubts I had as to my future were put to rest when Edgar asked me to come to his suite and in the presence of Mrs. Kaiser told me that if the project was a go he would name me as Director and General Manager of the new company. I was, of course, extremely pleased at this vote of confidence and I told Edgar that I was confident of the potential that IKA presented and would accept the assignment with enthusiasm. The next morning, before the first Commission meeting, Edgar told San Martin of my appointment and the Brigadier took me aside and gave me a big "abrazo" (hug) and assured me of his complete support. For the remainder of his tenure as Minister he took a personal interest in IKA's progress and was always available if I needed any help.

We weren't supported in all quarters though. Most of the Argentine engineers that I worked with in IAME had a lot of antipathy toward our program. While they supported the production of the Jeep utility vehicle line, they felt that the Kaiser passenger car was too big and heavy, the Continental 226 engine obsolete and that only new equipment should be imported. In the ideal sense they were correct on all counts. A lighter, more compact car would have been more in keeping with the Argentine requirement, there were more efficient power plants, and I would have been delighted to start up a new plant with state of the art equipment. But we couldn't afford the Utopian approach. The products, whether you liked them or not, were the only ones we had available, they would do the job, and the whole point of the story was the deployment of surplus machines and the development of automotive manufacturing in the country with the foreign exchange savings that would ensue to the benefit of everyone. Else there was no deal. And there were no other manufacturers willing to step forward and take the lead and risks involved in what would be the first venture of its kind in Latin America.

On Monday, October 11, the first meeting of the Mixed Valuation Commission took place in the Air Minister's office. Introductions were made all around and we were given the Valuation Instructions by Mr. Kaiser and the Brigadier in Spanish and English texts. The Commission then moved to the IAME offices were we had our first official meeting.

We reviewed the instructions and had a long discussion on the details of the Kaiser proposal wherein I answered a lot of questions put forth by the Argentine members. For their benefit as well as for Burpee and Drumm I described all of the background and planning for the venture. The conversations were all in English with Barcezat and Rubin translating once in a while for the benefit of Gaudioso, who was not completely fluent in English but understood practically everything. We came to the conclusion that the focal point of the survey and appraisal would be the Kaiser investment, since the IAME machines, together with the work that it would do in building dies and tooling, would be fairly straightforward from a valuation standpoint. A lot of time was spent discussing the phrase, "replacement value less wear and tear due to use." The Argentines, particularly Gaudioso and Rubin, accepted this concept very reluctantly. They, and Barcezat to a degree, argued that age was the all-important factor while my position, shared by Burpee and Drumm, was that a machine properly maintained could literally last forever. It was evident to me, however, that when this criterion was applied to the Kaiser passenger car dies and assembly tooling, valuations much greater than those we had proposed for investment credit would result. With the replacement value being the original cost, and since there was practically no wear and tear due to use, the valuation of the Kaiser assets under the formula would probably be double that which we had proposed. The Argentines, on the other hand, maintained that dies and tooling for a vehicle that had been discontinued were worth nothing more than scrap value. It was evident, notwithstanding the instructions that we had received, that we were starting our task with a wide disparity of opinions.

Due to my familiarity with the project I was asked by the other members to act as secretary and arrange for the inspection schedules and recording of the sessions. With the bulk of our work to be done in the States, it was decided that I should return immediately and prepare for the surveys there.

Back at the Engine Division on Wednesday, October 13th, I issued rather detailed instructions to Bill Heard for the Detroit and Dowagiac listings and to Homer Kelley in Toledo who was developing the listings for dies and assembly tooling. This was a very demanding job and it was lucky that we had started most of this work during the preparation of the definitive proposal. By working all out we finished the report, which was voluminous and which contained all of the valuation data as well as the location of each item, by late Sunday night for presentation to the Commission, scheduled to meet in my office at the Engine Division the next day, Monday, October 18.

To eliminate any potential language problem as well as provide accurate English and Spanish minutes of the proceedings, I arranged for the services of a translator, a Mr. F. J. Bakker, who was present at all of our meetings and surveys.

In the report prepared by Bill Heard and Homer Kelley, asset items were listed by the part manufactured and the operation performed. In addition to value, the estimated packaging cost and freight to New York were included in order to obtain the investment value of the item at the port of embarkation. The methodology used in determining 1954 replacement values varied greatly. In some cases we had to obtain statements from the original vendor. In others, especially tools and fixtures, we adjusted the original cost by applying known material and labor increases to bring the item up to its 1954 value. All purchase order records and other data used in arriving at valuations were made available to the Commission as well as photographs of typical machines and tooling.

The replacement value estimated for the Kaiser-furnished assets amounted to well over U$S 15 million. This figure included the U$S 3 million worth of machinery that Kaiser would be selling to the new company, and it didn't appear that we would have any serious disagreement on these latter items since they were all in excellent condition and the Commission could see them in operation at the Engine Division. The concentration of the Commission therefore would be on the items to be invested which, according to our study, had a replacement value at port of embarkation of approximately U$S 13 million. This compared to the U$S 10 million that we had shown as an investment value in the definitive proposal, the difference being in the deduction to be made for wear and tear due to use. Realistically, using the criteria, there was no logical way that the wear and tear concept would reduce the value by U$S 13 million since these items were practically new. But arbitrarily we made the reduction and it was our position that the 30% reduction was more than fair. However I found out that others could be arbitrary also — but before I disclose the final valuation that the Argentine members arrived at let's proceed with the surveys.

As scheduled, we had our first meeting in the Engine Division on Monday, October 18, and proceeded to analyze the report that had been prepared. Inspections were made of the items at the Engine Division, Willow-Run, the Dowagiac Foundry and several vendor plants. We spent well over a month on surveys interspersed with meetings wherein we attempted to finalize and come into agreement on each group of items as we inspected them. It became evident that the Argentines, particularly Gaudioso and Rubin, were not even close to the recommended investment values that we on the Kaiser side were proposing. The upshot of all this was that we agreed to disagree and submit two different opinions.

We completed our work in the U.S. by late November and the Argentine members returned home. In the opinion they submitted to Kaiser and IAME, a valuation was arrived at by using an arbitrary depreciation factor for body dies, fixtures and special tools that was based on year of manufacture and ranged from a depreciation of 60% on items purchased in 1946 to 35% for new items bought in 1954. This methodology bore no relationship to our instruction to base the depreciation on "wear and tear due to use." But this was their opinion and it had to be reckoned with. Using their formula, they came up with a recommended value for the Kaiser investment of U$S 4,588,000 — about a 45% reduction when compared to our proposed valuation. This was untenable and Edgar so informed San Martin.

In the various communications that went back and forth between the U.S. and Argentina, Cutler and Mario Bermudez in the main were in contact with Diaz Bialet who kept the Minister informed. Edgar was adamant. His position was that we had depreciated a realistic replacement value of U$S 13 million down to U$S 10 million — roughly 25% — compared to the completely unrealistic Argentine reduction of over 65%, and he refused to budge. There was a lot of talk that Jorge Antonio through Rubin had intentionally caused this impasse. I have no way of proving this. It's possible that Antonio may not have wanted the deal to go through but I doubt it. The project would have offered no competition to the Mercedes Truck plant and while the lucrative vehicle import permits for taxis and the like would probably be discontinued it didn't seem possible that he would attempt the complete disruption of the project if the President and the Air Minister supported it. One had to keep in mind that in the Agreement in Principle, the Mixed Valuation Commission was required to render an "opinion" only. It was to be left to the principals to arrive at the final arrangement. I really believe that Gaudioso and Rubin and, to a degree, Barcezat were just trying to cut a better deal for their government and believed very strongly in their position.

In any event, we were advised in early December that Brigadier Diaz-Bialet and Dr. Luis Pelliza would be coming to New York to discuss the situation. I wasn't present at any of these meetings which were handled by Edgar Kaiser, Cutler and Bermudez, but finally, on December 16, an accord was reached and a Memorandum of Agreement was signed by Edgar Kaiser for Kaiser Motors, Diaz-Bialet on behalf of IAME and Dr. Pelliza representing the Secretary of Economic Affairs. The document recited that the Valuation Commission had completed its review of the Kaiser assets but had not reached agreement and had advised Kaiser and IAME of their respective valuation opinions. The Commission was instructed to continue its work and complete the valuation of the IAME assets and submit a final report in which the reasons for any differences would be stated. The New York negotiation resulted in a final valuation of the Kaiser investment of U$S 8,250,550, kept the value of the machines and equipment to be sold to the new company at U$S 3,000,000, and set up a short list of machines, die models and a few miscellaneous items whose inclusion was to be reconsidered — we later eliminated them reducing the total valuation to a minor degree. The parties stated they would exert their best efforts to sign the Articles of Incorporation for the new company on January 15, 1955.

The New York agreement reduced the value of the Kaiser investment by roughly U$S 2,000,000 and I know that as a matter of principle the reduction was hard for Edgar to accept. On the other hand, there was a benefit for the new company. By keeping the total planned capitalization at m$n 360,000,000, the reduction that Kaiser agreed to in asset valuation would be replaced by cash. The share offering to the public would be increased by an amount equal to the reduction or m$n 28,000,000 and, knowing how tight our estimates were, I welcomed the change. The fact that our equity percentage would be reduced from 38% to about 32% didn't bother me at all. We were a minority shareholder and if we didn't do a good job managing the company, six percentage points wouldn't protect us. Further, there was no change in the valuation of the equipment that Kaiser would sell nor was the right to import and sell the 1000 Kaiser Manhattans affected. Both of these elements were very important to Kaiser Motors. Its pre-contract expenses had been very heavy and we could see some heavy expenses down the line in dismantling equipment and support activities until the new company could stand on its own feet. I don't believe the Argentines — particularly the Commission members — realized, and appreciated, how serious the Kaisers were and to what lengths they would go in assuring the project's success.

I spent the remainder of December in Detroit working on organizational planning, primarily that which had to do with the positions that would be filled by North American expatriates. Before leaving Argentina I had Bob Rice come down from Detroit to ferret out answers to questions I was sure would surface from time to time. To assist him I hired Herbert Spradling. Herb's father had run the Armco Steel Company's Argentine subsidiary and Herb had lived there most of his life and knew most of the North American subsidiary company managers. One of the problems we had to solve was the development of an overseas payroll policy that would apply to the expatriates we would be bringing down. Between the work done by Rice and Spradling in Argentina interviewing various companies and the work done by Ralph Peters, Industrial Relations Director at the Engine Division, we developed the policy which would enable us to move people as soon as the company was organized. The overseas personnel policy that we produced received a lot of scrutiny in Oakland, since Argentina would be the first foreign job for the Kaiser Company since Cuba in the twenties and whatever we did would set a future precedent.

The policy we came up with provided for a twenty percent overseas allowance on the base salary that the position qualified for in Detroit. The company calculated and assumed the responsibility for the payment of Argentine income taxes on behalf of the employee but deducted from the employee's gross salary an amount equal to the hypothetical U.S. income tax he would pay if he were living in the U.S. and receiving his base salary. In essence this gave the employee a net income increase of about twenty percent. He signed a two-year contract, and if it were renewed, the company paid transportation costs for him and his family for a one-month home leave in the U.S. Other benefits included free schooling in Argentina, the maintenance of the employee's Social Security payments in the U.S., and subsidized housing — the employee was responsible for paying up to 10% of his base salary for rent but above this, if it was absolutely necessary and with house selection subject to management approval, the company subsidized the differential. He was allowed to ship a pre-set weight of household goods, and the initial complement of expatriates were permitted to import a personal automobile.

The policy held up with a minimum of adjustments during the twelve-year period of Kaiser management and I think that most of the people thought it a fair plan. We brought an initial cadre of about 100 but after the first five years this had been cut by more than half. When we turned the reins over to Renault in 1967 there was a total of 20 North American expatriates, some of whom stayed on with Renault. This was a great team and their loyalty to IKA was outstanding. Even though we couldn't assure them a position back in the States when their tour of duty was over, it didn't seem to bother them — they had a job to do in IKA and they did it. The expatriated employee, in my opinion, sacrifices a lot going abroad for a few years, even though the experience he and his family get is irreplaceable. When he returns home he has lost some contacts, things are done differently, he has a new group of associates to work with and perhaps if he had stayed home he would have advanced more rapidly. This might be conjecture, though, since it seemed to me that when our expatriates returned home after a few years of experiencing the responsibilities we challenged them with and living abroad, they usually landed on their feet, ready for anything, and got back into the mainstream with little or no difficulty.

By the end of December, after getting all of the preliminary planning done that was possible, I turned my responsibilities at the Engine Division over to John Banks, who would have the thankless job of moving the equipment out and shutting the place down.

The six years I spent in Detroit had been quite an education. Manufacturing was a far cry from construction and shipbuilding. Working with the gang in the Engine Division had been a privilege and I left with a deep feeling of appreciation for all of them.

Chapter II | 1955

On January 1st, Bill Heard and I left on a Panagra flight out of Miami bound for Buenos Aires. We would be followed in a few days by some others since we had a long work list to get resolved prior to the final closing of the agreement with IAME and the incorporation of the new company, which had been scheduled for January 19th. One of the most pressing items was settling all of the details relative to the importation and distribution of the 1000 Kaiser Manhattans. This operation would most likely be the source of our first peso income.

The day after we arrived we met with the Tiphaine organization and determined the degree of disassembly that would be required to satisfy Argentine customs. Jose Monserrat, one of IAME's top engineers, was assigned to work on this program with us. Pete Mapes, who would become IKA's procurement director, and Carl Olson, its chief engineer, arrived a few days later and began work on the local procurement and engineering required. As soon as Mapes and Olson were functioning, Heard and I went to Córdoba to finalize the selection and listing of the IAME equipment investment for review by the Mixed Valuation Commission, Burpee and Drumm arrived along with the Argentine members and the Commission had its last meeting. We had no disagreements on the IAME equipment and jointly signed a report recommending acceptance by the principals. We all flew back to Buenos Aires in an Air Force Bristol cargo plane in time to meet Edgar Kaiser and Lloyd Cutler who had just arrived from the States.

The next big question that we had to get agreement on was the plant location. Normally this would be a management decision but it was such a sensitive matter that Edgar and San Martin felt it should be settled by mutual agreement and appointed Brigadier Diaz-Bialet and George Havas as a committee of two to formulate a final recommendation. The Brigadier and Havas were both in favor of Córdoba but agreed with me to explore alternate sites before finalizing their recommendation. While I was in Detroit in December, I had the Fantus Factory Locating Service — a firm specializing in demographic and market studies — do a quick analysis of the Argentine. The Fantus report concluded that the Buenos Aires metropolitan area would be the most desirable plant location for many reasons, including the proximity of the port through which practically all of our raw materials and imported parts would come. The vendor industry, for the most part, was located in the greater Buenos Aires area and we would be selling 50% or more of our production within a radius of 100 kilometers from the Federal Capital. I favored Buenos Aires for another reason — organization. General management, procurement, treasury, sales and service, government and public relations would have to be in Buenos Aires because of the proximity of Federal Government bureaucracy and the important part it would play in our daily life. With plant management in Córdoba the organization would be split.

I have always felt that the closer everyone in the organization is to the production center the more they are able to contribute to over-all efficiency. While I respected President Peron's decentralization policy, I also had to protect our competitive position. The Fantus study gave Rosario as second choice. With its extensive port facilities and the two steel plants, SOMISA and Acindar, close by, it could become a major industrial center and one that would attract supporting industries. I reviewed the Fantus study with everyone, including San Martin, Diaz-Bialet and Havas but, while they were interested, Córdoba was the only word in their lexicon.

Having struck out with the Fantus study, I tried another tack. General Motors had an assembly plant at Barracas in the port area of Buenos Aires and Fevre y Basset, the Chrysler distributor, had one in the San Justo suburb. Both were idle and either one could serve as our head office and final assembly point. The final assembly point is most important because this is where most of the problems with shortages show up. Under this scheme the power train manufacturing facilities would have been located in Córdoba and the press plant either at San Justo or close to Barracas. Edgar and I met with the General Motors manager, Walt de Schryver, and separately with Luis Fevre, president of Fevre y Basset. Both were interested in some sort of deal. General Motors would consider a sale of Barracas since it had ample space in the San Martin plant. Fevre had a problem since a sale of their only plant would put them out of the assembly business if and when they could start up again. Fevre expressed an interest in coming in with us and investing his plant in the new company. This could have been a good combination but there were some complications in the various ownership percentages within Fevre y Basset that would have to be negotiated out. In GM's case, the Barracas sale would have to go to Detroit for decision with the resulting delays, the length of which we had no way of estimating.

Taking everything into consideration, Edgar said to me, "Jim, Córdoba is it," and I finally had to capitulate. At least we had a decision although we still had to determine where in Córdoba we could locate. This chore was handed to me, and San Martin proffered his help in getting us located. We had included a stipulation in the Definitive Proposal that the government would furnish the land required free of charge but we were negotiated out of this along the way. Another job to get done and one that we would have to get on as soon as we got the company incorporated.

The other important decision we took prior to incorporation was the appointment of the auditor. The Price Waterhouse firm had the capacity to handle the magnitude of accounting work that IKA would be generating and was the firm we selected. Ed Fletcher, the senior partner, and David Gordon, who became the IKA *Sindico* — Auditor Trustee — gave us a lot of support during the ensuing years and were always available to advise, at times on questions far removed from those associated strictly with the Auditor's responsibilities.

The attorneys finally got all the paperwork put together and on January 18 in the Air Minister's office the founding partners, Kaiser and IAME, signed the Articles of Incorporation. It was just six months previous that we had met in H. J. Kaiser's office and for the first time discussed a possible Latin American venture, and here we were organizing a publicly owned Argentine corporation which would become the largest in the nation. The following day in President Peron's office the final contract was signed by Brigadier San Martin on behalf of IAME, Edgar Kaiser for the Kaiser group and myself as Director and General Manager of IKA. At the same meeting Presidential Decree 737, signed by President Peron and others, was issued approving the foreign investment to be made by Kaiser, the production program, plant location and other factors, and setting up the Ministries of Industry and Aviation as the monitoring authorities to verify that the facilities, parts integration and production were carried out in accordance with the contract.

The final contract essentially restated the October Agreement and fixed the initial authorized capital of IKA at m$n 360,000,000 with Kaiser subscribing approximately m$n 112,000,000, IAME m$n 80,000,000 and a public share offering for the balance or m$n 168,000,000. These numbers would change slightly as the various assets were integrated into IKA and their final valuations known. The Industrial Bank loan to be extended to IKA was set at m$n 200,000,000. The first Board of Directors was named and included Henry J. Kaiser as President, Edgar F. Kaiser as Vice President and myself as Director and General Manager. The Directors representing IAME were Santiago Diaz-Bialet and Carlos F. Mauriño.

In Argentina, titles and responsibilities are different from the U.S. The President is in actuality the President of the Board and the title of Vice President exists primarily to designate succession to the Presidency. There were no C.E.O. (Chief Executive Officer) or C.O.O. (Chief Operating Officer) titles nor were there any divisional Vice Presidents. Operations were carried out by the General Manager directly with managers of the various divisions, in accordance with policies emanating from the Board or by Board approval of the Manager's recommendations. The first Board only reflected representation of Kaiser and IAME interests since there were no public shareholders as yet. Edgar told me his father wouldn't remain President very long. In fact, Henry never returned to Argentina after the October 1954 meetings, although he continued to monitor IKA progress from Oakland and Hawaii until his death in 1967. Edgar also told me that he thought that someone who was a prestigious figure, possibly an outstanding Argentine businessman, should be named as President eventually. This question would answer itself, I was sure, and we had so much to do that the identity of IKA's future President was way down on my "need to know" priorities.

We set up a temporary office in the Plaza Hotel and Allende arranged for the loan of a secretary, Suzanna Barbat, to help out. Dan Kelly, one of our first hires, became my personal secretary. Dan was later supplemented by Jackie Grant and the two of them very capably handled my outside office throughout my years with IKA.

Pete Mapes concentrated on finding office space that would handle the entire IKA Buenos Aires organization once it was in place. This took some time but he eventually located, with the help of Sr. Giudice, a realtor, a building at Paseo Colon 439 that was undergoing remodeling. We started moving in during February on the heels of the craftsmen doing the remodeling work. Meanwhile I had moved our crew from the Plaza Hotel, which was terribly expensive, into the City Hotel. It also had the advantage of being within a short walk to the Paseo Colón office.

The most pressing problem we had, though, was finding a plant location in Córdoba. Bill Heard, Juan Martin Allende and I went there in January to inspect potential plant sites in Barrio Flores, Bella Vista and Villa Revol. Ferro Sessarego and Jose Monserrat — Jose had become our principal liaison with IAME — had located the prospective sites and accompanied us on our inspection. As with all prospective sites, each had its shortcomings — worker accessibility, waste disposal, lack of power, entry roads — all in varying degrees. The next day we met with San Martin in his Córdoba office and stated our preference for Barrio Flores with Bella Vista second. We all felt that we should keep looking because there had to be something better. About two weeks later San Martin advised us of an offer he had received from Sr. Rogelio Nores Martinez to donate 30 hectares of land in Barrio Santa Isabel, located a few kilometers south of the city and adjacent to the paved highway that connects Córdoba with the town of Alta Gracia. The Nores Martinez family had extensive land holdings in the area and felt that with the IKA development, their surrounding property would surely improve in value.

Edgar had just returned to Buenos Aires, this time in the company airplane — a Lockheed Lodestar called the "Halcyone" — and we flew in it to Córdoba to meet Nores Martinez. Mike Miller, George Havas, Juan Martin and Jack Hughes, who was to head up Kaiser Engineers' construction forces, were along also. After looking the property over it became apparent that this, by far, was the best site we had seen. I thought we should have more than just 30 hectares so as to allow for future expansion, and we finalized a deal with Nores Martinez that provided for a donation of 30 hectares and a purchase of 45. A couple of years later we had an opportunity to acquire more adjoining land and I authorized its purchase, thus increasing IKA's total property to 225 hectares — about 550 acres.

The following Monday, February 14, we met with President Peron, San Martin and Gomez Morales to report on progress since the organization of the company. In addition to George Havas and myself, Edgar brought Vince Rodriguez along. Vince was Cuban by birth and an attorney with Sullivan and Cromwell in New York. He was extremely helpful and worked with us during the first month or so of IKA's existence.

The President received us very warmly and was pleased with the progress we had made in getting the plant site pinned down. He stated that the National Railroads would build the three kilometers of spur line into the plant site and that EPEC — the Córdoba Provincial Power Authority — would provide the electrical requirements. This was a big assist since our energy load would be substantial and we had been worrying that we might have to provide our own power, which would have required a substantial investment. We were also told in the meeting that the IKA public share offering could proceed without the one year waiting period normally required of newly formed companies. This was also welcome news because cash availability would be the real pacesetter for our progress. This was a very productive meeting and one that demonstrated the personal interest that the President and San Martin were taking in the project.

During the early days of IKA our biggest problem was to get enough cash flowing in order to hire staff, start design and engineering and get moving with the construction. If the Kaisers had not supported us with substantial advances we never would have made it. Gradually peso income started coming in with the sale of the imported Kaiser Manhattans and on April 1st another milestone was reached when IMIM (Instituto Mixto de Inversiones Mobiliarias) released the IKA public share issue of m$n 164,934,100. The revenue was assured since the issue was underwritten by IMIM but our advisors were also confident that the issue would be sold. None of us was prepared, however, for the public support that was manifested. I was in the IMIM building the day the share offering was released to the public and when the doors were opened, crowds of people started streaming in. I stood on a balcony overlooking the main hall and watched the people below filling out the subscription application forms. In a matter of a few hours the issue had been over-subscribed and the taking of applications stopped. At that point there had been well over m$n 200,000,000 subscribed and a pro-ration would have to be made. IMIM favored the small shareholder and no pro-ration was made for share subscriptions in amounts up to 300 shares or m$n 30,000. The initial organization started to take shape. Joe Reis, Chief Financial Officer for the Kaiser organization, sent "Spike" Massaglia down to become IKA's first Controller. Joe came a little later when we were moved into the Paseo Colón offices and helped Spike get the accounting procedures established under the watchful eye of Price-Waterhouse, our auditors. Reis was also instrumental, along with Lloyd Cutler, in recruiting Dr. Jorge Hayzus for the position of Treasurer. Jorge, or George, as everyone called him, was a graduate not only of the Buenos Aires Law Faculty but of Yale Law School as well. Cutler, who was also a Yale Law graduate, probably located Hayzus through the alumni network in Buenos Aires. Hayzus strengthened IKA's management and we were indeed fortunate that he joined us.

Ken Flood, whom I appointed Plant Manager, had been my immediate superior during the Shipyard days and also at the Engine Division until he left to take on the Tinkertoy project in Arlington,

Virginia. While I was in the States with the Valuation Commission I maintained contact with Flood by phone and kept him up to date on what I was doing. He indicated a lot of interest and as he was finishing the Tinkertoy contract, I asked him if he would like to join the team and he accepted. As Plant Manager reporting to me our normal roles were reversed but Ken, great person that he was, never had a problem with this and did a fine job in Córdoba.

IKA's first Sales Manager was Larry Daniels. Larry had lived in Argentina for years. He first came to Argentina with the U.S. State Department, then went to work for General Motors Argentina in sales. After some years with GM he became a partner in Bosch Motors, one of GM's principal dealers in Buenos Aires. We needed someone well trained in sales and distribution, with a good knowledge of the various dealer organizations countrywide. Larry qualified on all counts. Bosch Motors had no new car business due to import restrictions and it was convenient for Larry to take a leave of absence. I made a deal with Larry — although no contract was signed — whereby he would get the IKA Sales Division organized and the initial and most important dealer appointments made and when IKA's production got underway, Bosch Motors would be considered for an IKA dealership. At that point Larry would return to his own company.

Eduardo Juan Jones, whom everyone called "Jack," ex-RAF and an Argentine of British descent, hired on as Personnel Manager. He was assisted by Anita Crinigan, an Argentine of Irish descent. But I must say that the two got along together very well. Their department not only satisfied the manpower needs of the various departments but also handled the many details associated with the incoming expatriate families.

Pete Mapes and Jules Lussier, along with the early local hires, Claude Deschamps, Mike Harris-Smith and Mike Crawley, began sourcing vendors and preparing for the customs clearance of the vehicles, machinery and equipment, and component parts that would soon be arriving from abroad.

With the initial nucleus of IKA management in place and with the move into Paseo Colón, it wasn't long before we started functioning as an organization.

Ken Flood and Bill Heard set up the manufacturing group on one of the floors in Paseo Colón and began detailed layouts of the engine, assembly and press plants along with ancillary facilities such as cut and sew, maintenance, tool room and cutter grind. The production team worked side by side with the Kaiser Engineers plant design group that Jack Hughes organized along with Bill Ball and Bob Hammersmith. George Schumann was Chief Design Engineer and Wright Price was Construction Manager. About this time Natalio Lucioni joined KE and played an important role in construction. After KE completed its assignment, Lucioni became IKA's Construction Chief Engineer and handled all of our expansions. We originally retained the Dodd's architectural firm to advise on local code and ordinance restrictions and to check and stamp all design work for submittal to the various authorities as required. Later, Architect Nicolas Emaides joined Lucioni's team and we handled our own building permits.

As areas were released by the manufacturing groups, KE would design the building and facilities to suit the production requirements. Some of the production facilities, such as the paint system, material handling conveyors, bridge cranes, vehicle conveyors and the like, which were readily available in the U.S. as "off the shelf" items, had to be designed and built from scratch. We had neither the time, money nor import permits required to buy these items in the States and bring them in. If it had been possible we would have imported all the mechanical gear for the paint system. But we couldn't and we suffered with the marginal quality of our homemade one for years. In reviewing the various design criteria produced by Kaiser Engineers, there were three areas that I took a personal interest in. In the engine plant and machine shop areas, I specified that the floor be at least 12 inches of heavily reinforced concrete. This requirement was a result of my Detroit Engine Division experience. There, because of a fairly light concrete floor, whenever we had to change machine locations, each move usually required the pouring of a special foundation with the resultant delay and disruption of production.

With the 12-inch floor we could reset production lines, moving virtually any machine at will without worrying about tearing up the plant. The extra initial cost would be saved many times down the line by having this flexibility. Also, to promote even greater flexibility, I requested a basic truss design that would allow the widest column spacing possible, within the limits of practicality. The third area that I was specifically interested in was the press plant. There, instead of unitized foundations for each press, which was the normal way, I had the engineers design a pitlike structure for each of the press lines that supported movable beams on which the presses were erected. This would permit changing press spacing and allow the insertion of additional presses in the future as vehicle models changed and required different stamping sequences.

Working under budgetary constraints as we were, anything that was an additional cost was difficult to approve but we knew that future flexibility was worth money also. One of the cost cutting measures we did take was the elimination of an administration building at the plant. The original KE layout called for this building to be erected in front of the assembly plant. I have always felt that plant management should be strategically located within the plant. All this administrative building would do, in my opinion, was encourage more overhead. And Flood agreed with me. So we took one bay out of the assembly plant and turned it into offices for management and administration, and located line supervision, Plant and Works Engineering in various areas throughout the plant.

In just a little over a month after Kaiser Engineers had moved in, bid packages were developed and we began requesting competitive proposals from local contractors. Wright Price, Construction Manager, had moved to Córdoba and set up a temporary office in the Bristol Hotel. I believe that Barsanti Brothers was the first major contractor we had — and probably the biggest. At least there is a photo of Wright Price and Señor Barsanti breaking a bottle of wine over a bulldozer blade, dated March 12, 1955, which must have marked the start of construction. Just a few days before, we had completed the transfer of property from Rogelio Nares Martinez.

Wright Price, who soon got the nickname "Correcto Precio," erected some temporary construction offices which allowed Ken

Flood, and the part of his organization which wasn't required to support Kaiser Engineers in Buenos Aires, to move to the jobsite and provide the owner representation needed by the construction forces. Ken also had to establish relationships with the provincial and municipal authorities, the power company, IAME and lay plans for the installation of the hundreds of tons of equipment that would soon be arriving. Ken had no Spanish then and he never really became proficient in the language. But his personality was such that he didn't need it. One of our first Córdoba hires, Luis Melnick, who was bilingual, was his staff assistant and, under Flood's guidance, did a fine job in the early days, handling a lot of these details. The work that IAME was doing on the tooling for the 4-cylinder engine and the Jeep dies and assembly fixtures also required a lot of supervision and technical information and was supplied from Flood's Córdoba organization.

Back at the Detroit Engine Division, John Banks had taken over and was arranging for the export packaging and shipping of all the Kaiser invested equipment. It was important that the prioritizing and scheduling of the items match our installation schedules as well as the sailing dates of the Argentine State Line vessels. We had agreed, in our contract, to ship via the State Line which, not having frequent sailings, made it doubly important that the export packaging be carefully planned and coordinated. There were thousands of tons of machinery of all sizes, shapes and descriptions that had to be gathered up from any number of locations in the U.S. In the case of the Shadyside presses, it was a major disassembly project to get the presses broken down into components that could be freighted.

For the most part, the export packaging was done by Morelli Bros. in New Jersey and loaded out there. Some shipments went out of New Orleans, but the New York area was favored because of more frequent sailings and the fact that New Orleans is actually a greater distance to Buenos Aires. Customs clearances in Buenos Aires were processed expeditiously by Colin Campbell, our customs broker. The whole process was helped, no doubt, by the distinction of IKA as a project in the national interest. The Procurement Division under Mapes had the prime responsibility for all traffic movement, and Traffic Manager Mike Crawley had his hands full. In some instances where heavy lifts were involved, we had to unload in San Nicolás which had cranes available. The move of the equipment to Córdoba was fairly straightforward but in a few cases some of the bridges enroute had to be temporarily reinforced.

The 1000 Kaiser cars were also arriving and Larry Daniels set up his initial organization to handle their distribution. Jose Massana in Sales and Bruno Ossowski in Service were early entries along with Bill Sussex, Joe Noonan, Clemente Nowakowski and Esteban Retali. It would have been easy to merely turn the whole job over to Tiphaine y Cia., the Kaiser-Willys distributor, but we wanted to start developing a dealer organization. In addition to getting a rather generous allocation of cars to retail, the Tiphaine organization handled the installation of the Argentine manufactured components and delivered the vehicles to the rest of the dealer body.

We had to manage the operation very carefully. The cars were sold to persons who had received a purchase certificate from the government at the predetermined price of m$n 92,500 — approximately U$S 6500. In the open market the cars would be worth much more than this, so the distribution of the certificates really amounted to political patronage. In many cases the holder of the certificate didn't need, or want, a car and would try to sell the certificate. But we insisted that the original holder had to be the buyer and initial registrant. Afterwards, if he wanted to sell the unit, that was his business. As one can surmise, in an operation of this sort all kinds of side deals could take place which were impossible for us to police. Although the price and delivery parameters were laid down by the authorities, we still had a lot of people clamoring for cars and a lot of questions to answer.

In the long run, the income from the imports is probably what saved IKA. I don't have the exact figures but we probably cleared about U$S 2500 per car after preparation costs, dealer discounts and original cost — say about m$n 35,000,000 in the whole operation. Although not a large amount of money in the overall scheme of things, it was stopgap support that allowed us to get started. If we hadn't been as far along as we were when the

Peron government was overturned, it is possible that IKA would have ceased to exist. Of the other two sources of cash that we had planned on during the pre-production period, the sale of stock was the only one that came through on schedule. The development loan from the Banco Industrial, a Government obligation in the contract, experienced one delay after another and placed IKA in a very delicate cash position in late 1955.

In December we had to stop all payments to contractors in order to make payroll and I called an emergency meeting of the Board to consider declaring bankruptcy. It was then we began to see some action and in January 1956 we started receiving advances from the Bank that were documented by partial chattel-mortgages on IKA's machinery and dies. The 200 million peso 10 year loan was disbursed almost entirely in this manner with each advance in the order of five million pesos each and issued by the Banco Industrial principally during the year 1956. As the advances were on account of the global loan, they carried no maturity and although IKA was not called upon to repay them since they were on account, there were times when the Banco Industrial money, in George Hayzus' words, seemed "too little and too late." I must reiterate, though, the serious cash problem we were faced with in 1955, during the plant construction period, and the fact that we were so close to bankruptcy that even today I wonder how we managed to survive.

On the heels of the successful stock issue, there was another event in April that could have, for better or worse, dramatically changed IKA's future. I received a call from Edgar Kaiser to tell me that he and Mrs. Kaiser were coming to Buenos Aires and were bringing General and Mrs. Matthew B. Ridgway with them. Edgar told me he was trying to interest the General in moving to Argentina and assuming the Presidency of IKA. I never did find out where the inspiration for this idea came from but Edgar had a lot of Washington connections. More than likely Chad Calhoun or Lloyd Cutler had gotten Edgar interested in Ridgway and had convinced him of the feasibility of the idea. There were a lot of intriguing possibilities that might have emanated with the General in Argentina. Not only would IKA's prestige have been enhanced, but the Peron government, at least extra-officially, might have improved its relations measurably with the U.S. A General Peron talking to a General Ridgway might open up a much broader horizon for the Kaiser interests because there were, and are, many other opportunities in Argentina besides just building automobiles.

This was the first time that I was aware of the Kaiser organization's even considering "going outside" to fill a top level position. But Argentina differed from the normal run of things and Edgar was determined that IKA would be a success.

The Kaisers and the Ridgways arrived in Buenos Aires about the middle of April. The General was then 60 years old and looked like he was good for another 60. He had just retired as Supreme Commander of the North Atlantic Pact Forces, a position to which he was appointed when General Eisenhower resigned to run for the Presidency of the United States. Prior to NATO, General Ridgway was Commander, United Nations forces in Korea.

The itinerary for the Ridgways included a couple of receptions, meetings with the IKA organization, such as it was at the time, and meetings with President Peron, Brigadier San Martin and other public figures. Peron manifested a real warmth in the meeting with Ridgway and the two conversed at length, through interpreters, about Argentina's need to conserve foreign exchange and provide work opportunities for its people through industrialization. All in all a very successful meeting. I conducted an intensive briefing in my office for the General and reviewed construction progress, organization, production planning and financial projections. Although he was very interested and asked a lot of questions, it was evident that this was far from the type of subject matter he would normally be addressing.

The Kaisers and the Ridgways returned to the States and I followed in a few days to attend a conference in Washington that Henry J. Kaiser, Jr. had organized, where managers from all the Kaiser subsidiary and affiliated companies gathered to spend a couple of days discussing plans and current events affecting the various businesses, and listening to speeches on business and governmental trends. At the closing banquet held in the Shoreham

Hotel, Gus, who was still in Detroit, flew down to join me. We sat with the Ridgways and this was the last opportunity I ever had to be with him. The General was a real motivator and I'm sure that working for him would have been a worthwhile experience.

During the campaign to recruit the General I had found it hard to believe that he would move to Argentina and assume the Presidency of IKA. I don't want to belittle IKA but here was a world famous figure, still in the limelight, only 60 years old. As a civilian he was receiving a myriad of offers, any one of which probably contained responsibility and opportunity levels much greater and less risky than what IKA offered, and all of which would keep him on the U.S. scene. Leaving everything and moving to Argentina would remove him from the center stage. So when Edgar called a few days after the Washington Conference to tell me the General had decided against the offer, I was disappointed but not surprised.

It was now June and I had been in Argentina continuously since January with the exception of a few quick trips to the U.S. Gus and Kim, my oldest son, then seven years old, had made a trip to Buenos Aires in March with Mrs. Edgar Kaiser and two of her sons, Henry and her youngest son who was also named Kim. Even with my visits to the States and Gus's to Argentina, I had seen little of the family and missed them tremendously. In retrospect, it was a mistake not moving the family to Argentina when IKA was incorporated in January. Despite the uncertainties and problems surrounding IKA, it would have been better for the family as a whole to experience the challenges of the new venture. Anyway, in mid-June, when the school year in the U.S. ended, I returned to Detroit, arranged for the shipment of my household goods and left the sale of my home in the able hands of Ralph Peters, the Director of Industrial Relations at the Engine Division. Ralph had been a good friend and colleague during my six years in Detroit.

Gus, Kim, Kelly, then two, and Mark, one, and I took off from Detroit for Miami and Buenos Aires on June 16. When we landed in Lima the next morning we were informed that Argentina was closed to all incoming traffic because a revolution was taking place. This was the aborted June 1955 revolution. We were advised either to return to the United States or remain in Lima until matters cleared up in Buenos Aires.

I opted for the latter and we went to the San Ysidro Country Club in the Lima suburbs. Needless to say this had a profound effect on Gus and the boys and even I began to wonder what we might be getting into. After we got to the Club and read some newspapers, we learned that a group of rebel pilots from the Argentine Naval Air Force had attempted to bomb the Casa Rosada (Government House). According to the news accounts there was a lot of street fighting and everything was out of control. We spent the weekend in Lima when Buenos Aires finally opened up and were able to take off on Monday, June 20th.

We landed at Ezeiza that afternoon and after we disembarked and went into the station I saw Ken Flood and others of the organization waiting for me outside the Customs Area. I wondered, at the time, why the welcoming party. As soon as we cleared customs and I met Flood I could tell from his face that something was wrong. He proceeded to tell me that Graham Tune, one of our expatriate engineers from the Detroit Engine Division, had been killed during an aerial bombardment directed at the Casa Rosada on June 16 by the Naval Air Force. Our office was within a block or so of the Casa Rosada and Graham was returning to work from lunch when he was accidentally killed. Graham and I had worked together at the Engine division and I knew him very well. Not only was he an important asset to IKA as its Chief Industrial Engineer, but he was a conscientious and personable individual respected by all who worked with him. When I was transferred from the Shipyards to the Engine Division, I first worked in the Industrial Engineering Department and Graham helped indoctrinate me into the automobile business. It was a terrible blow to Mrs. Tune, who was still in the U.S. and was scheduled to leave for Argentina in just a few days.

When something like this happens all one can do is do the best one can. We had a funeral mass for Graham which was attended by everyone in IKA at the time. Bob Scheuerle accompanied the remains to the States and did all he could to comfort and assist Graham's family. The incident had a marked effect on the IKA organization and brought Argentina's political unrest very close to home. But we had a job to do and got on with it.

At the end of June, IKA completed its first fiscal year, which was a partial one of six months duration. We had about 200 people on the payroll and 600 more working on construction which was starting to take on momentum in Córdoba. I had my family settled in a home we rented, was learning how to drive in Buenos Aires traffic and was making some progress with my Spanish. Machines and equipment were arriving in the port, being cleared through customs and transported to Córdoba. As soon as there was a section of roof up that could provide some protection for operators and equipment, machines were installed and temporary power hookups made. Within six months after groundbreaking there was a sizable machine shop in operation, which together with the shop at IAME was producing the special tooling for the 4-cylinder engine and the Jeep, using tool designs produced in our Buenos Aires office.

IKA's activities for the remainder of 1955 and well into 1956 were dominated, in the main, by the changes that took place following the revolution that finally ousted Peron in September.

During the latter part of August, rumors had been circulating that President Peron had resigned. A climax was reached on August 31 when mobs gathered in Plaza de Mayo and all businesses in the downtown area were advised to send their employees home. Conditions remained unsettled for the next two weeks. Edgar, who was at heart a trouble-shooter, decided to come down to personally investigate the situation and try to get our loan formalization moving in the Industrial Bank. He, Lloyd Cutler and Mike Miller arrived Tuesday evening, September 13.

Edgar couldn't have chosen a worse time to come. Martial law had been invoked and he was like a caged lion. Edgar Kaiser was one of the most humane persons I have ever known but when things weren't going the way he wanted them to he wasn't a pleasant fellow to be around. With martial law in effect, all business activity had stopped and the streets were practically vacant. I was home monitoring the radio on a Saturday morning with Mike Lawrence translating for me when Edgar called and wanted to know why I wasn't at work. He had strolled out of the Plaza Hotel, looked around and saw what he considered to be a completely pacific situation. What Edgar told me and what I had been hearing on the radio were two different portrayals, but rather than argue — you would always lose with Edgar anyway — I told him I would be at the office as soon as I could get there. About two hours later, after maneuvering around the Army barricades situated at the main approaches to the Federal Capital, I finally arrived at the office where Kaiser, Miller and Cutler were waiting for me. The streets were all quiet — hardly any traffic or pedestrians. We were the only ones in the building with the exception of Jack Jones and two or three of his people in the Personnel Department who were manning telephones and answering queries from employees.

We were well into our review meeting when bombs started exploding in the port area, just a few blocks from the office. At that point Jack Jones came into the office and in no uncertain terms told Edgar he had to leave. And we left immediately without any argument on Edgar's part. I put the three of them in my car; by this time the Plaza Hotel area was closed off and again, with much maneuvering on side streets to avoid the barricades, I finally got them to my home in San Isidro where they spent the night.

At home things were further complicated with my son Kim down with the mumps. At last, on Sunday evening, there was an announcement on the radio that the government had capitulated to rebel army forces in Córdoba under the command of General Lonardi. The rebel Navy forces, led by Admiral Isaac Rojas, had ships stationed in the River Plate with guns trained on Government House. On Monday I was able to get Edgar and the others back to the Plaza Hotel and then to the office. All the shops were still closed but there were crowds in the streets celebrating the rebel victory. It wasn't until the following Friday, September 23, when General Lonardi was sworn in as provisional president, that the country began to normalize and in a day or so we were all back at work.

Finally we were able to get a call through to the Córdoba office. Flood reported that while there had been a lot of troop movements in the area, the only noteworthy event affecting IKA had been the confiscation of most of the plant fleet of Jeeps and pickup trucks by the Lonardi forces. They were returned later, some of them a little beat up. Everything was back to normal and the construction workers were back on the job.

IKA's situation in Buenos Aires, though, was far from normal as the new government swung into action. On the Monday following the Lonardi take-over, IKA's shares were suspended from trading on the exchange. Having been organized during the Peron regime, IKA was suspect and the new government tried to ferret out proof of any acts of collusion, bribery or misrepresentation in the organizing of the company. Our relations with shareholders fell to a low ebb since we had no way of knowing when trading would resume. George Hayzus had his hands full trying to answer the many questions from individual shareholders.

Immediately following the Lonardi appointment, we had a meeting with Brigadier Abrahim who had been named to replace San Martin as Air Minister. He assigned Brigadier Pedro Rosas Dominguez to replace Diaz-Bialet as our contact with the Air Force and IAME and I spent a lot of time with Rosas Dominguez tracing IKA's history and getting him up to date on our immediate priorities. The last time I saw Santiago Diaz-Bialet was when he came into my office a few days later dressed in civilian clothes to tell me that he was going into exile. He was very upset and felt that he was in immediate danger.

On the Thursday following the transfer of power, Edgar had an audience with Lonardi that I attended together with Allende, Hayzus, Cutler, Miller and Jack Hughes. This most likely was Lonardi's first meeting with someone from the foreign business community, and he stated that his government would respect any and all commitments made by the previous one and he recommended that we carry on. Needless to say, our spirits coming out of the meeting were better than they were going in.

Around the first of October, Manuel Ordoñez joined IKA as manager of public relations, but quickly assumed much more responsibility than this job alone entailed. He, together with Allende and Hayzus, became my prime advisors on matters to do with the administration of the business and with community and governmental relations. The four of us, as an unofficial committee, bore the load of the endless contacts we had to make with the new authorities as well as the preparation of answers to questions that were being asked as the investigation of IKA by the Ministry of Economic affairs proceeded. A voluminous report was prepared at the request of Dr. Raul Prebisch, one of Latin America's leading economists, and an advisor to the new government. There was a new set of authorities in the Industrial Bank that we had to work with for our loan formalization and this required documentary evidence of construction progress and machine and equipment import validation. Ernesto Gaudioso, a member of the Valuation Commission who was on the staff of the Industrial Bank and knew more about IKA than anyone there, became one of our main proponents in trying to resolve the matter. There also was the question of the Kaiser second investment. I had located several precision machines in the Engine Division's tool room that were going to be sold and was able to persuade Edgar to make them a second Kaiser investment in IKA. They were valued at about one million dollars, and we proposed to IAME that their final valuation be made by the Valuation Commission after we had delivered them to the Córdoba plant. This was a demonstration of faith that I believe impressed the authorities.

On October 31, we had our first annual shareholder's meeting. The principal item on the agenda was the election of nine directors. Henry J. Kaiser was re-elected as President, Edgar as Vice President and myself as Director-General Manager. The new Directors were Juan Martin Allende, Jorge Hayzus, Alberto de Ridder, the principal owner of Tiphaine y Cia., Angel Miguel, a nominee of the Air Force, Brigadier Mayor Pedro Rosas Dominguez and Comodoro Medardo Gallardo Valdes. Medardo Gallardo had to resign from the Board in December when he was appointed Interventor of the Province of Córdoba by the new government. As Interventor — Governor of the Province in actuality — he continued to take a great interest in IKA's progress and helped us in solving problems that cropped up from time to time with the provincial authorities.

The other item of importance on the agenda for shareholder approval was our proposal to set up a stock bonus plan, similar to the one we had in the Kaiser companies, as an incentive for managerial personnel. More than likely stock bonus plans existed in other Argentine companies, but I don't believe they had as broad a range of management participants as ours proposed. The plan was well accepted by our people but through the years it never resulted in the remuneration we had hoped for due to the dilution in share value brought about by inflation and the resultant dilution of the value of the Argentine peso. But at least our people knew we were thinking about them.

On the production side, it was becoming apparent to Pete Mapes and his procurement organization that the primary items that were going to give us problems in achieving our local integration goals were castings, forgings, transmissions and differential axle assemblies. The final resolution of the problem was a long way off but we had to start studying what alternative we did have. It was in the final months of 1955 that we began seriously considering setting up a gear division within IKA that would produce all our transmission, transfer case and differential axle requirements. Two events took place in late October and November that defined the course we would follow.

Joe Reis felt that IKA should have a direct relationship with U.S. banks and he and Henry Drath, vice president and head of the Bank of America's Latin American division, made a trip to Argentina in late October. His visit and our initial discussions led to an agreement wherein the Bank of America backed up IKA's program of deferred payment on imports of parts and supplies by extending letter of credit facilities to the Banco Industrial which enabled Kaiser Motors to collect 100% of the FOB value upon shipment. The Bank of America-Banco Industrial financing of parts and supplies became the major source of working capital for IKA during the early years of production. The Reis visit also led to IKA's first direct line of credit, from the Eximbank, for U$S 1,000,000 of Gleason Hypoid Gear Generators that were required for differential axle production. This was the first of several direct loans that IKA received from banks in the U.S. and Europe for the various expansions it undertook. All of our loan agreements were direct with IKA and in no case did we ever have a back-up guarantee by Kaiser in the U.S.

The second event that focused us on gear making occurred when José Monserrat called our attention to a company called Vianini Argentina, SRL. This company had been working out a contract with IAME to set up a gear-making company before the revolution, and now found itself with a sizable quantity of imported gear-making equipment in the port but no plant to put it in or capital to start up with. Negotiations with Sr. Vianini took quite some time but in the end — as we will see later — were fruitful.

As 1955 wore on we continued bringing North American supervisory and technical personnel to Córdoba as fast as our construction of facilities became available to work in. As the families moved in we began accumulating a sizable population of boys and girls of all ages. It soon became apparent that we would have to do something about their education since there were no bilingual schools in the Córdoba suburbs where our people were settling in. Schooling was an item completely overlooked in all of our planning and plant location studies. The North Americans in Buenos Aires could attend the American Community School there, which offered both Argentine and U.S. curricula in both primary and secondary grades, and there were other excellent bilingual schools as well. We had provided the families that went to Córdoba with the Calvert System of Extension Studies, an excellent course of instruction that can be administered at home to children living in remote areas where no school facilities are available. This was not a long term solution however. Another facet of the problem was the Argentine requirement that primary school aged children residing in the country had to study the Argentine curriculum. This was mandatory whether or not the curricula of other nationalities were studied concurrently.

The only solution was to organize our own school. We bought a large old mansion, vacant for some time and pretty run down, in the Argüello suburb. It was located on a large piece of property that would allow for outside sports activities and future classroom expansion. Our personnel department located a retired British headmaster, Mr. Chivers, living in the Sierras de Córdoba. I made an appointment and drove up to see him. He was a wonderful person and I liked him immediately.

After a little discussion it was apparent to me that Chivers had the qualifications to direct our school. As I recall, he was also a mathematician. Chivers was interested in the position but indicated that he didn't want to stay active too long. He would help get us organized and would direct activities for at least the first school year. Following this initial contact we visited the old mansion together and, with some of our construction people, decided on the renovations necessary to provide for classrooms, administrative offices, locker rooms and the like. This was in November; by the start of the school year in March, 1956, Chivers had a faculty organized and a bilingual curriculum in place.

We also opened the school to the local community and had an initial enrollment of around 100 students. Down through the IKA years the school was expanded to triple its original size with the addition of classrooms, a library and additional playground facilities. A new library building, beautifully conceived by Nicolas Emaides, IKA's architect, incorporated many features I had noted in the Webb School of California, which my sons attended before going to college.

In early 1958, with the help of the Interamerican School Service, located in Washington, DC, Paul Becker was recruited to replace Chivers and remained as headmaster for the entire span of our management of IKA. Paul also played an important role in setting up and administering our other educational activities in the plant, such as the supervisory training courses and the IKA Technical Institute, of which more later.

Argüello Academy grew from its initial enrollment of about 100 to over 400. The majority of the students were Argentine with about 100 or so representing other nationalities, including the North American. It had a kindergarten, primary and secondary schools that followed both the Argentine and U.S. curricula. The secondary school was accredited by the University of Nebraska, enabling graduates to qualify for admission to U.S. universities. In parallel bilingual educational programs like Argüello's, students not only learn another language but get a profound understanding of two cultures. In the morning, in Spanish, they study the history of Bolivar and San Martin — in the afternoon, in English,

George Washington. In effect they go to school twice in subjects such as mathematics. The Academy always had more applicants for admission than it could accept. Although tuition was charged, it still needed some subsidization from IKA, but it was worth it.

On November 13, a little over a month after he had taken office, General Lonardi resigned and General Pedro Aramburu was appointed President by the Military Junta. Admiral Rojas remained as Vice President.

Dr. Julio Alizon García was named Economics Minister and IKA was high on his action list. We met with him soon after his appointment and he told us that he was setting up a special commission to analyze the IKA program from both the technical and economic points of view. He also stated that he had asked Ing° Bruzzone, a private Argentine industrialist, to be the chairman of the commission. I got the impression that Alizon García was somewhat dubious of our ability to carry out our contractual commitment and felt that an investigation might disclose good reasons for the cancellation of our contract. His attitude certainly didn't appear to be supportive and the role of the commission, as far as I was concerned, was more to engage in a witch hunt than anything else.

We had to continually provoke questions from the Bruzzone Commission and when we did get them, in typical Kaiser style we overwhelmed the Commission with volumes of material which was too much for it to digest. We were somewhat at a standstill, and I suggested to Allende that he try to arrange a meeting with the full Commission and have an open dialogue on IKA. In preparation for the meeting we designed a series of large charts that graphically portrayed the salient points of our program. Duane Gowland, one of Olson's engineering team who was good at chart work, helped me set it up. With Allende translating (he did more than that since he knew the subject matter as well as I did) I made the presentation to the full Commission. There were a lot of questions, a thorough discussion of the manufacturing processes we were installing, our forecast of exchange savings, Argentina's transportation requirements and the unit costs we projected. This was our only meeting with the full Commission and a few weeks later Ing. Bruzzone told me that he had no need for any more information and stated that he was satisfied with the technical aspects of our program and our ability to carry it out.

We changed Dr. Alizon Garcia's attitude toward IKA as well. Months later, when he resigned as Economics Minister and after we had gone through the interdiction process, the Prebisch report, the Bruzzone Commission and the Special Commission set up to renegotiate the Kaiser-IAME-IKA contract, he and his associate Dr. Roberto Verrier became IKA's financial advisors and remained in that role during the years of Kaiser management. With the professional standing of García and Verrier, IKA had to be spotless or this association would never have been possible.

Chapter III | 1956

The newspapers on December 26, 1955, announced that IKA had been placed on a list of interdicted companies by the National Council for the Recovery of Property (Junta Nacional de Recuperación Patrimonial). This was quite a Christmas present, coming on top of all the other problems we were having at the time. Interdiction (interdicción) literally is a deprival of civil rights and was, for our organization, a very serious state of affairs. We weren't the only company interdicted; there were several others including Fiat, which had two plants in Córdoba.

We worked until midnight the evening of December 26 preparing a document that dealt with every aspect of IKA's formation and its subsequent development, attempting to demonstrate that in the origin and disposition of its assets, no acts of bribery or collusion had been committed. The brief and supporting files were presented to the National Council the following morning. Placing IKA on the "black list" was manifestly unfair but the only resort was to fight back and get it removed from the list. I remember commiserating with Dr. Aurelio Peccei, Fiat's head of Latin American operations, and Dr. Oberdan Sallustro, President of Fiat Argentina, but they had no solutions either.

Following the notice of interdiction, the National Council informed us on January 23 that it had decided to intervene the company, which meant that an Interventor would be appointed to control and audit IKA's ongoing operations.

I didn't accept this notice very gracefully, in fact I was mad as hell since it was going to demoralize our employees and shake the confidence of our shareholders, suppliers and contractors. Edgar was also irate when I reported the event and he told me that if we were intimidated in any way we should just get up and leave. This, of course, was an impossibility. I knew we were clean and with the wise guidance of Allende, Hayzus and Ordoñez, we settled down and proceeded to develop a campaign of contacts and information dissemination.

In a day or so Dan Kelly came into my office, somewhat agitated, to announce that there was an Admiral in the outer office who wished to speak with me. Admiral Eliseo Vila was shown in and he presented me with a letter wherein the National Council officially appointed him Interventor. I must admit I was somewhat rude. I asked him how he intended to run the company and if he wanted to sit in my chair. He smiled and said, in perfect English, "Listen, Mr. McCloud, I am not here to ‹run the company' as you put it. My mission is to confirm that the interests of the Argentine Government and its citizens are protected. Once this has been satisfactorily concluded your company will be removed from the list and I will leave." This put a different light on things and I calmed down. We proceeded to work out a modus operandi that provided for an information flow that kept him abreast of all major developments. I set him up in an office next to mine and apprised him, on a daily basis, of anything of importance. He was invited to attend all Board meetings, and when an operations meeting of any importance took place he was notified of the subject matter to be discussed and invited to sit in should he so desire.

The Lord must have been looking down upon us with love and understanding when He guided the deliberations that resulted in the Vila appointment. If a dictatorial type had been selected who demanded to see and approve every purchase order, every new hire and every check written — which he probably had the legal authority to do — IKA's momentum would have ground to a halt. Admiral Vila, an engineer who had attended postgraduate school at the University of Michigan, immersed himself in our affairs and became completely informed of our program and supported it. We were not privy to his official reports; I assume there must have been several, and I have to further assume that he believed our program a good one and in the best interests of the country. Vila did tell me, confidentially, that he had been advised by the Ministry of Justice that the differences in valuation that were contained in the reports of the Valuation Commission, and an allegation that Peron had received shares in IKA, were the prime reasons for the interdiction.

The National Council lifted the interdiction six months later on June 21 and a Presidential decree confirming this was issued on July 31. The fact that we were the first company to be removed from the list not only demonstrated that we had been organized legally and correctly but was recognition as well of the importance our program had for the country.

However, there was still another obstacle that had to be removed. There were parts of the January 19 contract that the Economics Ministry wanted changed and this meant a renegotiation of the contract.   .

The Executive Power named a special commission on February 10 and we were given a list of the modifications to the contract that it wanted us to consider. A working group was organized with the Ministries of Air and Economy represented and Edgar had Lloyd Cutler come down to represent Kaiser Motors. It should be noted here that Kaiser Industries Corp. was organized in March 1956 and absorbed all the holdings of Kaiser Motors and the Henry J. Kaiser Company, as well as the holdings in the aluminum, steel, cement and other wholly or partially owned companies. Lloyd brought Eddie Miller with him to assist in the negotiations. Eddie, a lawyer in the Adlai Stevenson firm in New York, had served as Assistant Secretary of State for Latin American affairs during the Truman administration, spoke Spanish fluently and was well acquainted in Argentina.

The negotiations went on intermittently over a period of two months and the special commission submitted its recommendations to the National Council which approved them in May 1956. I don't know why it took so long but the revised contract between IAME, Kaiser and IKA was not signed until October 1956. Comodoro Julio Cesar Krause, who had replaced Brigadier Abrahim, signed for IAME, Lloyd Cutler for Kaiser and I for IKA. The principal changes to the January 19, 1955 contract consisted of the following:

a) Definition of the rate of exchange applicable to investments with original valuations in dollars:

The original contract specified that all of the Kaiser and IAME invested equipment that was valued in dollars be converted to a peso value at the "free market" rate of exchange in effect on the date of customs clearance. Prior to October 27, 1955, the free market rate was 14:1. After the imposition of an "official market" rate by the new authorities after the revolution, which was pegged at 18:1, the free market rate rose to over 30:1. With the bulk of the Kaiser and IAME investments clearing customs after October 27, the two founding partners' equity in IKA would have increased substantially and to the detriment of the public shareholders whose peso cash investment had already been integrated. While both founders had a contractual right to the increases, all parties agreed that the equitable solution was the application of the official market rate — 18:1 — on all invested assets that cleared customs after October 27. The conversion of asset value to pesos at the free market rate would also have had a large impact on amortization charges with a resultant increase in production costs.

b) Second investment of Kaiser Motors:

The second investment of Kaiser was approved, with the final dollar valuation to be made after arrival at plant site and converted to a peso value at the rate of 18:1. Kaiser waived its right to have the valuation made in the States to avoid causing any delay in IKA's schedule. The second investment had an estimated valuation of approximately U$S 1,300,000 and actually increased slightly in value after it was surveyed by the Valuation Commission. Kaiser also extended a credit to IKA for a period of three years and with no interest charge, for the payment of over U$S 500,000 in costs it had incurred in supplying IKA with the technical assistance it needed. Most of this was related to the moving costs of expatriates.

c) IKA second stock issue:

The new contract made provisions for a second stock issue that would allow the public shareholders, on a preferential rights basis, to increase their individual share holdings in the same proportion as the combined increase in Kaiser and IAME equity.

d) Production program:

In the original contract we had agreed on a five-year production program together with the value of the imported parts that we would be allowed to import each year. In the revised contract this was changed to require IKA to apply each year for the exchange required for parts importation.

After having experienced delays in dealing with Argentine government bureaucracy, particularly in the Industrial Bank, the change requiring annual approval of our complementary parts importation bothered me but there wasn't much we could do about it. As we proceeded through our first five years we did have problems in getting our annual import permits released on schedule but we always seemed to muddle through, even in 1957 when the government required that parts importation be made with foreign credit and on a deferred payment basis.

At last we were finished with all of the post revolution investigations and we all heaved a sigh of relief. Now we could get back to the business of building automobiles.

During the first quarter of 1956 construction progressed on schedule. In the machine shop and assembly plant, floor slabs, columns, trusses and roof were erected in sequences that permitted machines and assembly line equipment to be installed in accordance with the priorities laid down by IKA's Works Engineering Department. The Press Plant, because of the massive foundations it required, would not be ready for press erection to start until September. When completed, it would be the biggest plant of its kind in Latin America. But construction never seemed to stop in IKA. In my years with the company we were always building new additions. What started out as some 1,500,000 square feet of covered space grew to over 2,000,000 in Santa Isabel alone, not counting the construction that took place in IKA's subsidiary plants.

There were several working groups that had to be coordinated. Kaiser Engineers designed and managed all construction. IKA's Plant Engineering Division was responsible for permanent production installations such as conveyors, secondary electrical distribution, cranes, material handling and related items. The

Master Mechanic's Division developed the operational processes, designed and built tooling and fixtures. Product Engineering built and was testing the first prototype Jeep, which was given model designation JA1 to differentiate it from the U.S. built CJ5 which had a different engine. Procurement and Expediting was shipping sample parts of Argentine origin to the plant, where Quality Control set up inspection criteria and worked with the vendors to get their parts qualified. On the production floor, the mechanical parts had to be nursed, machine by machine, through the try out process, the sub-assembly fixtures in the body shop had to proven out, the body went into a paint system that started up for the first time, the trim shop started its production of seats and tops and all of this output started converging on the final assembly line.

On April 27 at about 5 pm the first Jeep rolled off the final line and Ken Flood presented me with the keys. It would be followed by about 2500 more by the end of the year. In recognition of the contribution that Lloyd Cutler had made in IKA's formation, we dedicated the first Jeep to Louisiana Winslow Cutler, Lloyd's daughter, who had been born just a day or so before in Washington, D.C.

I came close to missing the event. Ordoñez, Esteban Retali from the Sales Division and I were flying around the interior of the country in an old Waco biplane we had leased, inspecting dealer candidates. The plane had passed its prime and then some. This particular airplane's cruising range didn't depend on its gasoline carrying capacity; instead it burned so much oil that we had to land frequently to fill the crankcase. It also had battery problems and we finally limped into Córdoba the night before in time to be put to work helping round up materials for the first Jeep.

The first Jeep was not only built in a plant on which construction had started only 13 months previous, but, more important, its engine was the first ever produced on a production line in Latin America. The national content was about 50% and would have been much greater if the Press Plant had been in full operation.

The Jeep was shipped to Buenos Aires and was used as the centerpiece for a large reception that Gus and I hosted in the Plaza Hotel ballroom for dealers, Directors, government officials and the local business community. Dr. Alizon Garcia arranged for me to take the Jeep to the Presidential quinta in Olivos where I gave President Aramburu a demonstration ride around the grounds with my oldest son, Kim, who was then eight years old. The General was delighted with the ride and later examined the Jeep in minute detail as I showed him the parts that were of Argentine origin.

By the end of June we had produced about 200 vehicles and began having some quality problems that would not have occurred if we had had the time to do the field testing we should have done in the interior of the country, where most of the secondary roads are unimproved. And it is precisely in these areas that four wheel drive vehicles are needed. This was the risk we took when we had no choice but to put an experimental engine into production without extensive field testing.

We began getting reports of bearing failures from dealers in the interior that rang the alarm bell in Product Engineering and Service. Investigations disclosed that the engines were aspirating very abrasive dust, usually with a high silica content, causing abnormal bearing wear and bearing failure. Engineering responded overnight and set up some makeshift test cells, running engines in a dust environment to determine how it was entering the engine. New air filters were designed, better sealing of the engine was provided and, in a short space of time, the vehicles leaving the factory, at least, were OK. We still had the field problem since there were about 100 odd vehicles in circulation that needed attention. Ossowski and Olson organized several teams of service mechanics and engineers who would take a kit of new parts and repair procedures to a dealership and have the customer bring his vehicle in for a "factory inspection" with the promise that it would be returned to him in a day. The team would disassemble the engine, drop the crankshaft, replace all main and connecting rod bearings, in some cases the crankshaft as well, change over the filters and seal the engine in accordance with the new specifications that had been developed. There were any number of these "midnight overhauls" and most of the Jeeps were caught before failures had occurred. If we hadn't remedied this situation as expeditiously as we did, IKA would have been labeled with a bad quality reputation that we never would have lived down.

The other major problem we had at the time was with Jeep sales. The Jeep is a specialty vehicle and in our forecasts we never had more than 5% to 10% of it in our production schedules. I'm talking only about the four wheel drive military type Jeep. The only reason for a Jeep, other than military use, is passenger mobility for off-road conditions — not cargo carrying. There weren't many Argentine buyers, as a percentage of the car buying public, that required and could afford this type of transportation. Our inventory of finished units started to grow and Edgar, who was becoming concerned with our cash position, called me to New York. He and Mike Miller thought we should stop production long enough to let sales catch up. A shutdown would have brought with it some severe labor problems and I argued strongly against it. There is no unemployment compensation in Argentina and any short-term layoffs bring about a lot of labor strife and should be avoided to the extent possible. Knowing that the JA2 Jeep halft on pickup would soon be in production, to be followed by the Willys Station Wagon, I was able to convince Edgar that we should keep production going. Luckily I was right, and as the pickup models and the station wagons came on line in September, production of the classic Jeep was scaled back to a level commensurate with its demand.

The JA2 pickup was developed literally overnight in answer to Sales' demand for an economical truck in four and two wheel drive options with an enclosed cab. In addition to the engineering development time, a quantity of dies for the side panels, pickup box, cab and frame extensions was necessary and the tool shop turned these out in record time. The half ton pickup, particularly in the two wheel drive version, became one of our most popular utility vehicles.

Another sales obstacle was the lack of adequate retail financing. At an October meeting with principal dealers from fill regions, it was apparent that demand exceeded credit availabilities. Santone in Mendoza had over 500 firm orders but only 3 percent were cash customers. The others were in the process of applying for credit from the local Banco Industrial branch. Daniel Tiphaine, the principal spokesman for the dealer body — most of our original dealers had been part of his distributor network with Willys Motors — stated that the major problem was the lack of uniformity among bank managers in credit procedures. Private credit facilities existed but their interest charges were too high. Julio Alizon Garcia and Roberto Verrier had just started as our financial advisors and they, with Bill Sussex, who had replaced Larry Daniels as Sales Manager, worked on alleviating the problem through their many contacts in the Banco Industrial organization. This focused my attention on retail credit and the fact that we had better do something about it or lower our production goals considerably.

IKA closed its second and first full fiscal year in June. We didn't report a profit since we had only just started production. In September, however, we closed the third quarter of the calendar year with a positive cash flow, 21 months after the founding of the company. John Greenwald, who had replaced Spike Massaglia as controller, was all smiles when he brought me the figures. It was good that IKA had a controller like Greenwald. He was a tough nut when it came to handing out money. Every time I wanted to build something new it was like pulling teeth to convince him that it was a necessary project. With cash positive, at least we were heading in the right direction.

The annual stockholder's meeting, IKA's second, was held in October at the service training center we had established in a large shop building on Migueletes Street, not far from the main office. The principal items on the agenda requiring stockholder approval were:

a) Increase in the authorized capital of the company from m$n 360,000,000 to m$n 800,000,000.
b) Issuance of additional shares to Kaiser and IAME to cover the additional investments made by the two founding partners.
c) The changes to the original Kaiser-IAME-IKA contract that had just been renegotiated.
d) The special share issue to Vianini, SRL, in exchange for its investment of gear making equipment.

e) A special share issue on a preferential rights basis to the public shareholders, which resulted from the additional equity that Kaiser and IAME received due to the change in the rate of exchange used for valuation purposes.

f) The election of a new Board of Directors for the 1956-1957 fiscal year.

In the new slate of Directors, Edgar replaced his father as President, I was named 1st Vice President and General Manager, Martin Cairo, an IAME nominee, became 2nd Vice President, Stephen Girard, President of Kaiser Jeep Corp., was named to replace Henry J. Kaiser, Alfredo Paladino was another new IAME nominee, Allende, Hayzus and de Ridder were re-elected and Eduardo Huergo, an outstanding Argentine engineer and executive, was elected to represent the private shareholders.

At the end of the year, we had a total payroll of about 2000. The number of expatriates had been cut back substantially as Argentine supervision replaced them. Practically all of Kaiser Engineers' personnel had returned home with the bulk of construction completed.

Chapter IV | 1957

The first of several expansions of inhouse production capacity, primarily to increase local content, started with the investment, by Vianini, SRL, of a group of 50 or so gear-making machines. This was the nucleus of IKA's first gear plant which was the springboard into transmission and transfer case manufacturing that began in the second half of 1957. The production of differential axle assemblies followed about nine months later. The incorporation of these major components not only brought about substantial foreign exchange savings but the engineering and mechanical skills of our work force were broadened as well.

As I stated previously, we began negotiations with Sr. Vianini in late 1955. The Vianini equipment was already in the country, having been imported originally as an intended investment into a gear-making combine, in partnership with IAME. Vianini, like IKA, had interdiction and financial problems, and his project was at a standstill. In our first approach we asked Vianini to consider investing his equipment into IKA, on the basis of a mutually agreed to valuation, in exchange for shares at par value. Instead, he wanted to form a separate company in which he would invest his machines and IKA would supply the remaining equipment, tooling and cash necessary for the buildings, installation and working capital. He wasn't concerned with IKA's having the majority ownership and management but did not want to invest directly into IKA. Vianini was a very dynamic fellow, somewhat explosive, and our meetings were punctuated with very emotional and dramatic discourses in a mixture of Italian and Spanish. We remained firm and he finally realized that IKA represented the best solution to his dilemma and agreed to accept a package of roughly 25 million pesos par value of IKA stock in exchange for his equipment. The Vianini equipment, together with selected machines from the Kaiser and IAME second investments, made it possible for us to get into transmission and transfer case production. By rearranging the machine shop lines a bit we were able to locate the Gear Division alongside the engine plant.

During the course of the negotiations, Mapes and I, with the help of Leo MacKay, Procurement Manager at Kaiser Jeep, concluded a license agreement with Borg Warner Corp. that gave us the knowhow for manufacturing the transmissions and transfer cases. Getting the Vianini equipment was like finding gold.

Once the transmission project was under way we decided we might as well manufacture the differential axles also. Once you have a gear plant, a lot of things are possible. The key element in the production of the differential axle assemblies was about 3 million dollars of Gleason Gear generators. These are the machines used in manufacturing the ring gear and pinion, the heart of the differential. Gleason gear equipment was, then at least, only manufactured in the U.S. and in order to get an import permit, one of the requirements of the Central Bank was a long-term financing program. With Joe Reis's and Henry Drath's help this was arranged through the Bank of America with an Eximbank guarantee, directly with IKA and no Kaiser Industries co-signature.

In order to produce the Spicer differentials that were used in the Jeep utility vehicle line as well as the Kaiser passenger car, we had to negotiate a license agreement with the Dana Corporation of Toledo, Ohio. Jack Martin, then the Dana chairman, was very supportive of our program and a license agreement was concluded that not only enabled IKA to manufacture for its own use but permitted sale to third parties as well. The differential axle assembly was the last major power train component that was being imported and when it was integrated into IKA's production facilities, it, together with the transmission and transfer case, accounted for exchange savings in the order of 10-15% of the value of two wheel drive vehicles and much more for four wheel drive. We still had a ways to go because the import list still included major forgings and castings, stampings that we hadn't completed dies for as yet and some miscellaneous parts, including the foundation brake assembly, which we started producing ourselves in 1958 under a license agreement with the Bendix Corp.

IKA's first profitable month was in January 1957, two years after its founding. For the last half of the fiscal year that ended in June 1957, IKA's profit was about m$n 47,000,000. The exchange rate at the time was 42:1 so this amounted to a little over U$S 1,000,000. After deducting the losses of the first two quarters, the profit for the fiscal year ending June 1957 amounted to m$n 19,300,000.

In April we held our first Dealer Convention at the Sierras Hotel in Alta Gracia. At that time we had about 125 dealers in our network and we had representatives from every firm. We encouraged them to bring their wives since we wanted the conventions to be a social affair as well. IKA's management and sales personnel with their wives provided an atmosphere of conviviality and warmth. The annual convention became an affair that everyone looked forward to and it was always well attended.

The hotel was the hub of conference activities with meetings and tours at the plant. We had just started building the Jeep station wagon and had quantities being shipped which impressed the dealers since the vehicle would be released to the public in May and they could see for themselves that they would have the product to sell. Most of the dealer representatives had not seen the plant before and I think the best description of their reaction was that they now finally saw IKA as a reality. They were staking their resources on us and their confidence was bolstered when they saw presses stamping out panels, machines producing engines and vehicles rolling off the final line. In the automobile business, good products alone are not enough. You must have a dealer organization that has the financial capacity to carry an inventory of vehicles and service parts that together with a well trained service organization can attend to a customer's requirement professionally and efficiently. The factory's obligation is to support the dealer with competitively priced quality products, insure adequate selection by maintaining adequate factory inventories, provide training for service personnel and handle warranty claims fairly and expeditiously. Above all, the dealer must feel that he is an integral part of the organization. Dealer loyalty is the cliche used generally to describe what the auto company wants but I prefer to look on the relationship as a partnership. It can't be conducted on an arm's length basis. The dealer has to feel that he is an extension of the company and can voice his opinions on the same level as anyone else in the organizational hierarchy. This was the relationship we encouraged and the IKA dealer organization ultimately had more than 250 outlets around the country.

The Jeep station wagon was released for delivery to the dealers on May 2. The factory had started production in late March and we wanted to accumulate a big enough pool of vehicles so that every dealer in the country could have an inventory on the day it was announced to the public. Simultaneously with the launching of the station wagon we brought out a new Jeep that was designated the JA3B. This was a sport version of the regular Jeep; it had a convertible top, small doors and was offered in two-wheel drive only. But the real lift in sales would come from the station wagon. Ordoñez called it the "Estanciera" from the very beginning and the name stuck. The Estanciera was a full size five passenger station wagon with a lot of cubic capacity, plenty of power with the L6-226 engine and was offered in two and four wheel drive options. It was not a stylish vehicle and wasn't intended to be. It was square, boxy and devoid of frills. It had easy access, locks that worked, plenty of power and ease of maintenance. To digress a moment, the Kaiser passenger car was to have started production prior to the station wagon, in accordance with our original contract, but in the renegotiation with the Provisional Government, we were requested to give priority to the production of utility vehicles. This was actually an advantage for IKA because I don't think we would have been able to build a sophisticated passenger car in 1957 and still accomplish the percentage of local content as we did on the Estanciera.

Advertising started becoming a very important part of our sales thrust. Ordoñez brought Marcos Bullrich into IKA as advertising manager and we switched from McCann-Erickson to a combination of Pueyrredon y Cia. and Lino Palacios. McCann technically was very capable but it didn't have, in our opinion, the real feel of the Argentine automotive market. Ricardo Pueyrredon and Lino Palacios gave us a better insight into the Argentine consumer. The Pueyrredon agency did all the layouts and Palacios, the outstanding caricaturist in Argentina at the time, served as a consultant on format and portrayals. Lino also produced the annual IKA calendar which caricatured life in Argentina with one of IKA's products serving as the centerpiece each month.

Television was growing as an advertising medium and as it grew, IKA grew with it. I think the best TV show we did was the nightly news hour — "Telenoches IKA" — co-anchored by Monica Mihanovitch and Andres Percival. Andy Russell came down from the States and put on some great shows for us and another that was given top ratings was the Bishop Fulton J. Sheen lecture series. We arranged for him to come to Buenos Aires two years in a row and he gave the same programs, with simultaneous translation, that he gave in the U.S. For each of the years that he appeared, Sheen donated his fees to various poor parishes selected by the Archdiocese of Buenos Aires.

We felt TV was going to be so important as a medium that we even tried to set up our own TV station. When the government announced that it was going to award some TV channels to the private sector we formed a new subsidiary, Permanente, S.A., that submitted a proposal in the competition. We weren't selected for the award of a channel but the Permanente corporate structure later was used for our finance company.

As a result of the revised contract that was finally approved by the National Council and signed by Kaiser, IAME (in 1957 IAME's name was changed to DINFIA — "Dirección Nacional de Fabricaciones e Investigaciones Aeronáuticas) and IKA in October 1956, a second stock or "rights issue" was required that would allow the public shareholders to exercise their preferential rights to the increased capitalization of IKA that resulted from the increased valuation of the Kaiser and IAME initial and secondary investments. At its June 1957 meeting, the IKA Board authorized the issuance of m$n 56,000,000 par value in shares to be offered to the public shareholders on a preferential basis.

At this point in time, Argentina was a relatively undeveloped capital market and the IKA rights issue of 1957 was the first test of this type to be applied to an existing shareholder body which also was one of the largest in the country following the first public offering of IKA stock in 1955. For many of IKA's shareholders the reasons for and ramifications of the pre-emptive issue were unclear. IKA's bearer share certificate contained a coupon which had to be clipped and identified by number, calculating the number of new shares to which the holder was entitled, presenting a subscription form to the company's agent and paying in the shares prior to the expiration date. To the inexperienced shareholder, this is a task which might not seem worth the effort.

The rights issue had been underwritten by Argentaria, S.A. de Finanzas, a division of Deltec International. Deltec had been active in Brazil for a number of years and had concentrated on developing a market for shares in the interior of Brazil — away from the principal commercial centers of Rio de Janeiro and Sao Paulo. With logistic support from IKA's staff and much cooperation on the part of IKA dealers, a nationwide campaign to explain the mechanics of the issue was undertaken, with the result that a substantial portion of the issue was subscribed by existing shareholders. Coupons were also traded on the Buenos Aires Stock Exchange. The unsubscribed balance — about 15% of the total issue — was taken up by Argentaria and placed through its traveling salesmen, which relieved pressure on the Exchange and also made IKA better known in the interior of the country. Julio Nuñez, Argentaria's Managing Director, later became a member of IKA's Board.

The success of the rights issue was also noteworthy in that the public shareholders had still to see IKA's first dividend which was paid the following year — and was reflective of confidence and loyalty. The company's policy of regular reporting contributed to build and maintain a good image. In addition to the Annual Report, IKA provided quarterly summaries of its accounts in leaflet form which also contained updates on its progress, a practice which was not employed by other listed companies at the time.

The Kaiser commitment to IKA's shareholding public, originating as it did from the original structure of the company, earned recognition as the company became one of the ten market leaders on the Buenos Aires Exchange. The IKA formula was unprecedented in that the foreign investor was the largest minority shareholder, whereas in the few other cases of publicly owned companies with foreign partners, the foreign investor usually held the controlling interest. By and large, direct foreign investment in Argentina took the form of wholly owned subsidiaries, out of view from public scrutiny.

In this sense, IKA inaugurated a fresh approach to business organization in Argentina. The flexibility of an "open company" served the purposes of sustained expansion, as successive projects, as we shall see in following chapters, brought in new participants on mutually acceptable terms.

In mid 1957 we started an investigation that would, through licensing or inhouse development, give us a vehicle to compete in the 1000cc to 1500cc market. The Kaiser car that would go into production in 1958 was not the vehicle to satisfy the demand that existed for a small, economical unit. While the Kaiser was a beautiful automobile and would have its niche in the market, its size and price would put it out of the volume market range.

I went to Europe in July and had meetings with the Rootes Group in England and in France with Simca, Renault and Peugeot. All had a decided interest in the Argentine market and these preliminary discussions and plant visits gave me a good understanding of the products, manufacturing methods, management principles and, to a point, how far they would be willing to go in supporting the investment necessary to put a new car into production. I also went to Stuttgart, Germany, to visit the Porsche operation, a low volume producer with methods more aligned to IKA's volume than the methods in play at the big producers' plants. Although more labor intensive, we could sacrifice direct production manhours for a lower toolup cost and we learned a lot from Porsche body building processes as they were then.

We maintained contact with the three French companies, finally working out an agreement with Renault. In retrospect, we took too long working out the details and should have been in small car production two years before we actually were.

But, it is also necessary to recall that during the pre-Frondizi period all our planning had to be based on a policy of rigid import substitution. The extreme pressure brought to bear on us to lower the foreign content in IKA produced vehicles caused such high cost estimates for the tooling and equipment required in each new program we studied that it became the prime reason for our procrastination. The hybridization of the Alfa Romeo 1900 into the Bergantin — of which we'll talk in length later — was a result of seeking the lowest cost reduction of imported content per dollar of capital investment. The point is that the Automotive Decree effected by Minister of Industry Tedin during the Frondizi regime and which provided for high ceilings and low surcharges on imported parts was a complete reversal of the policy that IKA had been required to work under for five years. The Bergantin program was the last to be conceived under the general philosophy of our 1955 contract whereas the Renault program that IKA undertook later was framed within the dictates of the Frondizi Automotive Decree.

The third annual shareholders meeting, for the fiscal year ending June 1957, was held at the end of October. There were no changes made on the Board of Directors and the fact that we reported a profit for the fiscal year — our first — did much to inspire shareholder confidence. At the end of December we had 3200 employees on the payroll and produced almost 12,000 vehicles during calendar year 1957, with an exchange savings for Argentina in excess of U$S 20,000,000.

Chapter V | 1958

The first Kaiser came off the final line in April 1958. It was the first passenger car to be integrally built on a production line in Latin America. Called the Kaiser Manhattan in the U.S., we had originally intended to call it the Metropolitano in Argentina but just prior to production, Ordoñez and the advertising people came up with the name "Carabela" — Caravel in English. The name had some significance since the caravel was the ship Columbus used in the discovery of America and the opening up of the New World while we, albeit in a modest way, by producing the first passenger car, were opening up new vistas for a lot of people also. The Kaiser Manhattan, styled by Howard Darrin, was first introduced in model year 1951 and in my opinion was the most attractive U.S. car in the immediate post-war period. The Carabela we built was a better finished car than its U.S. predecessor. It had luxurious leather upholstery, a beefed up suspension and improved roadability. Henry Kaiser was so pleased with it that he ordered one for his personal use in Hawaii where he had moved after his so-called retirement — so-called because he never stopped building. Henry's favorite color was pink and we built an all pink car — including the leather interior — and shipped it to Honolulu where he drove it around for a few years, causing quite a stir whenever he was seen in it.

The greatly broadened supplier base that was needed for passenger car production required a demanding effort on the part of the Procurement and Engineering divisions. We worked with well over 2000 suppliers. Most of them were concentrated in the Buenos Aires area initially but gradually Córdoba, Rosario and other inland centers became sources as well. For parts that were unique and where special tooling was required, we would either provide the tooling or assist the vendor in getting it engineered and built. In many cases IKA interfaced with the U.S. vendor and brought about a relationship with him and the Argentine company via a licensing arrangement or some form of knowhow exchange.

But buying parts is one thing, getting them with the quality we demanded was another thing. In the early days we spent double or triple the receiving inspection labor than was normal. Product Engineering set up an Experimental Division that concentrated on vendor quality and worked in support of Inspection. Mechanical and electrical testing devices were developed to statically and dynamically test parts for function and durability — from generators, voltage regulators, batteries and other electrical components to wheels and seat springs, shock absorbers, bearings, radiators, water and oil pumps, windshield wipers and on and on. This investigatory work developed the sampling criteria that was used in receiving inspection. It was necessary to functionally test some parts 100%. If the circuitry in a wiring harness for a passenger car was faulty and this fault wasn't discovered until after assembly of the car, we would spend hours disassembling and rewiring the vehicle. We virtually had production lines in receiving inspection with operators on special fixtures checking parts before releasing them to the assembly line. As quality improved less of this rigid control was needed and inspection gradually reverted to statistical sampling. But in an automobile plant no matter how careful one is, something will slip through and a vehicle will wind up in the "repair hole." One must do everything possible to keep a faulty car out of the new vehicle delivery lot. Engineering and Procurement printed a book of standard specifications that was distributed to all vendors and clearly spelled out our inspection procedures, tolerances, metallurgical and other norms. The IKA Norms contributed to developing a quality consciousness in the vendor body.

Vendor pricing was also a problem. There just didn't seem to be any consistent relationship between the Argentine supplier's price for a part and the price we paid for it in the U.S. By bringing in second sources whenever possible we began to get some competition and prices started to level off. We even had problems getting the proper prices on such mundane items as tires. The Argentine subsidiaries of two U.S. tire manufacturers would not give us the OEM (Original Equipment Manufacturer) price. In the U.S., manufacturers of high volume items such as tires, batteries, sparkplugs, etc., give a substantial volume discount to the car maker and it's in their best interest to do so. On high mortality items in particular, if a given manufacturer has his product in the vehicle as original equipment, the chances are that when the owner has to replace the part he will select a replacement made by the original manufacturer. We finally did get OEM prices but we had to go all the way back to the home offices. In cases like this we got a lot of support out of the Kaiser Jeep purchasing department.

The production teams in the plant also had their challenges. This was particularly true in the Press Plant, Body and Final Assembly areas. This is where the task of segregating, rehabilitating and installing, in proper sequential order, the thousand or so special tools, dies, jigs and fixtures took place. The Kaiser tooling had not been used for years and getting it all in working order was a time consuming job. Much of the tooling had been used in Kaiser-Frazer vendor plants and our tool engineers and assembly plant supervision had never even seen them before. IKA produced the Carabela chassis and body in their entirety, whereas Kaiser -Frazer produced about one-half of these items, subcontracting the chassis assembly, doors and deck lids. In the machine shop the job was much easier because — with few modifications — the engines, transmissions, axles and steering gear were the same as in the Estanciera.

The imported content in the early Carabelas was about U$S 400 per automobile — about 15% of the vehicle wholesale value; this was reduced by half in 1959. The major items that stayed on the import list consisted of the large chrome plated die castings — grille, head lamp rings and hood vent intake. There was no diecasting equipment in the country big enough to handle these parts and we couldn't justify buying the equipment to produce them ourselves because of the low volume. Later as the usage of aluminum in the vehicles we built increased, particularly in the case of engine and transmission parts, we did set up a die casting facility. But by then the Carabela had been discontinued.

With the production of the Carabela, all of the commitments we had made were satisfied. From the date of its introduction until it was phased out in 1962 there were about 11,000 Carabelas produced. This was not a lot of volume for a set of special tooling and we had to write off a portion that was still unamortized. But the Kaiser Carabela left its mark on the Argentine industry.

I took one of the first Carabelas to the Presidential Quinta to show it to President Aramburu as I had done the previous two years in succession with the first Jeep and then with an Estanciera. This was just a few days before May 1 when General Aramburu would be turning the Presidency over to Dr. Arturo Frondizi. This visit gave me my last opportunity to thank the General for the support we had received from him and the Provisional Government. We had gotten off to a rough start back in 1955 with the interdiction and other harassments but had pulled through.

In June we held our second annual Dealer Convention, again in Alta Gracia. We were honored with the presence of Dr. A. Zanichelli, the newly elected governor of Córdoba province, who addressed the convention. The high point of the three-day meeting took place at the plant where we presented the lineup of new Carabelas. The public announcement was programmed for July 25 — about a month later. The dealers, which were now in excess of 200 locations, were astounded at the progress we had made during the year and each one was given an opportunity to drive a Carabela. By this time I was on a first name basis with a lot of them and I shared their satisfaction in finally getting a passenger car to sell.

Before we stopped Carabela production in 1962 we had put a lot of time and energy into various styling changes. We commissioned Toledo to develop some new body designs that were facelifts that minimized new tooling requirements. Dutch Darrin came up with some good ideas that concentrated on the front end of the car. The new styled Carabela that I liked best was a creation of Jim Angers that changed the roof line, producing a squarer superstructure and more side glass area. This blended with the lower body and gave the impression of a shorter, more compact vehicle. In Argentina, Experimental built prototypes of a two door hard top coupe and a two door convertible. Both of these were very good looking cars.

But we finally had to conclude that the volume market just wasn't there for a car with the weight and size of the Kaiser.

I can't let 1958 go by without relating how close we came to entering tractor production. The idea of producing tractors had intrigued me since 1956 when we were first approached by the Oliver Tractor Co. of the U.S. to consider manufacturing its products. The Oliver was a quality tractor and had an excellent reputation. It would have been able to compete very well against the Fiat, which was the principal tractor produced at the time.

IAME also produced one but it was an old gas engine design. The Fiat had a high degree of imported content which led us to believe that we could get into production very quickly if we were allowed the same import content. We submitted a joint proposal to the economic Ministry in April 1956 but it didn't go anywhere. We were on the interdiction list and had little time to devote to anything but IKA's principal business. Although the timing was wrong, the Oliver tractor would have blended in very well with our automotive manufacturing and marketing capabilities.

In 1958, we again got interested in tractors. This time, however, the proposed concept was a three-way proposition that involved Perkins Engine of England and Massey-Ferguson of Canada. Perkins, a diesel engine designer and producer, with its main plant in Peterborough, saw an opportunity in Argentina for its engines and wanted IKA to join with it in setting up an independent engine plant that would sell to tractor and truck manufacturers. Monty Pritchard, the Managing Director of Perkins, and I had several meetings. On one of my trips to Europe I visited Peterborough and toured the Perkins plant. Perkins had developed a fine line of engines and had a good reputation. As a commercial engine producer and without a proprietary vehicle that used its engines, Perkins, like Cummins Engine in the U.S., had to sell the vehicle manufacturer as well as the end user. While both Perkins and Cummins had been very successful in their respective spheres of influence, setting up a commercial engine plant in Argentina in 1958 when the only possible users were Fiat tractor and Mercedes truck — and both had their own engines — didn't seem to me to be a good proposition.

Pritchard suggested we talk to Massey-Ferguson which used the Perkins in its tractors. We met with Al Thornbrough, President of Massey-Ferguson, and we organized a joint team that did a complete feasibility study. The results of the study were positive but the investment required was substantial. The only way that I could foresee the project going ahead was through an investment of all the production equipment required by Massey and Perkins into IKA, which in turn would take the responsibility for plant construction, machinery installation and startup costs. Understandably neither Perkins nor Massey wanted to be a division of IKA even though they could have designated the management of the division if they had wanted to. More than likely, if we could have foreseen what the Frondizi Automotive Decree that was released in March 1959 entailed, we would have pursued the project more aggressively. It was, indeed, an opportunity missed. Later as IKA developed its general manufacturing in forge, foundry, tool and die making, gears and the like, the tractor and engine would have been large end-users.

In April we had our first serious labor problem when we could not come to agreement with the union representatives on wage issues during contract renewal negotiations. Given a little more time I'm sure that we would have been able to reach a settlement but the new union representatives wanted to flex their muscles and used a strike threat to try to drive us into a corner. We had several meetings in the office of the Provincial Labor Mediator but to no avail. The strike was finally called and serious harassment of management personnel occurred.

One of the worst incidences took place when a gang of workers forced some supervisors into the paint ovens and locked them in, threatening to light the burners if the company continued to refuse the union's wage demands. IKA paid the best wages in the Córdoba area, had medical plans, insurance coverages and other benefits in excess of what was legally required and provided a workplace environment that was safer and cleaner than any other industrial plant I had seen in the country. The SMATA (Sindicato de Mecánicos y Afines del Transporte Automotor) leaders misjudged IKA management when it called the strike. They believed that the teamwork we had espoused and the working relationship we encouraged between supervision and hourly personnel bespoke of weakness.

Practically every one of the North American shop supervisors we had brought down were men who had started as operators, had been union members and had come up through the ranks as group leaders, foremen and finally superintendents. They not only knew the production process from A to Z but, what was more important, they knew the capabilities and temperament of each individual working in their area. We encouraged direct communication between the operator, his foreman and his superintendent. If the operator had a job problem we wanted to know about it. The operator probably knew more about the operation he was assigned to than anyone else and could suggest innovations to improve quality and output that wouldn't occur to the process engineer or tool designer. The teamwork principle was antipathetic to union leadership in U.S. auto plants where, over the years, the insertion of departmental stewards discouraged direct communication between the operator and line supervision. Instead, the union leadership did all it could to promote the steward hierarchy as the intermediary between management and worker to the detriment of cost and efficiency.

In Argentina we did all we could to discourage this ambiance. By no means, however, did we try to take away from the individual worker his right to stewardship representation and/or to present a grievance if that was what he wanted. But, again, if a good working relationship existed the supervisor involved could usually handle the problem on the shop floor. Unfortunately there are some union leaders who consider the union as an independent entity — competitive with the company that employs it — and who are more concerned with the political aspects of unionism than they are with the individual well-being of the workers they represent. This was the driving motivation of the SMATA leadership in 1958 when the first strike against IKA was called. It believed that we would back down and agree to an exorbitant wage increase that had no relevancy in the Córdoba area and no basis in either cost of living or production trends.

As we progressed through the year our dealer body continued to grow and we added some important ex-General Motors and Ford dealers to our roster. We also had to cancel franchises in some instances for reasons varying from lack of service to bad commercial practices. One of the cancellations, and the one that disturbed me most, was Tiphaine y Cia. — our first dealer. The sales department was adamant on this one and I had to go along with it despite my personal relationship with Daniel Tiphaine and Alberto de Ridder. There were serious disagreements on sales policy and conformance with IKA procedures and there wasn't anything I could do to resolve the matter. A lawsuit was filed against IKA by Tiphaine y Cia. and it was years before it was finally settled out of court.

IKA closed its fourth fiscal year in June with a profit of U$S 5,500,000 on net sales of U$S 42,500,000 computed at the then current rate of exchange. For the fiscal year production totaled some 16,000 units, starting at a daily rate of about 45 and closing in June with an average of 95 units per day. At the annual shareholders meeting held in October, a 10% cash and a 20% stock dividend, related to par value, were declared. The Board was increased from nine to eleven members. Two of the new members were Julio Nuñez of Deltec and Charles Smith, Jr., Chairman of the Steel Improvement & Forge Co. of Cleveland, Ohio, with whom we had just concluded a technical assistance and investment agreement. Three other directors, Martin Cairo, Alfredo Paladino and Alberto de Ridder, had resigned and were replaced by three nominees from DINFIA: Comodoro Jaime Bayon Vago, Comodoro Vicente Villafañe and Luis Delpini.

Chapter VI | 1959

IKA passed another milestone in 1959 with the startup of its forge plant. But first let's trace the steps that were taken to bring this about and why we had to do it.

Forgings made up a large part of IKA's import content. With the exception of a few small forgings, the major items such as crankshafts, camshafts, gear blanks, connecting rods, suspension and steering components were imported — and we didn't see any local solution on the horizon unless we ourselves solved the problem. While the value of the imported forgings as a percentage of content was substantial, there was also a scheduling problem we wanted to eliminate that in itself was very costly.

Kaiser Jeep was IKA's source of supply in the U.S. and either purchased or manufactured the materials and parts we required, monitoring the deliveries to adhere to the schedules laid down by IKA. There were, essentially, two classes of production parts that Kaiser Jeep procured for us: parts peculiar to IKA's vehicles such as forgings and castings, and common parts such as stampings, electrical components and others that Jeep used in its own production. In the latter case, IKA could take advantage of Jeep's inventory if scheduling changes required either a cutback or an increase in requirements. With the parts that were peculiar to IKA, as was the case with forgings, it was an entirely different, and costly, matter. The forging vendor in the U.S. required at least four months lead time prior to delivery to a U.S. port of embarkation. He needed this time to book his steel orders, get steel delivery, produce the parts and ship. Allowing at least a month for transport by ship to Buenos Aires, another month for customs clearance and delivery to Córdoba plus the required one-month finished parts inventory in the plant, IKA, at any given time, had committed or paid for at least seven months of forging inventory. Procurement, freight and

"

inventory carrying costs added together were close to the value of the forgings themselves. Castings were somewhat the same problem but we were making good progress in procuring castings from Argentine foundries and the final solution — the acquisition of the majority ownership of Metalúrgica Tandil — will be related later.

The only solution we could see to establishing a local forging supply would be through the importation of the forging equipment necessary and either expanding an existing plant with it or setting up a completely new forge plant. It didn't take us long to convince ourselves that the latter course would be best in the long run. MacKay and Mapes came up with the names of two companies they thought might be interested in an Argentine venture: American Brake Shoe in Chicago and the Steel Improvement and Forge Co. (SIFCO) in Cleveland. In September 1957 I was in the U.S. and MacKay and I took a trip to Chicago where we met with American Brake Shoe management and determined there was no interest on their part. SIFCO was a different situation. In October, Mapes met with SIFCO management and a definite interest in Argentina was expressed. Mapes's meeting was followed by a visit to Argentina by Charles Smith, Jr., the Chairman and CEO of the company.

We were fortunate in being able to deal with a man like Chuck Smith. He was about my age, liked challenges and taking SIFCO international appealed to him. SIFCO was not a high production shop on single run items but concentrated instead on short-run, high quality forgings. SIFCO had also diversified and forgings was but one of its profit centers. As a result, it had some surplus forging equipment. During Smith's first visit, in late 1957, he was able to get a good understanding of our requirement and most important, get confidence in our ability to put the project together. Smith returned to Argentina in February, 1958. In the interim we had made a feasibility study of the forge project that included buildings, equipment layouts, cost estimates and project description. The total project value came to U$S 4,000,000 of which U$S 1,250,000 represented the estimated value of the equipment to be invested by SIFCO. Since this was used equipment, valuation criteria acceptable to the Argentine authorities had to be agreed to by SIFCO. The obtaining of import permits for used equipment, albeit a foreign investment, was difficult and a detailed project plan involving the SIFCO investment, forge plant construction, die sinking, heat treating and other auxiliary equipment required to support forging production was submitted to the Minister of Industry and the Central Bank for approval.

President Arturo Frondizi was inaugurated May 1st, 1958 and on May 7, Allende, Hayzus and I had a meeting with him and his immediate staff to review IKA's progress in general and the pending Forge Project in particular. We were assured of his support and the SIFCO foreign investment, more than likely, was the first to be approved by the Frondizi Government. The authorizing decree was issued in July.

Following the Frondizi meeting, Allende and I went to Cleveland and together with Lloyd Cutler and Sam Stern, an associate of Lloyd's, we met for a couple of days with Chuck Smith and his team and finalized the SIFCO-IKA contract. Smith and I signed it in the Kaiser Industries' New York office on May 20, 1958. In addition to the equipment investment, the agreement covered the technical assistance we would need during the construction and production phases as well as the seconding of a qualified manager to direct the startup and operation of the Forge Division for the first two years. George Gottschall, Chuck Smith's brother-in-law, with many years of experience in SIFCO, was the first manager of the Forge Division.

Plant design and construction started in about June. I remember that we started before receiving the authorizing decree. It was a "fast track" program with design staying just slightly ahead of construction. There were three main buildings initially: production, maintenance and administration. The production building housed the forging hammers, presses, raw material preparation and storage, and the maintenance building contained the heat treatment, die-making and die-maintenance facilities. Unlike the U.S. where there are innumerable die-making shops that a company like SIFCO could use for support, we had to provide enough die-making equipment to handle not only our maintenance needs but new die building as well. The initial rated capacity of the

Forge Division was 12,000 tons per year of finished product. While construction was proceeding, the SIFCO equipment was being dismantled and shipped. The first shipment arrived in Córdoba during March 1959 and the first forgings were produced in June. The official inauguration of the new plant took place on October 11, 1959 with President Frondizi and Governor Zanichelli present.

Even before the plant inauguration we were already planning to add heavier forging capacity and the second SIFCO investment was approved by Presidential decree in August 1959. The heavy forge building was the fourth major building in the complex and housed the heavy presses and hammers that produced the 6-cylinder crankshafts and other heavy forgings, particularly for the petroleum industry. As an example of the quality produced, the Hughes Tool plant in Argentina used forgings produced by IKA and I was told that they were the first ever produced outside the U.S. that Hughes had approved for the drill bits it made.

With the addition of the heavy forge facility, the total rated capacity more than doubled to 25,000 tons per year and the IKA Forge Division became the largest single forging entity in Latin America. Forgings were produced for industry in general, and practically every vehicle built in Argentina had an IKA-produced forging in it.

The two SIFCO investments translated into a 4.5% equity in IKA and Charles Smith was elected to the IKA Board at the annual meeting in 1958. The SIFCO support was always available and of top quality. George Gottschall managed the Division for a couple of years, was replaced by Sid Sheridan for a short period, and finally Bob Stich took over for the remaining years of Kaiser control. IKA's chief metallurgist, lng° Eduardo Abril, played a very important role in forging quality control and the integration of locally produced steel billets which was another important source of exchange savings.

The long awaited Automotive Decree 3693/59, promulgated by the Frondizi regime to regulate the industry, was issued in March 1959. We had assumed that the decree would provide for a scheduled integration of local content at least equal to what IKA had to accomplish in its five year plan. On this basis we welcomed the competition that would come in and the overall industrial development that would come about. The Frondizi decree however, did not take into account the capacity of the vendor industry that had been developed during IKA's three years of production nor did it require, insofar as production controls and integration schedules were concerned, compliance even close to what IKA had already proven was possible. The decree encouraged, to a degree, a decreasing imported content by applying a surcharge on the amount of imported content that exceeded the base amount per vehicle in a given year. The surcharge started at 300% but was reduced by a second decree, 6216/60, to 200%. The decree allowed an imported content of up to 60% of the vehicle's approved value for as long as four or five years of the specifically authorized program. All of the parts and assemblies requiring heavy investments in tools and machinery could easily fit within the 60%, thereby allowing the company involved to postpone the investments necessary for local production. IKA was producing a Jeep at the time the decree was issued with only U$S 75 in imported parts and was averaging about 10% import value over its entire line. With the latitude the decree offered there was no wonder why so many automobile companies and private entrepreneurs presented applications. Some 21 programs were approved, as absurd as that may seem, with 10 that actually came into being.

The IKA organization suffered a severe loss in April when Ken Flood passed away in Córdoba. Ken was one of my best friends; our relationship started when I joined the Kaiser organization in 1941. During the construction of Richmond Shipyard #2, Flood was Superintendent of Electrical Construction and I was a young junior engineer working out of the General Construction Superintendent's office handling whatever spot assignment came along. I was asked one day to go over to the electrical construction shack and coordinate some concrete slab work that Flood needed for his transformer substations. This was my first meeting with Kenny. He was short and wiry, of Welsh descent, had worked underground as a coal miner in Montana, learned the electrical trade and worked as an electrician on Boulder Dam, Grand Coulee and other major construction projects in the western states with various joint venture companies that Kaiser had either sponsored or participated in. I was able to get the bottlenecks out of the way of the electricians by coordinating the other crafts involved and I guess Flood thought I did a pretty good job because when we completed the construction of Richmond Yard #2, Flood was appointed Outfitting Superintendent of that yard and took me with him and placed me in charge of the graveyard shift. When he later became General Superintendent of Yard #3, where we built the big C4 troopships, he made me Superintendent of the Outfitting dock there. I was 24 years old, two years out of university, and making me responsible for a 5000-man operation, with all the complexities that the C4 outfitting entailed, took a lot of faith on his part.

Flood was the most open and honest man I ever knew. His door was always open for anyone who had a grievance or needed help. I could talk to him without reservation and, although we might have disagreement at times, we were always able to settle whatever differences we had. When Gus and I were married in 1944, Kenny was our best man. He was the main instigator of my going to the Detroit Engine Division and later, despite the fact that our roles would be reversed, supported my appointment to General Manager.

During his four years in Córdoba, Flood developed not only a fine facility but a lot of good supervision as well. He was a fine judge of character and, as the North American expatriates returned to the States after completing their tour of duty, the quality of their Argentine replacements was a tribute to Flood's judgment.

A farewell service held for Ken at his home in Alta Gracia was attended by hundreds of people. Although Ken wasn't Catholic, the services were conducted by a Catholic priest. Ken had a close relationship with the local Catholic hierarchy and in particular with Brother Juan, a member of the order of Don Orione. The order had a home for disabled children a few blocks from the main plant in Santa Isabel and Ken supported the home with donations of food and other necessities. Ken would never admit it but I was positive that he had built a line from IKA's boiler plant to the orphanage to keep it heated. Ken was a member of the Masonic Order and it was somewhat incongruous to see Ken in his casket with his Mason's apron and other emblems of the order, but with a Catholic priest in attendance. He would have loved it. The people of Alta Gracia named the street that he lived on in his honor. When the hearse pulled away to take Ken to Buenos Aires for a plane to take him to Oakland for burial, people along the way threw flowers on the street in front of the procession.

Bill Heard replaced Flood as Manager of Córdoba operations, Carl Olson continued on as Director of Engineering and New Product Development, and Gordon Woods as Manager of Production Engineering, which included Tool, Plant and Industrial Engineering. George Martin replaced Heard as head of all production operations in the Main Plant, which included Engines, Gears, Assembly and Press Plants. With the increasing aggressiveness of the SMATA union leaders, we needed more strength in our handling of industrial relations as well as our community and provincial government relations. Manuel Ordoñez moved to Córdoba and became responsible for these functions and performed in exemplary fashion.

This left a void in Buenos Aires and D. L. "Pete" Mapes became General Administrative Manager. Tibor Teleki, who had joined IKA in 1957, was appointed to the position of Public Relations Director. The naming of Jess Delaplain as Commercial Director was another important organizational move in 1959. Jess had been Vice President of Export for Kaiser Jeep. He had also been active in the American Automobile Manufacturers' Association and was well grounded in manufacturing and commercial practices around the world.

Plant configuration was constantly changing and I never ceased to be amazed at the amount of new construction we had going on at any given time. Although we had good cash throw-off from profits and non-cash charges, we always managed to find enough in the way of new projects to use it up. In addition to the new forge plant, 1959 saw the completion, as well as the startup, of several other major additions to the Córdoba plant.

In our original planning we had not considered the necessity of a dining room big enough to handle all employees on a given shift.

We were used to the common practice in the States of a short light lunch that most workers brought from home and ate at their workplace. The extent of company provisioning was mobile carts that sold sandwiches, cold drinks and other fast food items. Argentine practice was different and it was customary to provide a full meal at a low, subsidized price. We designed and built a dining room that could accommodate all the employees with cafeteria style service. Before the start of each shift the dining room was open for those who wanted a breakfast. The facility could serve up to 1500 at a serving and was also used as an auditorium, basketball court, movie theater, etc.

IKA's requirements for new tools and dies was growing as we added new vehicles to our lineup and a large building — bigger than the press plant in area — was constructed next to it to house all die maintenance and new tool and die making. Since the beginning, we had continually added tool-making equipment to the original cadre of machines invested by DINFIA and Kaiser, buying most of our new equipment in Europe, utilizing the favorable credit terms offered in France and Germany. Kaiser and DINFIA made additional investments of tool room equipment and a new building was necessary to relieve the pressure on the press plant. We were now, practically speaking, self-sufficient in all our tooling requirements.

Covered storage areas for new cars ready for delivery were constructed after we experienced a major hailstorm. The storm was of such intensity, and the stones so big, that the plant's corrugated aluminum roofing and its sawtooth windows were virtually demolished. Finished vehicles parked outside awaiting delivery had windshields broken, moldings ripped off and suffered a lot of paint and sheetmetal damage. Losses ran into the millions of dollars and while insurance paid a lot of the costs it never pays it all.

Another new building was constructed to handle new car preparation and delivery. Sales and Service was responsible for running this operation. A lot of customers preferred coming to the plant to take delivery of their new car and we encouraged the dealers to recommend this to their clients. The customer would get a plant tour, take delivery of his car and drive home. The freight savings helped pay for his vacation. We also trained service mechanics for the dealers in this facility, stressing a quality job of new car preparation.

As IKA grew, its insurance requirements also grew and the volume of our insurance premiums reached the point where we could justify setting up our own insurance brokerage company. IKACOR, SRL, a limited partnership, not only eliminated the expense of maintaining an insurance department but enabled us to build up a technical capability for insurance placement that included the valuation of insurance rates, selection of the best insurance plan for the risk or asset involved and claims representation. Dr. Jorge Hayzus's Treasury Division had the responsibility for insurance matters and Nicolas Clover was IKA's Insurance Manager. IKACOR was formed in July 1959 with Clover as General Manager. It handled not only IKA's brokerage but most of IKA's dealers' as well. A year or so after launching IKACOR, we went into insurance underwriting and organized Aseguradores Industriales, S.A., and Clover was made Managing Director.

We had begun selling bare engines and, in some cases, engines and transmission sets, to manufacturers of harvesting machines, lift trucks, railroad maintenance cars and other types of self-propelled and stationary power units. Each of these orders, which usually came from our dealers, required special handling and, although the sales were important — we had delivered over 2000 units — it was disruptive to production activities in the main plant. We bought a building in a locality called Pajas Blancas, on the road to the Córdoba airport, and created the Industrial Products Division (D.P.I., which stood for Division Productos Industriales). Stan Reis was appointed General Manager and Ing° Amilcar Romeo handled Industrial Product sales, working out of the Buenos Aires office. License agreements were signed with Gorman Rupp Pump Co., Schramm Compressor and Hobart Welding.

Together with the licensors, portable pumping units, welding machines and air compressors that incorporated our 4- and 6-cylinder engines with the elements we imported were designed and built by D.P.I. These units were much in demand by the construction and mining industries throughout the country and we enjoyed a pretty good business until some years later when diesel engines became available which were better suited to this purpose.

D.P.I. was given a lot of latitude, together with Product Engineering, in developing products for general industrial use and it relieved the main plant of small run items. One of the products it developed was a flat bed cabless truck for use in airports for baggage and cargo handling. A four wheel drive version was also produced for off-road use in the timber and mining industries. Called the Carguero, it was very popular and there are some of these units still in use today.

Two new utility vehicles were introduced in the last half of 1959, the Willys one ton pickup and a panel delivery version of the Estanciera. The pickup was named the "Baqueano" (scout) and the panel delivery was simply called the "Furgón," the Spanish equivalent. We later brought out a one-half ton version of the Baqueano that was dressed up with a two tone paint job and chrome bumpers and moldings.

Writing these accounts some 35 years later, and much from memory alone, I have to ask myself why we didn't produce these units at the same time that we brought out the Estanciera instead of two years later. There was much commonality in the three vehicles in frame and body parts, all the power train components were the same, and there would have been no problem in producing all three models simultaneously. Perhaps one of my ex-colleagues knows the answer — but I must confess ignorance. The Baqueano, in two or four wheel drive options, was a rugged pickup and worked in any type of terrain. The Furgón, as a closed commercial delivery van with ample cubic capacity, filled a need for many different businesses.

We finished the year with a production of over 24,000 units and a work force of almost 6000 employees. The Estanciera accounted for almost half of our output with Jeeps, Carabelas and the new utility vehicles dividing up the remainder. Our cumulative production since inception amounted to over 61,000 vehicles and at that point, one of every seven vehicles in circulation in Argentina was an IKA product. For the fiscal year ending in June we reported a profit of around U$S 4,500,000 on sales of about U$S 50,000,000 and distributed a 25% stock and 5% cash dividend to our share-holders. At the annual meeting all the Directors were re-elected with the exception of Comodoro Bayon Vago and Comodoro Villafañe who were replaced by Brigadier Generals Gustavo Hermansson and Antonio Parodi as representatives of DINFIA. I was elected President, replacing Edgar Kaiser, who continued on as a Director, and Steve Girard replaced me as 1st Vice President.

Chapter VII | 1960

1960 would be the first full year of production under the Frondizi Automotive Decree and we were somewhat concerned as to our ability to stand up against the competition. The competition would not only be offering their latest models but, because of the high amount of imported content the decree allowed, they could produce them at a lower cost. The decree was manifestly unfair to IKA, giving little, if any, recognition to the industrial capabilities that had been built up by IKA and its 2000 suppliers. The new companies had tremendous latitude in choosing to build locally or import. IKA did not enjoy this luxury of choice because for the five years of its existence it had dedicated its entire cash flow and a substantial amount of foreign debt to the creation of an inhouse manufacturing and vendor base that permitted it to comply with — even exceed in most cases — the local content levels established in our 1955 agreement. It would have been impossible, for evident reasons, to shut down our engine plant, lay off people and import engines even though it would probably have been more economical to do so and the imported engine would have been a more modern one than the engine we were producing. This same reasoning could have been applied to transmissions, axles, stampings, etc.

In addition to IKA, ten new companies would be producing vehicles. In addition to the ten new entities, two others, Mercedes Benz and DINFIA, had been operating for years and were not direct competition. Mercedes built heavy trucks, did very little manufacturing and operated under special provisions that allowed a high degree of imports because of Argentina's need for heavy truck and bus chassis. DINFIA produced a light pickup with a Borgward diesel engine that had just started to be produced locally. The DINFIA pickup, which was called the Rastrojero, maintained a fairly constant volume of around 3,000 units per year. Therefore, including IKA, there would be 11 major companies competing for the passenger car and light utility vehicle market.

Of the ten new entities, only four — General Motors, Ford, Chrysler, and Fiat — were essentially subsidiaries of the prime manufacturer. The exception was Chrysler, which had some local ownership by the Fevre interests but was managed by Chrysler. The other six companies — SIAM (British Motors), Industria Automotriz Santa Fe (Auto Union), Citroen Argentina (Citroen), Isard Argentina (Studebaker), Metalmecánica (De Carlo), and IAFA (Peugeot) — were local companies operating with license agreements and very little if any financial support from the parent. The government approval of this many companies was absurd to say the least. It was evident that there would have to be a restructuring of the industry because there was no way that 11 separate and directly competing companies could exist in a market as limited in absorptive power as the Argentine. But it would be a long time before bankruptcies, labor dislocations and general turmoil would bring about the consolidation needed. Meanwhile, IKA had to not only exist but progress as well. Today, over 30 years later, the bulk of the market is served by three companies, one of which is the successor company to IKA.

But IKA wasn't sitting still and watching the rest of the world pass it by. We had two new passenger cars that would be introduced in 1960. The other principal defensive action we took was the creation of a finance company to handle retail and wholesale credit.

Most customers do not have the ready cash to buy a car. Before our organization of a finance company, the buyer obtained credit through a combination of usually high cost sources. In some limited cases, credit came from commercial banks and the dealer to the degree that his working capital permitted it. In fact, the average dealer, with IKA's increasing production volume, was hard pressed to finance his ever growing inventory and needed wholesale financing.

In early 1959, Jess Delaplain, Hayzus, Allende and I talked with Joe Reis in Oakland about the credit vacuum in Argentina and began planning the organization of a finance company. Joe agreed to locate an experienced automotive finance manager and in a couple of months reported that he had found a man who had all the qualifications for the job. Platt Harburger, then working in an automotive finance company in San Antonio, Texas, had indicated an interest in the Argentine opportunity. Reis arranged for a meeting with Harburger in Kaiser's New York offices in July. I asked that Harburger bring his wife with him because if he was the right man for the job it was important that Mrs. Harburger be aware of what she would be facing in an overseas post. Expatriates who had problems usually had them because the wife was unhappy with the problems she faced in everyday living — language, customs, remoteness from family and friends. After meeting Mrs. Harburger, any concerns I might have had vanished. Jess Delaplain and I interviewed the Harburgers, reached agreement and in early September 1959 they moved to Buenos Aires.

We spent the next few months getting the finance company organized. We had an inactive corporation, called Permanente, that had been formed to bid on a television channel and we used it for the finance company. Permanente was a good Kaiser name also since it was the name of our cement company in the U.S. at the time. We bought a couple of floors in a ten story building at Belgrano 680 to get started in. As Permanente grew we acquired more and eventually owned eight floors there. IKA seconded some people to the finance company. Two of them that I remember were Juan Ponce from the accounting department and Juan Couceiro from purchasing, both with some previous finance operation experience. Ponce became office manager and was over accounting, while Couceiro was responsible for collections and the security pledges *(prendas)*. Under Harburger's guidance all the procedures and forms needed to operate a finance company were designed. An instruction manual was written telling dealers how to arrange credit from Permanente and outlining the method to be followed in discounting the prendas that the dealer offered as security.

The overriding question, of course, was where all the money would come from that Permanente would require for its credit operation. Harburger, together with Allende, Hayzus and Julio Nuñez, devised a financial plan that capitalized Permanente at m$n 200,000,000 — about U$S 2,500,000 at the time. Of this total, m$n 50,000,000 was in common stock and m$n 150,000,000 was in 15% participating preferred shares. IKA subscribed to all of the common and approximately 60% of the preferred. Deltec, through its subsidiary Argentaria, sold the balance of the preferred on the open market. The bulk of Permanente's working capital came from the sale of 190-day promissory notes or *pagarés*. These were marketed in Argentina by Argentaria and in the United States and Europe by Deltec.

The hard currency funds we obtained abroad were by far Permanente's major financing source. In order to make it possible for foreign corporations to lend to Permanente legally, we organized the Development Credit Corporation in the U.S., which borrowed from various corporate lenders and in turn loaned to Permanente. Renault and later American Motors agreed to address their royalties to Permanente until U$S 1,000,000 each was revolving. To avoid any devaluation exposure and to be able to know what our hard currency funds would cost in pesos when the note fell due, we covered all foreign borrowings with future exchange contracts.

There were times when, due to internal conditions in Argentina, people were hesitant to lend. We would then have to cut back on the amount of financing we could offer the dealers while we collected and met our obligations. Permanente never had a default. We instituted another safeguard by having our auditor, Price Waterhouse, maintain control of the prenda portfolio so that at any time its value was 30% greater than the total of promissory notes outstanding. Permanente reached its high point in 1965 when it had U$S 100,000,000 in total receivables of which U$S 75,000,000 were Permanente funds, raised as described above, and U$S 25,000,000 in wholesale financing which Permanente serviced for IKA. In other words Permanente did not invest its money in wholesale but made the collection from the dealer and turned the money over to IKA.

Permanente opened its doors for business on February 1st, 1960. At the end of June 1961, it completed its first full fiscal year and at that point was financing 35% of all IKA retail sales. It had a prenda portfolio valued at U$S 25,000,000 and reported a profit over U$S 750,000. The common stock — all owned by IKA — received a 19% dividend and the preferred share received its basic dividend of 15% and a 9% participating for a total of 24%, all related to par value.

IKA began producing its second passenger car, the Bergantin, in March 1960. The events leading up to its introduction provide an interesting story.

Before commencing production of the Kaiser Carabela in 1958 and watching the trend, particularly in Europe, toward smaller cars, we were cognizant of the fact that we would soon have to replace it or add a mid-size car to our line. The Kaiser, weighing well over 4000 pounds, with a 118-inch wheelbase and separate frame and body construction, was not the volume passenger car that the majority of buyers would want. We had been in contact with various automobile companies as far back as 1957, when we met with the Rootes Group in England, Peugeot, Renault and Simca in France. Alberto de Ridder, because of his many contacts in France, urged us to go in this direction. The biggest single problem we had to overcome with any of these companies and the reason we delayed so long in taking action was the magnitude of the investment required to tool up a completely new passenger car. In 1957, three years before the issuance of the Frondizi Decree, all our thinking was conditioned toward maximizing local content. As a matter of fact, we wouldn't have been able to get approval from the Aramburu government for any program that didn't measure up to IKA's own standards of local integration. Further, none of the small cars we considered would lend themselves to the standardization of any of our manufactured components that we had successfully accomplished between the Jeep utility vehicles and the Carabela. IKA, technically speaking, would have been able to develop its own car — and later did — but the exigencies of time and financial constraints weighed heavily against taking that course of action.

In 1958 we became aware of Alfa-Romeo's plan to discontinue its four door 1900 model. Memory tells me it was called the Berlina. We considered the 1900 to be an ideal size and type for the Argentine market. It was monocoque construction and we felt confident that we could adapt our power train components to it. Before approaching Alfa-Romeo to sound out its management to ascertain if it would consider selling the body dies and assembly tooling, we thought we'd better do some homework. We located a used 1900 and brought it to Córdoba where Olson and his team went to work on it. The project engineering team was led by Ing. Bascou and the production coordinator was Charlie Epps. The project team tore the vehicle down and rebuilt it with IKA components. Much of the Alfa-designed suspension components were retained but the power train, steering gear, brakes and all other components excepting the body were either IKA or its vendors. We disguised the vehicle with a false grille and some canvas and did some extensive road testing. The prototype proved out very well. It had good roadability and plenty of power — solid and comfortable for four or five passengers. We were now ready to go into design and with this preliminary work in back of us we were also ready to talk seriously with Alfa-Romeo.

Alfa, famous for its design and vehicle quality and with an origin that traced back to the early days of the automotive industry, was then owned by Finmeccanica, an entity of the Italian government. Alfa's principal offices and plant were in Milan. Ordoñez, who spoke pretty good Italian in addition to a few other languages, was given the assignment of making the initial contact with Alfa management and went to Milan in April 1958. When he arrived in Milan, it was decided in an initial meeting that the concept would have to be discussed with Dr. Igino Alloisio, Vice Director General, who was then vacationing on the Italian Riviera. As he later related to me, Ordoñez went to Portofino and located Alloisio sunbathing on a float offshore. I have a mental picture of Manuel swimming out to the float, introducing himself and telling Alloisio we wanted his 1900 tools and dies to build a car in Argentina. Although the first reaction was a bit cold — and it wasn't due only to the water temperature — Alloisio did say he would take the matter under advisement and get back to us. Ordoñez returned to Buenos Aires and maintained contact and, in a matter of a few weeks, we had a meeting date set in Milan. In the interim there were a lot of technical exchanges between Olson's team and its Alfa counterparts relating to our adaptation ideas. But nothing came out of Alfa indicating if, even in principle, it was seriously considering our proposition.

Ordoñez and I took off for Milan via New York in early September 1958. The only incident worthy of mention during the trip took place on the TWA flight out of New York, which landed in Paris before continuing on to Milan. After taking off from Orly, I noticed the number four engine — these were pre-jet days and we were flying in a Lockheed Constellation — starting to smoke. I called this to the attention of the stewardess because I didn't think the pilot could see it from his vantage point. She patted me on the head and told me to relax but sure enough, about ten minutes later one of the cylinders of the radial engine let go and came right through the cowl, hung up in plain view. We returned to Orly where we decided we had had enough of TWA and got on the evening train to Milan, arriving there the next morning, September 8.

After freshening up a bit, we went to the Alfa offices where I had the pleasure of meeting Dr. Alloisio, who was very warm and open, and I took an immediate liking to him. He suggested that we might like a plant tour and this took practically the entire day. The next morning we met again with Dr. Alloisio and after the usual exchange of pleasantries and a cup of cappuccino, Alloisio asked, "Have you ever been to Lake Como?" When I replied to the contrary, he suggested we take a ride there for lunch. This was alright with me but I kept thinking to myself that I'd like to get a positive response, one way or the other. We got into a car — there were four of us since one of Alloisio's staff, Ing. Vigo, was along. The one encouraging thing I noted was that Vigo was packing a bulky briefcase.

Como was beautiful and we had lunch in one of the magnificent hotels overlooking the Lake. Not a word of business during lunch, though, but finally when all the plates were cleared and we were having coffee, Alloisio said, "Mr. McCloud, I suppose you would like to know if we would be willing to let you use the 1900 dies." He then beckoned to Vigo who pulled out a thick three-ring binder from his briefcase and handed it over to me. The book contained a complete listing of all the dies and assembly tooling required for the production of the 1900 four door monocoque body. Alfa had done its homework. Alloisio stated that his company would sell IKA the set of tools for one million dollars with the proviso that the vehicle produced in Argentina would not, in any way, carry any Alfa-Romeo identification, nor could our advertising associate the firm with the Argentine product. Although an Alfa-Romeo association would have been valuable, it was not as important to us as getting the car. The body was Pininfarina styled and later we got Pininfarina approval to affix a label on the trunk lid. The price of one million dollars, which was non-negotiable, was a fraction of what it would have cost to design and build a comparable set of tooling. Alfa also made available its designs for seats, interiors, instrument layout, etc. An agreement in principle was finalized and we returned to Argentina.

Córdoba was released to commence engineering and the import permit applications were prepared and submitted to the pertinent authorities. As soon as we received the approvals necessary, I returned to Milan with Allende in December and we signed a definitive contract he had prepared. The final agreement provided for technical assistance from Alfa at cost, assistance in press setup, assembly fixture installation and initial body assembly operating procedures. Alfa complied to the letter of the agreement. The tools were delivered in good condition and the technicians who came later to help get us into production were all capable and dedicated individuals.

Engineering proceeded full speed on the adaptations and new designs required. We learned a lot from the exercise and the collaboration with Alfa was to prove of great value to us later on. The suspension system that was finally designed was a cross between Alfa and IKA due to the constraints of a fixed rear axle. In the adaptation of our engines to the body we followed the Alfa practice of a three point engine mount — two mounts, one on each side of the engine as close to the center of gravity as possible, and a third mount at the transmission. This system was later applied on all IKA products that used our 4- and 6-cylinder engines.

On March 22, 1960, Charlie Epps handed Bill Heard the keys to the first Bergantin that came off the new elevated final assembly line installed to produce the monocoque bodied car.

From the date of signing the final agreement in December 1958 to production took a total of 15 months. Following the nautical motif established by the Carabela, the vehicle was named the Bergantin, the Spanish equivalent of Brigantine. It was produced with both the Kaiser 4-cylinder and 6-cylinder engines. There was a taxi version produced in addition to the regular passenger cars for private use.

Assembling the Bergantin body was far more complex than the Carabela. Part of the problem was the monocoque construction but in the main the extra work was caused by the method the Italians used in die design. At that time in Europe there were several cars that were produced in relatively low volume and manufacturers would use more direct production hours per unit in order to minimize tooling costs. The die sets for the Bergantin reflected this practice. Instead of a single die set for a fender, the Bergantin might have two or three sets that were much simpler in construction but required the joining together of smaller stampings to produce the final part. Smaller presses could be used but more setup and run time was needed and in the body assembly shop, extra manhours were needed to weld and lead the joints in order to hide them and produce the desired finish. In today's plants this practice is not followed due to environmental health standards, but in those days leaded joints was common practice and also required a lot of skill.

We learned from the Bergantin experience, knowledge that was used later when we designed the adaptations of our mechanical components to the Rambler line, which replaced the Bergantin in 1962, and still later when we designed the Torino.

The total production run of the Bergantin amounted to slightly more than 8000 units — enough to amortize pre-production costs but nowhere near the volume we had hoped for. The developmental work on the Bergantin took place in the early days of the Frondizi regime and the new decree came out just a few months after we had concluded the Alfa-Romeo agreement. We were then beyond the point of no return.

It was evident that when the Chevrolets, Valiants and Falcons of the competition appeared in 1962 the Bergantin would be finished. Meanwhile we had finally concluded an agreement with Renault that would satisfy IKA's requirement for a small passenger car, and talks had begun with American Motors for a licensing agreement that would give us a vehicle line to replace the Bergantin.

From time to time we would have important visitors in Córdoba from the U.S., Europe and Latin America. I vividly remember the visit in March 1960 of presidential candidate and former Ohio governor Adlai Stevenson, accompanied by former Connecticut Senator William Benton. Senator Benton, who was then publisher of the Encyclopedia Britannica, wrote a book-length report on the two-month trip he and Governor Stevenson made entitled "The Voice of Latin America and Its Significance in Today's World." His views on the need for private capital formation in Latin America are still appropriate 30 years later. Because he so keenly understood what we in IKA were trying to accomplish, I think the following paragraphs quoted from the section of his book devoted to IKA are pertinent to this story.

> Kaiser Industries Corporation in Córdoba, Argentina, known familiarly as IKA (Industrias Kaiser Argentina), was the outstanding U.S.-created plant we visited. About 85% of all new cars sold in Argentina in 1959 came from this plant, the biggest single manufacturing enterprise in Argentina with a current annual volume of $ 100,000,000. Governor Stevenson and I were shown around the 1,600,000-square-foot plant by its manager, James McCloud, who told us its fascinating history.
>
> After the failure of Kaiser-Frazer cars in the United States, Henry J. Kaiser, Sr., took his old dies and equipment from his Willow Run, Michigan, plant and started up in Córdoba in 1955. One year later the plant was turning out cars. Thus far it has produced about 70,000 vehicles of various types — Jeeps, station wagons, etc. More than 40,000 units of 15 different models were scheduled for 1960. McCloud told us that there is an unfilled Argentine demand for at least 1,000,000 vehicles. (He says that the average

age of the cars on Argentine highways is between 15 and 20 years!) So, despite the fact that General Motors Corp., Ford Motor Co. and Chrysler Corp. are now opening plants in Argentina, McCloud hopes for a steadily rising production for Kaiser.

An important point is that, of the total outstanding stock of IKA, Argentine investors own 51% or more. Further, although McCloud started with 150 U.S. officers and employees, he has now replaced all but 32 of them with Argentines. I was told that IKA, including its Buenos Aires office for sales and finance, employs 6,000 people. (In my judgment the IKA ownership pattern is sound: U.S. companies, if they wish to "export capitalism" and protect their investments in Latin America, would do well to extend to citizens of the countries where they operate a wider opportunity to acquire equity shares in their Latin American subsidiaries and thus the opportunity to participate in earnings and dividends. This is one of the significant issues of private enterprise of the future.)

The plant has a strong labour union with the men working 44 hours a week and being paid for 48. The average man on the line earns about $22 a week while men in the forge, doing more skilled and more dangerous work, earn about $26. This latter group had been trained by men sent down from Toledo, O., during 1959. We saw them handling the hot metal with forceps and enormous 'hammers' seemingly with great skill, and we were told that these men learned at least as fast as U.S. workmen. One of the Kaiser directors said that within a year he thought their productivity would actually exceed that of U.S. workmen; he said that they try harder and are more interested in their work.

Here is an outstanding example of U.S. enterprise and industry working in co-operation with Latin-American capital and labour. I cite it as well as the other examples to show how constructive and important the investment of foreign capital and the importation of foreign business leadership can be to the industrialization of these underdeveloped countries.

Further on in his article, Senator Benton again addresses the role of private foreign capital:

> As I have suggested, a U.S. economic policy toward Latin America
> that consists solely or primarily of a policy of encouraging private
> U.S. investment in Latin America is at best singularly inadequate.
> At the same time it is critically necessary to recognize the crucial
> role that private foreign capital has played and can play. The IKA
> story illustrates this.

The Renault Dauphine, our second new car for 1960, came out in July, following the Bergantin by four months. The history of this development is not only interesting but the fact that it was carried out simultaneously with that of the Bergantin meant that a lot of us in IKA were pretty busy people during the two years — 1958 to 1960.

Alberto de Ridder had a lot to do with opening up our relationship with Renault. Alberto and I first met with Renault Export Sales personnel in Paris in July 1957. We had long discussions about IKA's need for a small car and its manufacturing capabilities. We were taken on some plant tours and were also shown into Renault Experimental and saw their future vehicle concepts. This was the start of IKA's "French Connection." About a year later I brought a survey team to France that included Claude Deschamps from Purchasing, Ing. Bascou from Engineering and Manuel Ordoñez. We had meetings with Renault, Simca and Peugeot.

In January 1959 we started to get serious in pursuing a Renault license. We were now aware of the activity in the Ministry of Industry directed toward the development of an Automotive Decree to promote new investments and regulate the manufacturers. It would have been impossible not to have been aware of the activity in the Ministry because there were delegations in Buenos Aires representing every car maker in the U.S. and Europe trying to negotiate a deal with the Government. This deluge of separate proposals was the trigger for the regulations that evolved into a decree. While every one of the aspiring new applicants had a hand, directly or indirectly, in the document finally promulgated by the Ministry, one would have thought that IKA's opinion also would have been sought — but it wasn't. The gleam of a deluge of foreign investments was in the eye of the Frondizi government and the steamroller couldn't be stopped.

Charles Bernal, Renault's export sales manager for Latin America, met with me in January 1959. Bernal was a good salesman and a good looking fellow. I remember giving him the nickname of "Cary Grant." Willys Overland do Brasil had just signed an accord with Renault and Bernal gave me a good summation of the Renault-WOB agreement and indicated that we could get the same basic terms. One of the most important aspects of the agreement was Renault's willingness to make a substantial investment consisting of most of the tooling and equipment required for the production of the Dauphine that would be brought in to coincide with the integration schedule contained in the decree. I had also received indications from Edgar Kaiser and Steve Girard that Kaiser Industries would support the Renault program and would be willing to make an additional investment in IKA of some equipment that would help round out our requirements. The program took on momentum and we began studying in earnest the unique features of the Dauphine that we would have to consider in our production planning. All of the pre-production work on the Dauphine would be taking place simultaneously with the Bergantin, producing a heavy work load for Engineering and Planning, but unlike the Bergantin, the Dauphine startup could take advantage of the liberal import facilities contained in the decree and not have to be completely dependent on inhouse manufacturing.

We received word that Bernal had arranged a meeting for me with Michel Maison, Renault's Export Director, in Paris on May 4. George Hayzus and I left Buenos Aires on a Panagra flight heading for New York where we would meet with Girard, Cutler and others before going on to Paris for the negotiation with Maison.

Our first stop was Santiago where I was greeted with a cable from Girard saying that Maison had postponed the meeting. We got on the next plane back to Buenos Aires, arriving there about three in the morning to be greeted with another cable that reinstated the meeting for May 4. There was nothing to do but go home, clean up and get back on Panagra again.

This was another memorable flight. After leaving Lima enroute to Miami we lost the number two engine and had to land at Guayaquil, Ecuador, where we would have to wait until a replacement engine was flown in and installed. Hayzus and I walked around the town and watched the coffee beans drying in the streets, then took a room in the Humboldt Hotel where we worked until we again took off about midnight, April 30, arriving in New York about noon the next day. We had an all-day meeting at the International Hotel at the airport (then Idylwild, now J.F. Kennedy) with Girard, Cutler, Allende, Lou Staelens, the Kaiser Jeep controller, and others. Bill Heard also came into the meeting, having just landed from Paris where he had been reviewing production planning with his counterparts in Renault.

The key issue to be negotiated with Renault was the amount of IKA equity it would receive for its investment and, secondly, the royalty agreement. IKA's book value per share at the time was about U$S 5.00 — substantially higher than the market value as quoted on the stock exchange. We set our negotiating target at U$S 4.50. The royalty agreement would have to be fairly similar to the IKA-Kaiser Jeep and WOB-Renault agreements so we didn't envision any real differences that could arise in this aspect of the negotiation.

With our position fairly well formulated we took off for Paris that evening on a Pan Am 707 — one of the first scheduled jet flights — to Paris, arriving there Saturday afternoon. We started our meetings Monday morning with Michel Maison and Charles Bernal, made good progress and arrived at an agreement in principle on Wednesday that would enable us to definitize our application to the Ministry of Industry for inclusion in the new decree. As expected we were negotiated down in our asking price to U$S 3.58 per share, which was still above market. The total agreed value of the Renault investment was U$S 3,800,000, which gave it a 7.3% equity in IKA. The complementary investment by Kaiser was valued at U$S 1,700,000. Kaiser's equity then rose to 30.3%. Provisions were made for Renault to nominate a director to the IKA Board and to appoint the Quality Control Manager for any products built under the license agreement.

I then returned to the States and got Edgar's blessing on the new program. I finally got back to Argentina in time for the third annual dealer convention which was held in Mar del Plata — we had outgrown the Sierras Hotel in Alta Gracia.

In June the IKA Board approved the Renault agreement and final government approval was issued in September. We had already released the Renault tool and die build program and we were already well along with the modifications to the plant layout. We still had some minor points to settle with Renault but everything finally came together and on the evening of November 6, Maison and I signed the agreement at my home.

Mapes, along with Jules Lussier and Leopoldo Tirel, went to Paris and with the Renault planning department worked out the imported parts and tooling shipment schedules. Tirel would stay in France as IKA's representative and Lussier was named coordinator for the program. Lucien Combes led the Renault team in Córdoba as Chief of Quality Control and Camille Gruau represented Renault in Buenos Aires and became a Director.

The pre-production work on the Dauphine was much simpler than on the Bergantin. We had a proven vehicle to work with, good product designs and specifications and were supported by a major producer with all the resources necessary. This was a much different situation compared to the Carabela and the Bergantin where we were completely dependent on our own organization. The production mentality at the plant underwent quite a transformation with the advent of the Dauphine. Everything that had to be processed was smaller and lighter than we had been accustomed to in our other vehicles. Tolerances, and quality as a result, were much tighter. The exercise was good for IKA and brought about a much higher degree of quality consciousness throughout the organization.

On July 12, 1960, the first Renault Dauphine came off the line and a ribbon with the colors of France and Argentina was cut by the French Commercial Attaché to Argentina, Robert Le Guyader. Two months later, at the Plaza Hotel in Buenos Aires, the official public presentation was made with Bernard Vernier-Paillez, General Secretary of Renault, and Michel Maison present. We built about 3800 Dauphines in 1960, which accounted for 11% of IKA's total production. In 1961 18,000 Dauphines were built — 42% of our total — which serves to illustrate the importance that Renault products had for IKA.

The Dauphine, a 31 hp rear engine, rear drive car weighing 1400 lbs was, in a sense, Renault's answer to the VW Beetle. With four doors it was a more comfortable car and although we never had to compete with VW in Argentina, I'm sure that we'd have given a good account of ourselves. Fiat came into the market in 1960 also, and had two cars — the 600 and the 1100 — that bracketed the Dauphine 850, but we always managed to capture our share of the market. In 1962 we introduced a sports sedan version called the Gordini — named after Renault's famous engine designer. This model had increased horsepower, a four speed transmission and better seating and trim. More than 85,000 Dauphines and Gordinis would be built before their discontinuance some years later, to be followed by the latest Renault models as they emerged. Renault became a dominant factor in our forward planning. We were kept updated on its various new vehicle developments and were able to plan future new model introductions accordingly — a luxury we had not enjoyed previously.

We had our disagreements from time to time but our relationship overall with Renault was good. Michel Maison did not like what he termed "heavy" production activities, meaning our forge, foundry and other integrated activities, that served industry in general. I think he would have been happy if we had concentrated our resources on our own in-house production only, and more specifically, the Renault line to the exclusion of utility vehicles and our other passenger cars. I saw things differently and wanted IKA to be more than just a car producer. Be that as it may, IKA was good for Renault and vice-versa.

One indication of Renault's respect for IKA took place in 1964 during the Illia regime when President de Gaulle of France paid a visit to the plant. We had heard a rumor to the effect that ex-President Peron, then in exile in Spain, had sent word ahead to "welcome General de Gaulle as if he were me." Large crowds were at the Córdoba airport and thousands lined the route from the airport to the plant. It seemed to me, though, that there was as much anti-Peronism sentiment as there was pro. On the way to the plant the side windows of the car Illia and de Gaulle were riding in were broken by rocks thrown by the mob. I remember giving President Illia my handkerchief to stem the flow of blood from a hand that had been cut by flying glass.

When the entourage arrived at the plant, somewhat shook up, I was at the head of the receiving line in the lobby and when I welcomed de Gaulle, I could see that he was somewhat taken aback by the fact that it was an American and not a Frenchman that greeted him. We had a cavalcade of open Jeeps to tour the inside of the plant and I drove the lead car, taking both Presidents and Córdoba Governor Paez Molina in it. Security guards walked on each side. Every once in a while a bolt would whiz by the Jeep. I was really concerned for the safety of the two Presidents and I'm certain that they weren't too comfortable either. Both were standing erect in the Jeep during the plant tour and de Gaulle had his hand on my shoulder for support and kept saying to me, *Marche!* — "keep going!" After we circled the plant and arrived back at the plant side of the lobby entrance I signaled to the guards to open the doors and drove the Jeep through the lobby and down the outside stairs to the waiting cars. If we had stopped in the plant I think we would have been mobbed.

After the plant visit Gus and I were invited to attend a luncheon in honor of de Gaulle given in his honor by President Illia at the Palace of Justice in Córdoba. Crowds had gathered outside and there was a riot during the luncheon that had to be quelled by mounted police with dogs and tear gas. General de Gaulle took it all in stride. It was evident that he had been through situations a lot rougher than this. He represented France at its best and his demeanor left no question as to the respect that was to be accorded to him as Chief of State.

1960 was the year that we, together with Kaiser Engineers, organized our construction subsidiary company, ICKSA (Ingeniería y Construcciones Kaiser, S.A.). Kaiser Engineers was responsible for the construction of IKA's original facilities and when this first phase was completed — in little over a year — Jack Hughes and his team returned to Oakland. Jack did a good job in developing the Argentine construction organization left behind and it was made part of the IKA Plant Engineering Division. The Construction department, headed by Natalio Lucioni, designed and constructed all subsequent IKA plant expansions. We had enough ongoing work to justify a small Architectural and Engineering crew, under Nicolas Emaides's supervision, and the construction work was performed either by direct hiring or by managing subcontractors. Usually, on any given project, it was a combination of both. Since it was part of our organization, the Construction Department was able to react much faster to IKA's needs, coordinate with the operating departments better and eliminate any production interferences. IKA's growth was so dynamic that we didn't have time to call in an outside architect and engineering consultant, go through an indoctrination process to get him up to speed and then watch over his work. It was more efficient and less costly to do it ourselves. Of course, when you have a construction group as energetic as ours you have to be careful that you don't overbuild. But this is what management is for.

When 1960 rolled around it looked like the bulk of our new construction, at least at the main plant, was fairly well completed and the question was what to do with the Construction Department. It was going to be difficult to sustain it on the work level we foresaw in the immediate future. I talked to George Havas and Jack Hughes about this. The concept of a jointly owned engineering and construction company evolved and we organized Ingeniería y Construcciones Kaiser, S.A. in September 1960. The new entity gave Kaiser Engineers an operating company in Argentina that would alert it to major projects that it might be interested in pursuing and IKA would still be able to call on its own construction arm, with the added advantage of being able to use KE's depth in engineering, project management and cost estimating expertise. We also expected a lot of foreign investment activity that could lead into steel and mining projects.

Al Hilleland, one of Kaiser Engineers' project managers, was just completing some work for Willys Overland do Brasil and, with his background and experience, was well qualified for the position of Vice President and General Manager of ICKSA, to which he was appointed shortly after ICKSA's formation. About 160 IKA employees were transferred to the new company. Nat Lucioni continued on as Construction Manager and Luis Allende, who had been working in the U.S. with Kaiser Engineers, returned to Argentina as Project Development Manager.

ICKSA closed its first fiscal year in June 1961 with about a million dollars worth of work for outside clients on its books and about the same amount for IKA. It reported a small profit for the year — about $50,000. ICKSA built a number of major housing projects, roads and industrial plants. At the end of the Kaiser management period — 1967 — ICKSA's yearly turnover was about U$S 5,000,000 and it was showing an annual profit of U$S 250,000. By this time IKA's own work had been reduced substantially and probably amounted to no more than 10-15% of ICKSA's portfolio.

Kaiser Engineers also benefitted from the association. It won several important projects: a major phase of the Somisa steel facilities in San Nicolas, a major expansion of the St. Joe lead mine in Jujuy and feasibility studies in various minerals projects.

The Kaisers encouraged their people to involve themselves in local community affairs. It was an unwritten credo and IKA was no exception.

In celebration of the 150th anniversary of the May 1810 revolution of independence from Spain, the City of Buenos Aires organized its International Sesquicentennial Exhibition in 1960 and invited IKA to construct an exhibit. IKA, at that time, was probably the largest manufacturing firm in Argentina and its exhibit would have to reflect the importance it played in the industrial community. The Kaiser Aluminum and Chemical Corporation, together with the noted architect, Buckminster Fuller, had developed a geodesic dome that was made up of interlocking tetrahedron stamped aluminum panels that could be erected to cover virtually any diameter desired.

At the Hawaii Kai development in Honolulu, Henry Kaiser had erected one to serve as an adjunct to the hotel for conventions, exhibits, and the like. It was a very efficient facility due to the completely unobstructed interior and, I might add, a very economical building cover in terms of cost per square foot. We concluded that the Kaiser dome would not only provide the space we would need for our exhibit but would also stand out on its own as an example of modern construction techniques. The firm that designed the original Kaiser Aluminum exhibit in Disneyland was selected to do the layout for the IKA exhibit. Using a dome with a diameter of 130 feet that yielded about 13,000 square feet of clear floor area, we had the outstanding attraction of the Sesquicentennial.

All of IKA's products were on display in the dome and, in addition, we included exhibits of Lockheed-Kaiser, Kaiser Aluminum, Kaiser Engineers, and IKA's subsidiaries — Permanente, IKACOR and ICKSA. Everyone who visited the dome was impressed with IKA's industrial potential. IKA was more than a reality; in the short space of five years it had become a dominant factor in the Argentine industrial community.

Our participation in the Sesquicentennial was but one example of IKA's community involvement and reflected the principles that the Kaisers — Henry J., Edgar and Henry J. Jr. — had always laid down. Wherever we happened to be, whether it was Australia, Ghana or Detroit, we were encouraged to become part of the community and to participate to the fullest extent we were able. With IKA, this guiding policy reached into several areas: educational, cultural, sports and social activities for our employees, financial support to charitable institutions and local civic projects.

Argüello Academy and the IKA Technical Institute were two examples of our support of education, but there were many others. Both at the plant and in Buenos Aires several courses of study were provided by the Company and staffed by competent educators. IKA's training departments, under Paul Becker in Córdoba and Julio Navarro Monzó in Buenos Aires, conducted supervisory training, business administration, English language with emphasis on technical terminology, and secretarial instruction among other curricula. Pablo Soultanian, Tool Room Superintendent, conducted on the job training for tool and die makers that enabled them to become masters of their trade. Extensive instruction throughout the plant on safety procedures was under the direction of Fred Stewart-Harris and prizes were awarded to the departments and individuals with the best safety records.

Another example of our policy to maintain cordial and direct relations with all our employees was the annual service award presentation. Every employee who completed five years of service was presented his five year pin at an annual dinner to which his immediate family was also invited. At the first award dinner held in 1961, some 900 employees were presented their five year pins. Subsequent years would see this number grow as more and more completed their fifth anniversary, then their tenth, etc. As the years wore on, the award dinners outgrew our dining hall and we had to go outside where we would have a massive barbecue for the 5000 or so awardees and their families.

IKA's internal activities included an extensive athletics program, chess, drama, fishing, target practice, weekend family excursions to the Sierras of Córdoba — everyone had something to participate in if they so desired. Eduardo Juan "Jack" Jones, Director of Personnel, did a fine job of organizing the activities program, getting a lot of people involved. IKA hosted the Inter-Industrial games, in which teams from other companies in the area would compete, and the annual soccer game between an all-star team from Córdoba and one from our Buenos Aires offices was the highlight of the season. Córdoba usually won but that didn't dampen the enthusiasm. The North Americans taught the Argentines softball and these games were really something to see. I think there was a good spirit in IKA and a mutual respect between the rank and file and supervision. We had labor problems from time to time — you can't employ the thousands of people that we did without having them — but in the main, these problems emanated from general politico-economic crisis in the country or from a few labor leaders who felt they had to prove their worth to their membership.

The annual art contests that we sponsored starting in 1958 were very effective community programs. The IKA Art Salon began as an annual affair and was held in Córdoba. Luis Varela was the primary motivator of this program and it was under his direction, in his role as Director of Public Relations for the Córdoba area, that the salons got started.

In the first IKA Art Salon, competition was confined to artists from the province of Córdoba and embraced painting, engraving, graphic arts and photography. At least two of the painters who won awards in our first competition became known internationally: Marcelo Bonevardi and Antonio Segui. I think we had two motives in sponsoring the competitions: as members of the Córdoba community we felt we should contribute to its cultural development and, second, promote the reputation of local artists who suffer a geographical disadvantage compared to their contemporaries living in the Buenos Aires area.

The following year, the II IKA Salon was limited to paintings, sculptures and ceramics. The area was extended to include artists living in the 16 interior provinces, excluding Buenos Aires. Over 350 works were entered with the jury accepting 82. The first prize for the II Salon was awarded to Leonidas Gambartes of Rosario for his work "Mito Arcaico" (Archaic Myth).

In the III and IV Salons the competition was limited to paintings only, due to the logistical problem of handling ceramics, and was open to artists from the 16 provinces as before. The positive results and experience gained from the Salons spurred IKA on to organize the I Bienal Americana de Arte in Córdoba in 1962. The Córdoba Biennial invited participation by painters from three neighboring countries — Brazil, Chile and Uruguay — and, of course, Argentina. The selection panel was composed of one representative from each country, and the well known English art critic Sir Herbert Read served as president of the panel. Top honors were awarded to Argentine painter Raquel Forner and Manabu Mabe of Brazil, while other prizes went to Ernesto Barreda of Chile, Jose Gamarra of Uruguay and Romulo Maccio and Antonio Segui of Argentina.

At the conclusion of the I Bienal Americana de Arte, Sir Herbert Read stated, "I am genuinely surprised and impressed by the high level of artistry in the countries represented in the Biennial, that can be compared to any paintings in any part of the world. The art of the four countries represented is at a par with the international art movement." One can imagine the invigorating impact an authoritative statement such as this had on the participating artists.

In 1963 the V Salon IKA included artists from all over Argentina except those living in the Federal Capital and metropolitan Buenos Aires. Ricardo Supisiche of Santa Fe was the first prize winner. The panel of jurors for this exhibit included Chilean painter Nemesio Antuñez and Peruvian critic and painter Juan M. Ugarte Elespuru. A selection of works from this competition was shown in Buenos Aires and the United States.

Under the direction of Dr. Christian Sorenson, who had assumed responsibility for the Córdoba Public Relations Department, IKA sponsored its II Bienal Americana de Arte in 1964. Ten countries — Argentina, Brazil, Bolivia, Colombia, Chile, Ecuador, Paraguay, Peru, Uruguay and Venezuela — were invited. This time the Jury had to contend with a total of 310 works by 106 artists selected by panels in each of the countries. The final awards were made by a jury presided over by Umbro Apollonio, Director of Contemporary Arts of the Venice Bienale. Other members included José Sicre, Director of Visual Arts for the Organization of American States, and a renowned art critic from each participating country. The II Biennial Grand Prize was awarded to Jesús Soto of Venezuela and the First Prize to Alejandro Obregón of Colombia.

Many specialists and critics came to Córdoba during the II Biennial: Paul Mills, director of the Oakland, California, Museum of Art, John Coplans, editor of *Art Forum* Magazine, Lawrence Alloway, curator of the Guggenheim Museum and Robert Wool, president and founder of the Inter-American Foundation of the Arts. Ambassadors to Argentina from all the participating countries came to Córdoba for the Biennial, which gradually emerged as not solely an art competition but as an international arts festival that had Córdoba in the spotlight for a period of two weeks. Several other events were held including a choir festival, an international engraving contest for Latin American art students, and an exhibition of Inca and pre-Columbian art with silver and gold collections arranged by Peru and Colombia. John Coplans and Paul Mills gave lectures and showed colored slides on art and sculpture of the West Coast of the United States.

On the last night a closing dinner was held in the aluminum dome at the IKA Technical Institute. After dinner everyone gathered outside around the Institute's soccer field and watched a performance given by the Diablada of Oruro, Bolivia. The Diablada, or Devil Dance, consists of 150 or so men dressed in garments adorned with stones, rich embroidery and silver fringes. All wear extremely heavy masks and for this reason all the dancers are men, even those that dance in women's roles.

The Diablada Ferroviaria de Oruro is one of the most famous in Bolivia. The Diablada had its origins in the XII Century and combines Catholic theological concepts with pre-Hispanic and some Asian folklore. The masks the dancers wear are the most important single element of the pageant — a true Dantesque fantasy which is evident in the reproduction of lizards, serpents, toads and spiders and in the spiral of corkscrew horns and bulging eyes which are ingeniously made from light bulbs. The pageant is made up of the Devils, which form the retinue, Lucifer, who commands it, the "Supay China" or wife of the Devil, St. Michael the Archangel and a group of men costumed as brown bears who act as guards for the dancers. The dance has to be performed in a large area such as a football field. In the following days the Diablada de Oruro paraded on the streets of Córdoba and gave several performances in a stadium we arranged for it in Buenos Aires and to which the public was invited, free of charge.

A selection of 32 paintings from the II Biennial was made by Paul Mills, Lawrence Alloway and Robert Wool for exhibition in the U.S. under the sponsorship of the American Federation of the Arts. It was so well received that it was held there for over a year and was viewed by thousands in several cities.

The III Biennial in 1966 was a repeat of the previous one except that artists from Mexico, Nicaragua and Guatemala were invited in addition to the ten countries represented in the II Biennial. This year there was a marked emphasis on quality, with fewer painters invited from each country. Again, it was a huge success with the attention of the artistic world directed on Córdoba. The selection panel was chaired by Alfred Barr, Jr., director of the Museum of Modern Art in New York, Sam Hunter, director of the Jewish

Museum of New York, Aldo Pellegrini, an Argentine art critic, and Carlos Raul Villanueva, a noted art critic and architect from Venezuela. Cruz Diez of Venezuela was the Grand Prize winner followed by Paternosto and Deira of Argentina, who won the first and second prizes respectively. The III Biennial also sponsored a festival of experimental and electronic music with works of John Cage and other composers played by the Center of Experimental Music in Córdoba. Earle Brown gave several lectures and conducted the orchestra in some of his own works.

In eight years the small Córdoba art show grew to a major Latin American cultural event that brought together diverse parts of the community. We were the main sponsor but had support and assistance from the University of Córdoba School of Art, the Province of Córdoba Cultural Department, IKA employees, workers and supervisors. Our mission was not that of an arts patron. In addition to being the medium for cultural appreciation and dialogue between various countries, we strove to project a corporate image that was willing to do more than its share in the betterment of its local community. We were also supported by the Instituto di Tella, a tremendous force in the art and literary fields, and the Fiat company.

At the annual shareholders meeting in October, Bill Heard was elected to the Board and appointed 1st Vice President, replacing Steve Girard who remained a Director. Bill had been one of the first of the North American expatriates to come to Argentina in early 1955 and had been instrumental in setting up the initial plant organization. He was an excellent production engineer and a good friend. Bill did an outstanding job in IKA but was never really comfortable in Argentina. Whether it was language unfamiliarity, customs or just homesickness for the Detroit Eastside I never could determine. In any event, he was in and out of Argentina a couple of times. Bill left IKA in 1964 permanently and became Plant Manager of the Kaiser Jeep plant in Toledo.

Heard's first line organization had Carl Olson as Assistant General Manager, Bob Beens as Production Manager, Pete Mapes as Manager of Material Supply and G. K. Woods as Works Engineering Manager. George Harbert, Chief Product Engineer at Kaiser Jeep and formerly at Willow Run, was transferred to IKA to replace Olson. The Olson promotion and the transfer of Harbert recognized the importance that new product development played in IKA's future. The Quality Control and Inspection functions, which were supervised by Lucien Combes of Renault, were moved into the Engineering Division. In Buenos Aires, Tibor Teleki, in addition to his duties as Manager of Public Relations, assumed the responsibility for two other important and sensitive areas — Government Relations and overall automotive industry coordination.

New construction and plant expansion never seemed to end. 1960 saw the completion of a service parts warehouse and distribution center. Until we completed this facility, we had parts inventories scattered around in about three different places with the resultant loss in efficiency in the handling of Dealer orders. There is nothing more frustrating than late delivery of replacement parts for a customer's vehicle. The new distribution center was designed and built for the express purpose of parts warehousing and distribution. We installed the latest in material handling, packaging and inventory control equipment with the then state-of-the-art IBM computers. Bill McFall, Administrative Manager of Parts and Service, was responsible for developing the new parts center and when it was completed and in operation we were able to lower the response time dramatically in filling orders. It was in this operation that we were able to offer employment opportunities to blind persons. We set up specially designed work stations for small parts packaging, and after a training period, a blind worker performed as well as a nonhandicapped person. It was always a moving experience watching these people work and sharing their happiness in being gainfully employed.

In 1960 we produced and sold a total of over 33,000 units, our best year to date. This, the first full year of the decree, saw a total industry production of 89,300 units including all categories — from heavy trucks to small passenger cars. IKA's total production broke down into the various categories stipulated in the decree as follows:

Category		
A	Jeeps and Pickups	13,274
B	Small Passenger (Renault Dauphine)	3,772
C	Special Vehicles (Estanciera, Furgon)	10,965
E	Large Passenger (Bergantin, Carabela)	5,194

In the Category A area, IKA's competition was primarily Ford, General Motors and Chrysler. Total Category A production of these three companies amounted to some 27,000 units. On this basis IKA's penetration of the light truck market was 33%. If one were to expand this category to include the Estanciera and Panel Delivery, which were really utility vehicles, our penetration would have been 47%.

IKA's Dauphine (850cc) competed in the small passenger car market against the B.M.C. Riley (1500cc) which was called the Di Tella, the Fiat 600cc and 1100cc models, the Auto Union 1000cc and the Peugeot 403. While all these different models were in Category C, the wide variance in vehicle size — from a Fiat 600 to a Peugeot 403 — complicated market analysis. Nevertheless, of the total Category C production of some 15,000 units, the Dauphine penetration amounted to 25%. In the large passenger car category E, IKA's Bergantin and Carabela were the only vehicles built. The Falcons, Valiants and Chevrolets wouldn't appear until 1962. We were already in pre-production planning for the Rambler line since there was no way that the Bergantin and Carabela would be able to compete against the new cars that the Big Three would be bringing out.

Although IKA accounted for 37% of the market in 1960, competing against 10 competitors, we were by no means complacent. With ten producers all scratching for market share it was going to be a hectic, if not chaotic, state of affairs in future years.

Edgar Kaiser signs the final papers of incorporation for IKA on January 19, 1955. President Juan Peron is seated at left.

Wright Price celebrates groundbreaking for the Santa Isabel plant on March 12, 1955 — with the traditional bottle of wine — as the contractor, Sr. Barsanti, looks on.

General Matthew B. Ridgway (fourth from left, in civilian clothes with hat) visits the plant in 1956.

Kenneth J. Flood hands McCloud the keys to the first Jeep on April 27, 1956.

Presidential candidate Adlai Stevenson checks out a car interior with McCloud during a visit in March 1959.

Paul Becker, Edgar Kaiser and McCloud visit the Academia Argüello.

An aerial view of the plant shows the Instituto Técnico in the background (top center).

In its more than 25 years of existence, the Instituto Técnico has graduated some 2000 well qualified technicians who are working in all branches of industry.

President Charles de Gaulle of France speaks to assembly plant workers in 1964 as the international press looks on.

The Carabela first came off the line in 1958 — the first passenger car to be integrally built on a production line in South America.

Chapter VIII | 1961

In February we produced our 100,000th vehicle. It was a Bergantin. Now, in automotive terms, building 100,000 cars is not a particularly noteworthy achievement but to us this milestone was meaningful. At the end of 1960 Argentina had a total of 850,000 vehicles in circulation which meant that one out of every nine vehicles in use was an IKA product — and this in the short space of five years since production began in Córdoba.

As a gesture of appreciation to our people, a raffle was held in which all IKA employees were eligible to participate to win the Bergantin. The drawing was held at the plant at shift change and thousands were present. Tickets with the badge number of each employee were in a cylinder and Horacio Masdeu, the first operator hired by IKA, turned the drum several times and withdrew a ticket. Molina Viamonte was the lucky winner and was so grateful that, on the spot, he announced that he would personally donate a motorbike. The cylinder rolled again and the winner of the motorbike was Juan Alberto Pizarro of the Paint Department. These were fun times.

The Fifth IKA Dealer Convention was held in Mar del Plata in March. We had grown to over 260 dealers — the largest and best in the country. Jess Delaplain had done a fine job in building strength into the dealer group, attracting over to IKA many dealers from the competition. Juan Lutteral, Delaplain's principal advisor on new dealer recruiting and a retired GM dealer himself, was very successful in attracting several ex-General Motors dealers into the fold.

The conventions were always great affairs and not only were they fun socially, they gave the dealers a good opportunity to meet a lot of IKA management that they normally wouldn't come into contact with in the normal course of business. This was a fine bunch of men. I always tried to be on hand for the inauguration of a new dealership, no matter where it was. While I admire and respect the production people and their ability to cope with some really tough problems, the products have to be sold and no one can appreciate more than I the variables that the dealer, a private businessman, is confronted with daily. At the Fifth Convention, Miguel Egaña, a dealer in Santa Fe, presented my wife, Gus, with a painting by Fernando Fader, a noted Argentine artist, on behalf of the IKA dealer body. The Fader still hangs in our home — one never forgets gestures such as this.

In April 1961, five years to the month after the first Jeep was produced, IKA's affiliated company, Aviones Lockheed Kaiser, S.A. (ALKSA), produced its first airplane — a CL402. At 11 am April 1, with Juan Carlos del Toro at the controls, the CL402 made its first takeoff from the plant's airstrip, carrying two passengers, F. Penn Holter, General Manager of ALKSA, and an inspector from Argentina's Civil Aviation Authority. It flew to the DINFIA field and made its first landing there in homage to the institution that has been predominant in Argentine aviation history. A short time later it returned to the plant strip and was met by the Archbishop of Córdoba, Msgr. Castellano, Brigadier Abrahim, Secretary of Air, myself as President of ALKSA and a number of government and company officials, after which a ceremony was held in commemoration of the event.

The CL402, designed in 1959 by Albert Mooney for the Lockheed Aircraft Corporation, was a single engine, high wing monoplane powered by a 250 hp horizontally opposed Continental air-cooled engine. It could carry six passengers, including the pilot — or the equivalent in payload. It was developed primarily as an economical air cargo carrier for Latin America and other areas where all-weather road networks were deficient. It had a flexible tripod landing gear that allowed it to land on rough fields with a landing speed that permitted landing on a 250 foot strip.

The IKA story wouldn't be complete without tracing the events that led up to its first airplane.

In 1959, W.A. "Bill" Cannon, an old friend from the shipyard days, was managing Kaiser Aerospace and Electronics Corp., which had headquarters in Oakland. Prior to joining Kaiser in the

Richmond shipyards, Cannon had worked for Lockheed. Kaiser Aerospace was a Lockheed supplier and Cannon maintained close contact with its top management, many of whom were close associates during his Lockheed tenure. Bill brought to my attention the fact that Lockheed had developed a single engined plane that had just received its airworthiness approval from the U.S. Federal Aviation Authority. It was just about this time that the Argentine Government had issued Decree 16911 which incentivized aircraft production in the country by setting heavy tariffs on imported aircraft. Lockheed had dubbed the CL402 the "Jeep of the Air" and wanted to produce it in Latin America. It was already working with a Mexican group and had selected Argentina as a target because of Decree 16911 and the industrial capabilities in aircraft production that had been developed there by DINFIA — ex-IAME.

Cannon advised that Dan Haughton, Lockheed's President and CEO, and Ken Hull, President of Lockheed International, would like to meet with me to discuss the project, when convenient. We had our first meeting in Lockheed's Burbank offices on July 10, 1959, and agreed to doing a joint feasibility study, subject to IKA Board and Kaiser management approval. Edgar Kaiser liked the idea and the IKA Board, particularly those members who represented DINFIA, were in favor of proceeding with the study. The existence of the aircraft production decree, of course, helped this decision along.

We had our second meeting with Lockheed International in Ontario, California, the following month. In addition to Dan Haughton and Ken Hull, the authors of the study, Scott McGilvray, Tony Chapman and others were present. Lockheed had put a lot of effort into their study of Argentina as a potential source. Hull laid out their thinking on the marketing of the plane and expressed the opinion, which I shared, that with IKA's infrastructure at Santa Isabel, a heavy investment would not be required to set up the assembly facilities.

In December Hull visited Argentina and we spent a few days together in Córdoba where he had an opportunity to see all of IKA's operations. Needless to say he was much impressed and became more enthusiastic by the hour.

We worked out an agreement that called for the establishment of Aviones Lockheed-Kaiser, SA, with an initial capitalization of 160 million pesos to be shared equally by each partner. With the exchange rate in 1960 at 80:1, IKA's commitment amounted to one million dollars, with Lockheed's the same. Most all of IKA's contribution was in the form of assembly tooling and fixtures that would be produced in IKA's tool room plus plant space that would be rented to the new company until its production requirements justified its own plant. The space that IKA could make available was located in the new spare parts warehouse that we had recently built, part of which wouldn't be required for a year or so. By then we would have a better handle on ALKSA's potential. Lockheed's contribution was cash. It would also supply management and technical supervision at cost.

The production goal we targeted in our agreement called for the production of 500 planes in the first five years with a gradually increasing Argentine manufactured content, arriving at 75% in value at the end of the fifth year.

The December 1959 agreement that Hull and I signed was approved by the respective Boards and its production program was submitted to the Government authorities for approval under decree 16911; it was granted in May 1960. This was the formal start date of ALKSA. Lockheed appointed John Kincaid as General Manager and he, together with two or three technical people from Lockheed, and Al Mooney, who worked as a consultant, formed the nucleus of the Lockheed personnel. They were supplemented by some IKA people, in particular Luis Melnick, one of IKA's earliest employees, who handled Public and Community Relations. Kincaid was replaced by F. Penn Holter about midway in our pre-production program. Penn managed the company through its first aircraft production and was replaced by Marc Worst in September 1961.

The first airplane produced in April did everything that Lockheed claimed it could do. Its payload capacity, slow landing and takeoff speeds and stability were all as advertised. Its cruising speed was comparatively slow, having to sacrifice speed to gain payload. Sales were slow. Clients wanted more speed and comfort than the spartan CL402 offered. The biggest problem we had that affected our sales was due to the radical changes the Government made in the aircraft production decree, which practically eliminated the tariffs applicable to importations. This is what caused us and Cessna, which was engaged in a similar program in the Mendoza area, to cease operations. In February 1962 we stopped production and established a new orientation for the ALKSA organization.

In retrospect, I don't think the CL402 would ever have been a success — at least not in Latin America. The marketing studies Lockheed developed and on which we based our decision to go into the venture were flawed. The need for the cargo service and the purchasing power to go with it just didn't exist, at least not in Argentina. And of all the countries in Latin America, Argentina probably was the likeliest candidate to have a successful venture. ALKSA had performed well, however. Starting from scratch it had produced an airplane in less than a year and had developed a quality conscious organization.

Our task now was to find something for this organization to do and recoup our losses.

About this time in IKA we were having real difficulties securing quality wiring harnesses, die castings and miscellaneous other parts such as carburetors, fuel pumps and the like. Marc Worst was a top Lockheed production man and we thought it would be a good idea to get ALKSA into automotive parts manufacturing. It took well over a year to liquidate all the aircraft inventory and associated equipment and when this was finished, ALKSA's cumulative loss amounted to 376 million pesos. In 1963 this amounted to about U$S 2.5 million. During the liquidation period we had started ALKSA on manufacturing wiring harnesses for IKA's needs and it was rapidly tooling up to be able to satisfy 100% of our requirements.

In this same time frame, IKA was concluding contracts with General Motors, Ford, Chrysler, SIAM and others to supply them our transmissions and axles. It was apparent that we could recoup the ALKSA tax losses a lot faster with the profits on transmissions and axles than we could by manufacturing wiring harnesses and other parts. As a result we concluded with Lockheed to form a new company for miscellaneous parts production, to be owned in equal parts. The new entity was named Industrias Latinoamericanas de Accesorios, S.A. (ILASA), and it became active in fiscal year 1963-64. The agreement with Lockheed provided for the transfer of the facilities used for the manufacture of wiring harnesses from ALKSA to ILASA as an investment from the two partners. In addition we both agreed to make the investments necessary for carburetor, fuel pump and die casting production by the new company. We acquired a factory building near the IKA Industrial Products Division on the Pajas Blancas road and ILASA was off and running.

The other basic stipulation in the agreement referred to the ALKSA tax loss. By setting up ALKSA as the conduit for the high sales volume of axles and transmissions, most of the losses would be recoverable in the time allowed for tax loss recovery.

We agreed with Lockheed that in exchange for its stock in ALKSA we would give it its share of the tax loss if we recovered it, but payments would not begin before the first fiscal year in which the new ALKSA was profitable, and no more than a third of the total tax loss recovery would be paid to Lockheed in any one year or such lesser amount as might result depending on the amount of profit earned. The corporate name was changed to Transax, S.A., and we moved our axle production facilities out of the main plant into a building we purchased from IN-DE-CO that was located at Kilometer 3 on the road to San Carlos, a Córdoba suburb.

I might add that while we felt it only fair that Lockheed participate — to a degree — in ALKSA's tax loss recuperation, I also felt very strongly that IKA should be the sole owner of Transax. To get this new company into the axle and transmission business, substantial capital investments would be needed and its success would be entirely dependent on IKA's organization and ability to market the product. Transax was going to be a successful company and I didn't need or want anyone else with us in the business. Lockheed was always a good partner, however, and in no way do I want to imply that it was not. There will be a lot more about ILASA and Transax later in this story.

Henry J. Kaiser, Jr. passed away in May. He and I had been friends since Stanford. He was a couple of years ahead of mine and I first met him when I played freshman football and he was the student manager of the team. I later joined the Delta Upsilon fraternity where Henry was a member. I remember taking a ride with "JR," which was his nickname, to the construction site of the Permanente Cement Co.'s first plant, which the Kaiser Co. was building at Los Altos, a short distance south of Stanford University. This was my first exposure to the Henry J. Kaiser, Co. Later, when I was close to graduation, JR suggested I might be interested in applying for an entry position as Junior Engineer with the company at its Richmond Shipyards where construction had just started. This was early 1941 and when I went to Richmond for an interview, Henry Jr. met me and introduced me to Clay P. Bedford, General Manager of Kaiser's Richmond Shipyards, which would eventually be four in number and employ about 125,000 workers during the war years. Mr. Bedford interviewed me and offered me a position upon graduation. I am indebted to Henry Jr. for the invigorating experience of the 42 years with the Kaiser Companies that I was privileged to have.

Henry Jr. left all of us who had been associated with him with a deep sense of grief and respect for his long and enduring fight against multiple sclerosis. It was during World War II that he first contracted the disease and he fought it for almost 20 years. After the war, JR directed the overall public and community relations efforts of Kaiser Industries and its subsidiaries even though in later years he was confined to a wheelchair. He was never too busy to see me when I visited Oakland and we would routinely keep Henry updated on the goings on in IKA with particular reference to our community and government relations work. Henry Jr.'s interest in IKA was unabated and he was a staunch supporter.

There was another interesting happening having to do with community relations that IKA participated in, this time in Uruguay, that should be related. DeLesseps "Chep" Morrison, former mayor of New Orleans, and one of the prime instigators of the Kaiser ventures in Latin America, had been appointed Ambassador to the Organization of American States by President Kennedy following his election in 1960. Chep, because of his founding of International House in New Orleans and his own close relationship with various countries in Latin America, was an excellent choice. Chep called me one day and asked if IKA could assist in a "Power Plant for Peace" project that he wanted installed in a small village near Punta del Este, Uruguay, during an OAS economic and social conference in August 1961. Vice President Lyndon Johnson was the main proponent of the concept that a cost effective and timely impact could be made by going into small villages that had no power or water supply and giving them a small, economic installation that would supply these basic necessities in short order. Thus was born the "Power plant for Peace" idea. Chep wanted to install the first one during the OAS conference as a demonstration unit for the delegates and media present to witness.

IKA and Fairbanks Morse & Co. of New York donated a Jeep with a power take-off plus accessories such as a well digging device and a mechanical saw; a gas engine power plant that produced 10 kw; a water well with a purification system and storage tank; in short, an integral package of electricity, potable water and transportation. We had to bring some of the equipment in by air in order to have the dedication during the conference. The well was drilled, the pump installed and potable water and power were available for the first time in this community.

The town that was selected had been built by the workers who lived in the community. President Eduardo Victor Haedo of Uruguay was the principal speaker and laid a cornerstone which officially named the community: PUEBLO OBRERO PRESIDENTE KENNEDY. The weather was perfect and some 3000 people attended including the media — TV, radio and press. Chep was the principal speaker representing the U.S. and the Governor of the Department of Maldonado, in which the community was located, also spoke. Two young men from the village had been given scholarships by the Cordell Hull Foundation which would enable them to attend our service school in Córdoba and be taught how to maintain the equipment. There was a dramatic point in the ceremony when President Haedo called for the oldest settler in the town, Doña Carmen Gutierrez, to draw a glass of water from the new well and bring it to him. He drank it on the platform, announcing that since the water was good enough for the President, it was good enough for everyone. Doña Carmen responded, "For us life begins today. We have lived here for over 20 years without these necessities and the Americans have brought them to us in 36 hours."

A document incorporating the village was signed by President Haedo, Governor Salazar, Edward Sparks, U.S. Ambassador to Uruguay, Chep Morrison and members of the town council. The document was inserted in a metal tube, sealed and placed in the large cornerstone that was then lowered into place by an A frame with block and tackle. Bishop Cavallero of Maldonado then blessed the town. Following the benediction there was native dancing and a big *asado* (barbecue) for everyone. I was impressed by the uniqueness of the affair — a chief of state naming a community in honor of another chief of state — and also proud that we in IKA helped get the program started.

1961 also saw the formation of an automobile manufacturer's association in Argentina. The old saying is, "When you can't beat 'em, join 'em." I had reached the point where I felt that all of us in the industry were so dependent on governmental dictates that we should have a united voice in our relations with the Ministry of Industry relative to decree interpretations. As a single industry we were the largest employer in the country, and the Ministry should certainly prefer a more coherent approach to the many questions that emanated from the various auto companies. Each of us had our own specific problems to cope with but we all should be working under a regulatory decree that was interpreted by the Ministry on a consistent and universal basis.

I met with Doug Kitterman, Ford's Managing Director, and we talked over the idea of an association. Between the two of us we contacted the other companies and invited them to join the association we were proposing. In addition to Ford and IKA, Chrysler, Fiat, General Motors, SIAM Automotores (BMC), Industria Automotriz Santa Fe (Auto Union) and Mercedes Benz agreed to join, but Citroen, DINFIA, ISARD (Studebaker), Metalmecánica (DeCarlo) and IAFA (Peugeot) declined. With the association accounting for 85-90% of total industry production, we were representative.

On September 5, 1961 at a meeting in the Plaza Hotel, the Asociación de Fábricas de Automotores, ADEFA, was officially organized. Dr. Jorge Richard Zorraquin was nominated by Doug Kitterman to be the permanent Director General and Dr. Alberto Puiggari was selected to act as Technical Advisor. The founding members signing the accord were: Dr. Oberdan Sallustro for Fiat, Dr. Enrique Ariotti, Industrial Automotriz Santa Fe, Guy Clutterbuck, SIAM, William Mosetti, Mercedes Benz, Howard Vange, GM, and Paul Archer, Chrysler-Fevre, in addition to Kitterman and myself. It was established that the presidency and other offices would be rotated annually and I was chosen as the first President in recognition of IKA's pioneering work in the industry. Guy Clutterbuck was named 1st Vice President and would succeed me in the second year. Guy was not only head of SIAM Automotores but was Managing Director of all of SIAM Di Tella's other operations which ranged from heavy electro-mechanical manufacturing to household appliances. SIAM Di Tella was Argentina's true industrial pioneer.

Over the years ADEFA has been a unifying element. It has provided the services that the industry as a whole needs. In addition, for government entities and the public at large, it is the single source for automotive statistical data that planners require. But this is where ADEFA's services ended. We each retained our individuality in product pricing, labor negotiations and sales policies. Never once was there even a hint of collusion between member companies in price or volume setting.

IKA closed out the year with a total production of over 42,000 units — by far the largest in the industry. SIAM was second with 14,000 — yet our market penetration dropped to 30% from the 37% we had in 1960. With a total of 11 companies in direct competition with each other, vying for market position and survival, the industry as a whole was in a very confused state and it would be years before any semblance of rationality would come about.

For the fiscal year ending in June, IKA did very well financially. We had a net profit of slightly over U$S 9,000,000 which was about 7% related to sales. At the annual meeting of shareholders, a 25% stock and a 10% cash dividend was declared.

Chapter IX | 1962

Pre-production work had already begun on the Rambler passenger car line and the first units were coming off the final testing rolls in January 1962.

The events that led up to this IKA milestone began in 1960. William "Bill" Pickett, AMC's export director, had formerly worked for the Kaiser Jeep Corp. and was completely informed on the extent of IKA's progress. He, together with Roy Chapin, then Executive Vice President of American Motors Corp., broached the idea of an IKA-AMC relationship to Steve Girard, and I was then brought into the picture. Pickett was well versed in the details of the Argentine Automotive Decree, the investments that Ford, GM and Chrysler were making and their production plans. He had concluded, as I had, that IKA would not be competitive in the market sector represented by the Chevrolet, Falcon and Valiant if we stayed with the Bergantin and the Carabela — two really old models versus three new ones. If we didn't get new cars we would have to abandon this category entirely. Another factor in favor of the Rambler, and most likely the most important, was the fact that AMC was using the Borg Warner transmissions and Dana axles — products we were already manufacturing — and would allow us to use our L6-226 engine as well. Our pre-production costs would be minimal and we would easily surpass — by a large margin — the local content quota called out in the Decree, even importing the body components for the first two or three years. There was an inherent advantage in timing also because we could direct our die building efforts to the new model line that AMC was planning for the Rambler. The conclusion was that a licensing agreement with AMC was definitely in IKA's best interests. But first let's retrace some of the steps that led up to a final agreement.

In the sixties the U.S. automotive industry continued the shakedown of companies that had started in the great Depression of the thirties. Kaiser-Frazer, Willys, Studebaker, Packard, Hudson all left the passenger car scene. Going into the sixties, in addition to the big three, there were the American Motors Corp. and Studebaker-Packard. AMC was the result of the merger organized by George Mason of Nash Kelvinator with the Hudson Motor Car Corp. Studebaker and Packard also merged but that was short-lived, at least as a passenger car manufacturer. This was a pity because with the demise of the Packard one of the finest motor cars ever built was lost. The Packard in its day could stand up to Rolls Royce and Mercedes Benz and was in as much demand, as a fine motor car, by presidents and kings the world over. There is a story told by Mike Scott in the magazine *Autoweek* that Ettore Bugatti preferred his Packard for long, fast business trips over his own creations. But now I am digressing — only because I loved the Packard.

George Romney followed George Mason as Chairman and CEO of American Motors a few years before we began our discussions with the company. Romney was dedicated to the production of compact, economical vehicles and was bucking the trend that the Big Three were then following in their development of bigger, heavier and higher horsepower units. George's appearances on TV during the AMC commercials were famous and his blasting of the "gas guzzling dinosaurs" produced by the competition is legendary. George was an evangelistic type and an excellent speaker. When he spoke you listened — and he sold cars. The personal appearance of "the man in charge" — and Romney exuded this profile — reacted favorably with the audience and was a big reason for AMC's popularity in the more conservative sectors of the car-buying public.

IKA's dilemma in 1960 was that it knew it couldn't compete with the outmoded Bergantin and Carabela, but the primary question was whether we shouldn't concentrate solely on the Renault and Jeep lines and forego the bigger car market. The solution was apparent when one considered that there was no way we could drop the Jeep line, and in order to keep them in production we would be producing the same power train components required for the AMC cars. There was just too much productive capacity that would have been idled if we had decided to confine IKA to Renault. Years later, under Renault management, the company was able to concentrate its output on the Renault line because the Jeep and AMC products became outmoded and Renault was able to replace them with new models it had developed, thus spanning the market and lowering production costs as well.

The category that the AMC vehicles competed in (over 2500 cc) accounted for approximately 50% of the total passenger cars produced by the industry in the first five years of full production under the Decree. In that same period the IKA-AMC line accounted for approximately 30% of the total produced in this category. This would seem to justify our decision to proceed with AMC in 1960.

American Motors was producing two vehicle sizes under the generic name of Rambler. Both used monocoque bodies. The Rambler American was the smaller of the two and was much older than the bigger car, which was produced and sold in two versions — Classic and Ambassador. The American was produced in coupe and sedan versions and the Classic and Ambassador in sedan and station wagon models. AMC would be bringing out new Classic and Ambassador models in the 1963 model year which would enable us to start with the current model, then follow with the new one later in 1963. The decree's generous import allowances would allow all the sheetmetal to be imported for the first model and make it possible for us to start our die build program on the new model body parts and be ready for their local production when the Decree required it.

Negotiating a license and investment agreement with AMC was another matter however. I found myself between two strong characters — Edgar Kaiser and George Romney. IKA needed as much capital input in the form of investment as it could get to help defray the new model startup costs. While Romney was in agreement with a substantial investment, Edgar Kaiser was adamant in his opposition to AMC having a large equity position at the outset in IKA. His concern was that in the long term, AMC, through incremental investments for new models or other reasons, would gradually surpass the Kaiser equity percentage ownership and take control. Edgar's position vis-a-vis AMC was somewhat ambivalent, however, because he had never voiced these same questions when we negotiated the Renault investment just two years earlier. Renault, with its financial resources and intimate knowledge of IKA through its presence in management and on the Board, would have been in a much better position to surpass the Kaiser equity position and take control. Edgar would also say to me at times that equity percentage was one thing but good management was another, and that if we couldn't run the job right then we ought to step down regardless of the amount of equity we had. Really, the root of the problem was the fact that Edgar didn't get along too well with Romney. I really believe, and this is with no disrespect for Edgar because he was a wonderful human being, that there was a tinge of jealousy on his part due to Romney's success in the business compared to — and let's face it — Kaiser's failure in the U.S. passenger car market.

Edgar decided to call a meeting in his father's office in Honolulu to settle our differences. This was scheduled for April 19, 1961. I flew to San Francisco where Edgar and Steve met me and we continued on to Honolulu.

One of the traits I admired most in Edgar Kaiser was the respect he accorded his father. Whenever an opportunity pre-sented itself to bring Henry J. into a discussion that he would have an interest in, Edgar did so. Henry was close to 80 at the time but his interest never flagged when the subject of IKA was brought up. It was great to see Mr. Kaiser again even if I had to fly about 15,000 miles to do it. It didn't take us long to come to a conclusion and with Henry nodding his head we agreed to pro-pose to American Motors that it invest U$S 1,750,000 into IKA to help defray startup costs, for which it would receive about 3.5% of the company's equity. Another U$S 1,750,000 would go into Permanente preferred stock and, in addition, a revolving credit to Permanente would be set up in the amount of U$S 3,000,000 which would be covered at all times by future exchange contracts as a guarantee of remittability. At least we had the Kaiser position established but we still had to negotiate with American Motors. From my standpoint I would have preferred the entire investment going into IKA, where it was really needed, than into Permanente.

The following month, on May 24, 1961, we signed a license agreement with American Motors that provided for royalties, technical assistance and financial support to IKA and Permanente. AMC agreed to the equity investments into IKA and the preferred of Permanente but it negotiated us down on the matter of the revolving credit that we wanted it to extend to Permanente, and would only agree to allowing its future royalties to accumulate to a maximum of U$S 1,000,000 as a revolving loan, which would, of course, be covered by future exchange contracts.

When the AMC investment was finally integrated, IKA's ownership was disseminated as follows:

Public shareholders	38.20%
Kaiser	28.65%
DINFIA	12.28%
Renault	7.30%
Banco Industrial	6.61%
American Motors Corp.	3.74%
Steel Improvement & Forge	3.22%

We had imported some Ramblers well in advance of our final agreement and had begun the adaptation engineering and installation of IKA power train components, brakes and suspension system. Extensive road testing had started and the experience we had gained in developing the Bergantin came to good use. In slightly more than six months after signing the agreement, Ramblers were rolling off the line. The successful launching of the Rambler was due, in no small way, to the support and cooperation we received from AMC. From George Romney on down — Roy Chapin, Bill Pickett, Dick Purdy, Bill Wey and the AMC attorneys, Joe Vieson and Dick Cross — everyone pitched in to make the Rambler a success. We produced 11,000 Rambler units in 1962 compared to the combined 1961 production of the Carabela and Bergantin of some 2600 units. For the first five years of the Decree — 1962-1966 — 186,000 cars were built by the industry in the Rambler category. Rambler led, with 60,000, Falcon was second with 55,000, Chevy third at 38,000 and Valiant last with 33,000. Despite the fact that it was still very much a competitor, Renault phased out the Rambler line in the '70s, replacing it with its own new models. Honors have to be accorded the Ford Falcon, however, for remaining in production for over 25 years.

George Romney was interested in IKA's development and visited Argentina two or three times. He spoke to various groups and was very well received. This was just prior to his successful race for the governorship of the state of Michigan. Romney was also a member of the Mormon Church and was very active in its affairs. No doubt it was his interest in Córdoba and his standing in the church that caused a Mormon Stake (a term used to designate a Mormon settlement) to be formed and a church to be built.

In March an old friend, George Havas, passed on, and it is only fitting that I recall George's deep involvement in the initial formation of IKA. George was a complete engineer. Born in Hungary and educated there and in Germany, he emigrated to Cuba and was working there when the Henry J. Kaiser Paving Co. started construction of about 250 miles of the Cuban Central Highway under subcontract to the Warren Brothers — a major highway construction company in the U.S. that had the prime contract for a total of 750 miles. George, then 25 years old, was recruited by Kaiser and quickly assumed the engineering responsibilities for the Kaiser section of the project. When the job was finished, Henry J. brought Havas to Oakland where he quickly became Chief Engineer of all of the Kaiser Co.'s interests. He played a major role in the organization and development of Kaiser's cement, steel, aluminum and automotive interests, while managing the engineering and construction division of the company.

During IKA's infancy, George's keen analytical and organizational attributes were instrumental in guiding us through the many obstacles that were in our path. Being fluent in Spanish, George was a key player during the early negotiations with the Peron government and I don't think we would have been able to successfully conclude the negotiations if George hadn't been around to keep us headed in the right direction. On every trip I made to Oakland I would give George a progress report. Gus and I will never forget the memorable evenings we would spend with the Havas's when George on the violin and his wife Judith on the piano would give a concert.

On May 2, 1962, the IKA Technical Institute opened its doors and the first class, composed of 112 students, began their studies. In three years the student body grew to over 300 as second and third classes entered. Thus began an entity whose graduates over the years have made an important contribution to Argentina's industrial growth.

During the six years I worked in Detroit I met many graduates from the Ford Trade School and the General Motors Technical Institute, who were spread throughout the industry. Tool engineering is the basic science of manufacturing and at the Ford Trade School, the one I was most familiar with, students were trained in the operation of the various machine tools and other equipment and in class rooms would receive their regular academic courses with an emphasis on pre-engineering subjects. Graduates could go directly into industry as junior tool engineers or entry level tool and die makers, or continue on into university for an engineering degree. The grounding that the students received in manufacturing processing and leadership training prepared them for scaling up the ladder into foreman, superintendent and management roles. In fact, a number of IKA's expatriate personnel were Ford graduates.

I commented earlier on my initial impression of Argentine industrial practices. There was a lack of process engineering knowhow in most of the plants I visited and it was evident that neither industry nor the engineering schools were producing the technical capabilities needed to attain low cost repetitive quality production. Now this isn't a criticism of the engineering training received in Argentine universities. The Argentine engineers who joined IKA's product engineering or works engineering divisions were well grounded in the basic engineering disciplines and rapidly assimilated automotive design fundamentals and plant engineering practices common to our industry. And there were some good industrial schools, but all of them visited were woefully short on equipment and had a curriculum that wasn't as responsive to the demands of the production line as, in my opinion, they should have been. There were no industrial schools that we knew of where tool engineering per se was taught and where engineer trainees were given experience in machine operation in order to learn the capabilities of the different types of production equipment and, more important, their limitations. In discussions at the plant there was universal agreement that the most important contribution we could make to the Argentine industrial community would be the creation of a qualified technical training center modeled along the lines of the Ford Trade School.

In addition to his responsibilities as Director of Academia Argüello, Paul Becker was also Director of Training at the plant and had done an excellent job organizing the various supervisory proficiency courses and other in-plant training that we made available to our people. He, together with Bill Heard and other Ford Trade School graduates, with the counsel of Manuel Ordoñez and Jack Jones, developed a plan of action. The Ford Trade School was contacted in the U.S. and it was very cooperative in suggesting curricula and facilities requirements. We also worked closely with the National Technical Education Council (Consejo Nacional de Educación Tecnica) since it would have to approve the curricula and the graduation certificates.

The Institute's facilities were designed to ultimately accommodate a total of 600 students and consisted of an administration building, two wings containing ten classrooms each, and the shop building, which housed well over 100 pieces of equipment — lathes of all types, mills, surface grinders, jig bores, radial drills, heat treating, inspection and control instruments, layout tables — in essence, a completely balanced shop. The centerpiece of the Institute is the geodesic dome we had imported from the U.S. for the Sesquicentennial celebrations in Buenos Aires, which was disassembled when the Fair ended and re-erected at the Institute. It serves as a multipurpose facility — auditorium, dining hall and indoor sports. The Institute covers about ten acres on the northwest corner of IKA's property.

Juan C. Mir was the first Director of the Institute with Horacio MacKinlay, Administrative Manager. Both reported to Manuel Ordoñez, then Director of Industrial Relations. Eventually the Institute became part of the Kaiser Foundation of Argentina, a non profit organization that acted as a conduit for our support to charitable and educational entities.

The original program that we started the school on encompassed the last three years of secondary school *(ciclo superior)* with students receiving machine tool operation training concurrently with the required academic courses. To qualify for admission, the applicant had to have successfully completed the first three years of secondary school, preferably an industrial type, and pass an entrance examination. Graduates received their regular high school diploma together with a Tool and Die Technician *(Técnico Mecánico Matricero Herramentista)* certificate. A uniform was supplied for classroom wear and coveralls for use in the shop. All classroom and shop supplies were gratis. A large percentage — more than half the student body — came from outside Córdoba city and from many different provinces. In cooperation with Córdoba authorities, we were able to locate housing for those who could not live at home. The boys worked hard and school hours were from eight to five. The Institute's program now covers the full six year secondary curriculum together with shop training, which has been broadened to include the operation of computer-controlled equipment, electronics and other modem manufacturing techniques.

Shop training wasn't confined to machine operation only. Specific projects were assigned to the Institute — the students produced and repaired dies, jigs and fixtures for the main plant. In cooperation with the Argentine association for the fight against infantile paralysis (ALPI), students designed and built special orthopedic braces for use by victims of the disease who could not otherwise afford them. Infrequently we would produce an engine in the plant that had a defect that could not be repaired. These were reworked by the students and donated to industrial schools around the country for use as demonstrator models in engine repair courses. Practical work projects such as these had a two-pronged benefit. The students could see a project through from start to finish, and the result was given to those who could not otherwise afford it.

Of the 112 who that started in the first class in April 1962, 76 graduated in December 1964. Most went to work in IKA's main or subsidiary plants, about 20 entered university and some were recruited by other companies. Four went to Canada for DeHavilland aircraft. One outstanding student received a scholarship for study in Germany. This was pretty much the pattern in subsequent graduating classes. It was our policy to offer a job to all graduates but a lot were attracted to other companies including many of our vendors. I remember visiting the Ford River Rouge plant once, and in its tool and die division I was hailed by two men who were Instituto graduates. In its more than 25 years of existence the Instituto has graduated some 2000 well qualified technicians who are working throughout industry.

We brought out the Gordini version of the Renault Dauphine in August 1962, and it became a very popular model, outselling the standard Dauphine by a ratio of about three to two. In response to the demand for a sports version of the Dauphine, Amadeo Gordini, Renault's famous engine designer, introduced several modifications to the original Ventoux engine and transmission used in the Dauphine. With an increased compression ratio, a new camshaft and cylinder head, and a new four speed transmission, the car's performance was improved substantially. The interior trim was upgraded, reclinable bucket seats were installed and exterior two-tone paint styling was designed. The Gordini was more than just a deluxe version though. Its performance was outstanding for its size and it was not only the first IKA vehicle to be entered in Argentine sports car racing but also the first one of wholly Argentine manufacture. The team of Gaston Perkins, Heriberto Bohnen and Roberto Odiol were first, second and third respectively in the first three stages of the 1962 Argentine Gran Premio. Even though the team didn't win the entire race, Perkins did place second in his category, and this was enough to prove that we could produce vehicles competitive with the best. Later in this story we will talk more about IKA's racing history.

In the automobile business one is always confronted with a "make or buy" decision and this was particularly true in the case of chrome plating that we purchased from a number of vendors. IKA had such a large volume of parts requiring plating that it seemed, on the surface at least, that an inhouse plating facility could be economically justified for cost and quality reasons. We confirmed this after a thorough feasibility study and started laying plans for the construction of this new facility. Practically speaking, 100% of the parts that required plating were manufactured by IKA and the vendors we had to depend on for polishing and plating were located in the greater Buenos Aires area. With plating inhouse we would not only eliminate the procurement and follow-up problem but we could cut back on the inventory of parts in transit at any given time.

Calvin Johns, one of our "old timers" from the Detroit Engine Division, pulled together a team of process engineers and designed the polishing and plating facilities, a big portion of which we built in our own tool room. INGALCO, the representative of the Udylite Corp., a major supplier of plating compounds and chemicals, provided assistance in sizing the tankage, laboratory facilities and process flow. The concentration, particularly in the polishing area, was on automaticity. The polishing and other operations that lead up to the final chrome plate are by far the largest consumers of manhours in the process. The chrome plate, which is applied in the final step of a long series of operations starting with polishing the piece, is the fastest single operation in the whole series. After polishing, the copper and nickel that follow are plated to a thickness about four times that of the final chrome. Throughout the whole chain of events, cleanliness is the watchword and the laboratory constantly controls solution cleanliness and chemical composition and the thickness of the three different plating deposits.

The construction and installation of equipment was accomplished in record time by ICKSA. Construction started in October 1961 and the first chrome plated parts were delivered to IKA's final assembly lines in September 1962 — just eleven months. The new plant had a plating capacity of 60,000 square decimeters per day, which is close to 1,000,000 square inches — or over 6500 square feet. That's a lot of plating. The quality of plated parts in our vehicles improved markedly and the cost savings resulting from lower inventory carrying costs and plant efficiency were noteworthy. The new facility, which covered about 45,000 square feet, was located adjacent to the Forge plant and was managed by Bob Stich, who also ran Forge. This was a good combination. Stich was a good manager and since Forge sold a lot of its output to third parties we could take advantage of Forge's sales force since we would also be selling chrome plating to others as well.

On September 2, 1962 we had a big celebration at the plant with over 8000 people in attendance. September 2 is Industry Day and commemorates the same day in 1587 when the first manufactured goods — blankets, cotton cloth and flour sacks from the province of Santiago del Estero — were exported from Argentina. Our program was officiated by Rogelio Nares Martinez, the Federal Interventor for the Province of Córdoba. Also in attendance were Engineer Fernando Mejide, Secretary of Industry and Mining of the Nation, the Archbishop of Córdoba, Dr. Ramon Castellano, the Commissioner of the City of Córdoba Architect Vito Remo Raggio and many others, too numerous to mention. The program for the day consisted of the official inauguration of the new IKA Technical Institute, the Chrome Plating Plant, the official naming of the street that borders the Press Plant as "Avenida 2 de Septiembre," and the initiation of the First Inter-industry sports competition in which 400 participants from 24 different companies competed in chess, basketball, bocci-ball, fencing, soccer, gymkhana, judo, ping pong and rugby. I can guarantee that we had a full day of activity.

Total production for the calendar year was about 40,000 units and though this was slightly below 1961's total, we maintained our market penetration of 30% since there was a proportionate drop in total industry output. It was hard to explain the total market drop because this was the first year that the Falcon, Chevrolet and Valiant compacts appeared. The Rambler more than held its own and was selected as the car of the year by the Argentine Institute of Public Opinion.

Financially we lagged 1961 also. For the fiscal year ending June 1962 our after tax profit dropped about 6% to 702 million pesos. When translated to dollars the drop was more than 40% which was due to a peso devaluation of about the same amount during the period. What this really meant was that we were not able to keep our car prices moving up in pesos commensurate with devaluation. Customers were buying vehicles in ‹62 at a dollar price substantially lower than in ‹61. In fact, I can remember at one point in time that the Jeeps we made in Argentina were cheaper — in dollars — than the ones built in Toledo, illustrating the problem one confronts in managing a company in a hyper inflation economy. This was the "third dimension" we faced in management that was on top of the two fundamental dimensions of production and sales.

Chapter X | 1963

During July and August we concluded sales agreements with General Motors, Ford, Chrysler and Studebaker (Isard) for our differential axle assemblies with deliveries starting in the last quarter of 1963. In addition we obtained the transmission business of General Motors, Ford and Studebaker. These companies, together with IKA, accounted for 60% of Argentina's total automobile and light utility production in 1962, having produced 70,000 of the 117,000 vehicles built. After concluding the above agreements we also obtained the SIAM axle and transmission business so that, in effect, we had 100% of the axle and transmission requirements of the vehicles produced that our products were applicable to. This had been a long sales campaign and when finally Howard Vange, General Manager of the GM operation, and I came into agreement, the other firms rapidly followed.

Finally, the Frondizi decree was starting to work in our favor. The competition, faced with complying with increasing local content, could not individually justify the investments required for the manufacture of the parts on a low volume basis, nor could they live with the piece price cost that would have resulted. I'm sure that the procurement managers of each of the companies had done all they could to attract one of the major producers such as Dana, BorgWarner or Eaton to come in and set up a plant, but they certainly weren't successful. Eaton did enter Argentina later but concentrated on heavy axles, and other than pirating some of our management and skilled workers away from us didn't offer any competition.

We had a big job ahead making ready to supply the demand which would more than double our current output of the two major assemblies. The main plant was getting crowded and since we would have had to build additional space to accommodate the additional production equipment, we decided to move the differential axle manufacturing to a building we purchased from Indeco-Minoli, located south of Córdoba and east of Santa Isabel at Km 3 on the road to San Carlos. It was about a 15-minute drive from the main plant. We wanted it as close as possible because there would be a high degree of dependency on the main plant during the startup phase. I also felt that our customers, all of whom were competitors, would be happier dealing with a separate corporate entity located away from IKA's central offices. They would get better attention and we didn't want them around the main plant anyway.

As I stated previously, we used the ALKSA corporate structure, changing its name to Transax, S.A. With the tax loss carry-forward in its books, using the ALKSA corporation would permit the first 376 million pesos in profit to be tax free, a tax savings of 149 million pesos which was a little over a million dollars at the time. We decided against moving the transmission production into the Transax plant because the Borg Warner T86 transmission and the Renault transaxles were so interdependent on gear cutting equipment we would have had to move all or nothing. Although IKA would continue to produce the T86 transmission, its sales and distribution would be handled by Transax.

A substantial investment would be needed for the organization and startup of the new company. The original Indeco plant that we bought contained about 50,000 square feet and cost some U$S 350,000. New forge shop equipment required to support the additional volume that Transax would require cost about U$S 1,000,000. When the forge's expansion was completed, it would be producing about 25,000 tons per year of forgings, of which about 50% would go to IKA and 25% each to Transax and other outside customers.

Additional axle and transmission production equipment had to be ordered worth about U$S 3,000,000, the bulk of which would come from Europe where we could obtain direct financing from the manufacturer's export credit institutions such as Hermes in Germany and Coface in France. The financing terms accorded by these institutions were 10% with the order, 10% upon delivery and the balance in 10 equal semi-annual installments. In those days machine tools were much cheaper in Europe. About U$S 600,000, primarily Gleason Hypoid Gear generators, had to be procured in the U.S., then the only place they were made. About U$S 500,000 of miscellaneous equipment would be procured locally. In addition we had a building expansion and machine installation cost at the Indeco facility of about U$S 1,000,000, bringing the total cost to over U$S 5,000,000. Our cash flow forecasting would also have to take into account the pre-production startup and increased inventory carrying costs.

The new customers wanted the Dana model 30 differential in addition to the model 44 that we had in production. Although this required more tooling, it was an advantage for us since it would allow IKA to incorporate this smaller axle in our lighter vehicles. In addition to the price per axle we negotiated with each of the clients we added a one-time set up charge of about U$S 30 per axle for the first 45,000 axles delivered — in total — that we delivered. The setup charge and quantity of axles varied with each customer but the net result was that we would receive about U$S 1,500,000 in premiums to help offset our investment and pre-production costs. In return we had to agree to a committed capacity that varied with the customer, but in total it meant that Transax would have to more than double IKA's current output. This would require an installed capacity to produce some 100,000 axles and 80,000 transmissions annually. This had an advantage also since it would lower unit production costs as well as allow lower piece prices on forging billets, castings, bearings, seals, etc.

The one-time premiums paid by the customers plus the tax savings to be realized would substantially lower our total investment cost, but these savings would only come in over a period of time. Meanwhile we had to put a financing plan together so IKA didn't run out of cash. Getting Transax up and rolling was a big drain but we made it. In addition to the European equipment financing, we were able to arrange a U$S 3,000,000 five-year loan from the Bank of America International. Russ Smith was head of the Bank's international division at the time and Henry Drath headed up Latin America. The Bank was always supportive and never required, although I'm sure it would have liked to have had, a back-up guarantee by Kaiser Industries. We collateralized the U$S Transax loan with a pledge of the Transax stock in IKA's portfolio.

Al Hilleland, who had managed ICKSA from its inception, was appointed General Manager of Transax. Al, a mechanical engineering graduate of the University of Wichita, Kansas, had done a good job starting ICKSA up and had it organized to the point where he could be replaced by Natalio Lucioni. Hilleland was a good manager and took Transax through its startup and ongoing operation, producing quality products and maintaining good customer relations. When Renault took over IKA's management in 1967 and sold Transax to the Ford Motor Co., Al remained as General Manager until his retirement some years later.

Jack Martin, Chairman of the Dana Corporation, on one of his visits to Buenos Aires came into the office to talk about Transax. He finally got around to asking if we would consider selling. I said we would but the price would be over 20 million dollars. And Transax was well worth it when one took into account the premium that IKA would have to pay on its axles plus the profit Transax made on third party sales. I don't think Dana got into any other license agreements with foreign companies that it didn't own or have a substantial interest in. When Mexico began manufacturing vehicles some years later, Dana installed its own plant.

ILASA (Industrias Latinoamericanas de Accesorios, S.A.), the Corporation that evolved from the partnership with Lockheed after IKA assumed control of the Lockheed-Kaiser (ALKSA) corporate structure, began operations during the same time frame that Transax started up. As we phased out aircraft production in the wing of our parts warehouse, we began the production of wiring harnesses there, then moved the operation to a building we bought on the road to the Pajas Blancas airport, very close to the IKA Industrial Products Division plant.

ILASA's initial capitalization was low, starting at some U$S 300,000. This was more than doubled in about two years through additional investments by Lockheed and ourselves. Under Marc Worst's leadership and Bob O'Neill's engineering, ILASA produced quality wiring harnesses at competitive prices and expanded into diecasting and carburetor and fuel pump production. The Carter carburetor was produced under license to ACF Industries and was the first carburetor to qualify as national under the Automotive Decree. ILASA also progressed into the production of large die castings for IKA and others as well.

When Worst returned to the States, Vic Berelejis, an IKA engineer, replaced him as General Manager. Two years after startup, annual sales volume was close to U$S 2,000,000, there were 275 on the payroll with assets of U$S 1,650,000.

ILASA saved IKA many hours of inspection and production labor. Before ILASA, the quality of harnesses we were buying was so irregular that we had to build special test fixtures in receiving inspection and test all incoming harnesses 100%. This was after we had gone through a period when, after completing a car and in final test, we would find short circuits or lack of continuity in the wiring and have to completely rip out the harness and install a new one.

The first Argentine foundry from which IKA purchased castings was Metalúrgica Tandil, located in the southern part of the province of Buenos Aires. It was the best in the country and the only one we could locate in the early days capable of producing "cored castings." A cylinder block, for example, is a cored casting, so named because of the internal passages in the block that are used for water circulation. Cylinder heads, intake and exhaust manifolds also fall into this category.

Santiago Selvetti, President and General Manager of the firm and a principal shareholder, had built Tandil from ground zero; it was literally a miracle that he was able to turn out the quantity and quality that he did. We had a fine relationship with Santiago, dating back to the time when Charley Read, our foundry expert, first worked with him in developing Tandil into our prime castings source. The time had come to get Tandil better mechanized, enabling it to achieve lower production costs and higher volume. This would require a large capital infusion which, on its own, Tandil didn't have the financial clout to do. The only way we could see getting the job done was to expand the capital base of Tandil with a new share issue that IKA would subscribe to.

Metalúrgica Tandil was then capitalized at m$n 260,000,000 and was traded on the Buenos Aires exchange. Our studies concluded that an investment of m$n 80,000,000 would be required to equip and mechanize the plant to lower production costs, increase capacity and make possible the production of nodular iron, a type of cast iron which was more malleable than "gray iron." Nodular was used in parts where greater tensile strength and malleability was required — in some cases substituting for forgings.

Tandil had two classes of shares in circulation: single vote and multiple (five vote). The holders of the multiple vote shares agreed to the transfer of multiple vote shares to IKA concurrently with the integration of its investment, receiving in turn single vote shares that emanated from the new stock issue. By the time IKA's investment was totally integrated, it had an ample percentage of voting rights, more than enough to exercise the management control it required. The agreement was approved by the IKA Board in September 1963.

Under the leadership of Selvetti and F.W. "Red" Bromley, whom we sent to Tandil to help him, the modernization program went smoothly and was completed on schedule. Tandil produced as wide a range of foundry products as one would see in any modern day foundry anywhere. In addition to IKA, the other major customers were General Motors, Ford, Fiat, John Deere Tractor and Perkins engines, with IKA accounting for approximately one third of the foundry's output. Its only major competitor was the Acinfer foundry, located in San Nicolás, an affiliate of the Acindar Steel Co.

In the last quarter of 1963 we began producing three new vehicle lines: the 1963 Rambler that had been introduced in the U.S. the previous year, the Renault R4L and the Gladiator pickup in half ton and one ton capacity models that replaced the Baqueano pickup we had been building since 1960.

The new Rambler was produced in three models. The top of the line was the Ambassador 990 four door sedan, a de luxe automobile that was the first car produced in Argentina to offer power steering and power brakes. The Rambler Classic station wagon and four door sedan completed the lineup. Dick Teague, AMC's

Chief Stylist, had developed a car with real eye appeal. It had a lower body profile than its predecessor, more inside room and trunk space, and featured curved side window glass. The body designers had been able to reduce the number of sheetmetal parts by 30% which, in addition to lowering the body weight by 100 pounds, simplified die building and body assembly. The Rambler was one of the oldest marques in the U.S., first appearing in 1902, and the 1963 models carried on the tradition of providing quality transportation.

The Renault R4L was first introduced in France in September 1961 and IKA began producing it in late 1963. The R4L, an economical, rugged five-door sedan with front wheel drive, was the start of a new trend in Renault. Every new car it has introduced since has been front wheel drive. Front wheel drive has a lot of advantages but also brings on service problems if the power transmission to the driving wheels isn't proper. In the early beginnings of Kaiser-Frazer, Henry J. favored front wheel drive and some of the first prototypes were built this way. But the added extra front end weight and the fact that the design state of the art hadn't reached the point where it inspired confidence caused the engineers to stick with the orthodox rear wheel drive.

As engines got lighter and more efficient and power transmission to the front wheels was perfected, front wheel drive became a competitive alternative and gave the body designers much more latitude since everything aft of the engine compartment firewall is a flat platform. This simplified body construction and provided roomier interiors. The R4L used the Dauphine engine which made it possible for us to achieve integration compliance under the Decree with a lot to spare. With features such as an easily removable rear seat and a fifth door, the car could be used as a light utility vehicle as well as a passenger sedan and performed almost as well as a four wheel drive Jeep in off-road use. With a lower price tag than the Dauphine, it was able to reach a much larger market. A closed delivery van version, the R4F, was also produced. In 1964, its first full year of production, the R4 was second to the Fiat 600, but not by much, as the highest volume single model produced in Argentina. In 1965 and ‹66 it attained the number one spot.

In December the first Jeep Gladiator pickups came off the final line. I was sorry to see the Baqueano go but the competition's modern styled pickups made necessary its replacement if we were to stay in the light utility market. The Gladiator was produced in one ton and one-half ton capacities and had good styling. The front end suspension was independent using a system of torsion bars and half axles which was somewhat advanced for its day and did provide a better ride, but also brought on some maintenance problems. In the pickup market our only competition was the Big Three, with the Gladiator selling on a par with the GM and Chrysler products, but the Ford F100 outsold any one of us by almost double.

IKA had done a tremendous job in bringing out three completely new vehicle lines, which strained both its financial and manpower resources. 1963 saw a total industry sales drop of 21% compared to 1962, with IKA dropping about 30%, which caused us to slip in market penetration. People still wanted cars and the dramatic drop in overall industry sales was caused by an economic situation in the country wherein inflation caused car prices in pesos to skyrocket while the peso/dollar exchange rate remained fairly constant. IKA's situation was even more aggravated by having to start up three new models practically simultaneously.

All of this had a negative effect on the IKA's financials reported at the end of our fiscal year. Compared to 1962, our sales volume in dollars remained about the same at the U$S 96,000,000 level but our profit nosedived from close to U$S 7,000,000 in 1962 to slightly less than U$S 1,000,000 in ‹63. But the dramatic effect was on car prices. Measured in dollars, prices rose just about 50% due to the Government's economic policy of maintaining a constant exchange rate while peso prices were escalating. And one can't drop production rates without laying off people. We had to reduce our work force by some 18% and this isn't done without a lot of labor strife.

Chapter XI | 1964

The year 1964 was to be one of consolidation rather than expansion. We had to regain the market penetration lost in 1963 and we had the products that would enable us to do it. The sales and penetration drop in 1963 caused by inflation, pre-production startup time, and the growing pains that are always experienced in new model introductions were behind us, and we now could concentrate on production and sales and regain the 30% market share that was IKA's norm. This objective was accomplished and in 1964 we produced over 50,000 vehicles, averaging over 200 per working day and spread over some 15 different models. The overall imported content average was less than 10% of vehicle value — far and away the best in the industry.

The automotive industry's recovery was, in the main, due to the economic health of the country which had begun to improve with the extraordinarily good performance in the agricultural sector's 1963-64 season. Comparably speaking, inflation was down and the peso/dollar exchange rate remained fairly constant. The industry's total output rose almost 60% compared to 1963, with IKA's production rising 80%.

For the fiscal year ending June 1964, IKA posted a net profit in the order of U$S 5,000,000, which was a great improvement but far short of our record year, 1961, when we netted close to U$S 9,000,000 on a sales volume of about the same number of units. As a percentage of sales our net profit in 1964 was 3.27% versus 7.15% in 1961. Contributing to the drop in profitability was the fact that our competition — mainly Fiat, GM, Ford and Chrysler — were now up to speed, fully organized and scratching for market share, with the resultant price squeeze. Secondly, there was a much higher percentage of larger passenger cars in our production mix, on which our margins were much lower due to the intense competition.

Automobile prices generally moved upward at a much slower rate than the Argentine wholesale price index. The IKA Board also had a hand in applying the brakes to price increases. It was always a struggle to get the prices recommended by the Commercial Division approved by the Board, which usually whittled away at the recommendations. Our financial advisors, Julio Alizon García and Roberto Verrier, would always have some reason to advise the Board to set prices lower than what management proposed. I would get caught in the middle because Edgar Kaiser, on the other hand, would be pushing to establish an even higher price level than what we in management thought the market could bear. It usually came down to the Argentine directors on opposite sides from the foreigners.

I can't recall ever calling for a Board vote on prices. The routine usually consisted of recessing, then long and painful telephone conversations with Edgar, meetings with the financial advisors and management with final Board resolutions about a week or so later. Understandably, what they were trying to prevent was an indexation of prices parallel to the inflation rate, but by the same token we had to keep the company healthy and I couldn't agree that IKA should be the "White Knight" in ameliorating Argentina's economic woes. That was someone else's job. But Alizon and Verrier usually came out the winners with our com-promised prices closer to what they wanted than what we in management had recommended. This is the only sticky subject that I can remember we had with the various IKA Boards over the years. In all other areas, such as management selection, labor negotiations, wage and salary policies and, in particular, our reinvestment and vertical integration program, the Boards were always unanimously supportive.

The top management of the Commercial Division always seemed to be in a state of flux. I can't say I'm proud of the fact that we changed Commercial Directors as often as we did, but there always seemed to be a good reason to make a change. Larry Daniels, our first Commercial Director, left after about two years to return to his own dealership, which was our original agreement. Bill Sussex, who was Larry's second in command, also wanted to get back into a dealership. Heinz Pulvermacher and Barney Keene, who followed in succession, just didn't have the depth of experience nor dealer relationships that I felt were necessary to manage the size of organization and marketing complexities that we had. Jess Delaplain, who transferred in from Kaiser Jeep, did a fine job in stabilizing and professionalizing the organization. Jess was the only one of all the managers we went through who had the experience of being in responsible charge of a similarly sized sales and service organization. Jess was a professional and together with John Lutteral built a lot of strength in the dealer body and greatly improved our mutual relationships. When Jess left IKA to join Hickman Price in a venture in Paraguay, his legacy was a professional sales organization.

At that point we combined the finance company, Permanente, and the Commercial Division, and put Platt Harburger over both with Juan Ponce as General Manager of Permanente and Bob Fischer over the Commercial Division. Then when Bill Cannon, who was running our two U.S. companies, Development Credit Corp. and Purchasing Services, Inc., retired, Platt replaced him in the U.S. and Fischer and Ponce continued on in their respective assignments until the transfer of equity to Renault in 1967.

For the last three or four years of our management we had the dealer body organized in five regions, each of which was headed up by a Regional Manager who had sales and service people under him and in direct contact with his dealers. Each Regional Manager had one executive in the Buenos Aires office who, in addition to his other duties, served as the principal contact for the region in getting action on problems of delivery, finance, warranties, etc. For example, Enzo Iannicelli, who was manager of Region III, had as his principal contact Jose Massana, who was assistant to Bob Fischer. Fischer himself served as one of the Regional Executive sponsors as did Bruno Ossowski, Juan Lutteral and Enrique Nyborg. This structure gave the dealer direct access, through the Regional Manager, to the highest echelons of the Commercial organization in getting the myriad of questions answered that are always popping up in the field. And the Regional Managers in the field — Iannicelli, Diego Bolster, Bill McFall, Edmundo Brennan and Luis Pedrique — had one person in Buenos Aires who could cut the red tape and get them some action.

The great variety of vehicles produced in Córdoba eventually made it necessary, in certain high-density areas, to separate dealer franchises into either the Renault or Jeep-Rambler line. This simplified the parts, service and distribution problem tremendously and gave specialized attention to the car owner. Not all dealers liked this move but most went along with it without too many problems. Some of the larger ones who wanted to retain both franchises set up separate show rooms and service facilities and retained both lines.

There were some other organizational changes in IKA about this time that were triggered by Bill Heard's resignation. For the second time in his IKA career, Bill Heard resigned his post as 1st Vice President and Manager of Operations to return to Kaiser Jeep in Toledo. Bill was never really happy in Argentina and missed his family and friends in the States. Bill made a great contribution, particularly on the production side, and was respected by all who came in contact with him. Carl Olson was named to replace Bill and was elected to the Vice Presidency of the Board and moved his office to Buenos Aires. Carl's range of responsibilities was such that we both felt he would be more effective working out of the Buenos Aires office. The principal operating managers who reported to Carl were Bob Beens in the Main Plant, Bob Stich in Forge, Jules Lussier in Procurement in place of Pete Mapes who had returned to the States, George Harbert as Chief Product Engineer and Gordon Woods, Works Engineering Manager. We would soon lose George in a tragic automobile accident and he would be replaced by Lucien Combes of Renault.

Olson also had the coordinating responsibility for the subsidiary companies — ICKSA, ILASA, Transax, Metalúrgica Tandil — and the two operating divisions that produced for third parties, Industrial Products, (DPI) and Tool and Die (DPM). Reporting to me were Olson, M.X. Ordoñez, General Secretary, Jacques Graviere, Treasurer, Jorge Hayzus, Legal Director, Bob Fischer, Commercial Director, Ernie Jones, Controller, and the managers of the affiliated and subsidiary companies such as Nat Lucioni,

ICKSA, Vic Berelejis, ILASA, Dick McGrath, DPM, Santiago Selvetti, Tandil, and Al Hilleland, TRANSAX. This was the IKA organizational structure from 1964 until Renault took over in 1967.

There were two interesting and potentially very important associations for IKA — had they been concluded — that we spent a lot of time on in 1964 and that should be related in this chronicle. One was with Volvo, the other with Peugeot.

Arne Lindquist, Latin American representative for Volvo with offices in Caracas, dropped into my office one day to talk about the industry in general and to get our point of view on the potential interchange of products between the Latin American countries should the free trade agreement (ALALC) then being discussed among the countries come into being. Volvo was interested in establishing a manufacturing base in Latin America and preferred Argentina. Also, from IKA's point of view there were many good reasons to consider the manufacture of the Volvo products. After a few days of internal meetings and cables back and forth to Goteborg, Sweden, the headquarters of Volvo, we agreed to organize a joint team to study the feasibility of the idea.

Stan Reis, Manager of IKA's Industrial Products Division, was given the assignment of leading the study team, with Lindquist responsible for all Volvo input.

The Volvo heavy truck and bus chassis had an excellent reputation in Argentina and would be very competitive with Mercedes, the only heavy truck and bus chassis in the country at that time. The projections that the study would develop had to be based on Argentina alone since it was the only known quantity. But Volvo, by getting established in Argentina, would automatically have a foothold in the Latin American Common Market when and if it came to pass. Aside from getting into the truck business with a product with a worldwide reputation, IKA's main interest — and perhaps the most important one — was the potential gear, axle, forge, foundry and die business that the project could bring. It would have represented a logical expansion of our capacities in these areas as well as representing a very profitable one.

I really enjoyed working with the Swedes. Gunnar Engelleau, Volvo's President and CEO, was extremely interested in the project's potential and supported the study in every way possible. During our involvement I went to Goteborg where Volvo's principal plant and home office are located. Everyone I met was most hospitable and eager to cooperate. All the operations I visited were well maintained and the quality of the production installations was excellent. I was particularly impressed with Volvo's paint system. It was completely independent of the assembly facility, located in a separate building of its own. Most of the floor area was covered with gratings, below which water was in constant circulation. This assisted in controlling atmospheric cleanliness throughout the building. Ventilation in the spray tunnels was very efficient, completely protecting the spray painters from any fume inhalation whatsoever. If nothing else we learned a lot from Volvo on quality control and processing.

Mr. Engelleau invited the IKA team and the Volvo executives working with us to dinner at his home one evening at seven. We arrived in taxis a little before seven and I noticed that our Volvo colleagues were standing outside the main gate to the estate and I wondered why. They explained that in Sweden you were never early or late — you were absolutely punctual. So we got out of our taxis and lined up with the rest of the guests. Precisely at 7 pm — not one minute before nor one minute after — we rang the bell and the butler came down the walkway and admitted us.

Mr. and Mrs. Engelleau were in the middle of a big reception foyer, standing below an immense chandelier, and formally welcomed everyone individually. When we pulled up in front of the main gate I had also noticed that everyone was arriving in taxis and I thought this a bit odd for people in the automobile business. But I soon had this question answered also. We had a rather intense cocktail hour with the usual scotch highballs and when we sat down at the dinner table the alcohol started to flow in earnest. There were twenty or so seated around an immense dining table and each of us gave a toast that concluded with a shot of Akvavit followed by a beer chaser. Dinner then started with white wine accompanying the first course, red with the main course, champagne with dessert and port wine with a bit of cheese to top everything off. We then adjourned to the living room for cigars and cognac. I then understood why nobody ever drove his own car to a dinner party in Sweden.

Volvo would have been a good partner and I was disappointed when we had to mutually agree that the economic feasibility for the project didn't exist. Actually it seemed to me there was more reticence on the part of Volvo than on our side. We continued to stay in touch with Volvo in the hope that conditions would change but after Renault took over the management of IKA, the relationship ended. Years later, Scania Vabis, the other Swedish heavy truck manufacturer, did enter Argentina and at last report was doing very well.

Our attempt to put a venture together with Peugeot is a story that should also be told. Early in 1964 I had a series of meetings with Sr. Richard, the principal owner of IAFA (Industria Automotriz Franco Argentina, S.A.). In 1965 IAFA changed its name to SAFRAR (Sociedad Anónima Franco Argentina de Automotores). A Peugeot licensee, IAFA was one of the several firms approved under the Frondizi Decree and started production in 1960. It had become evident — at least to me it had — that IAFA, like some of the other local companies operating with license agreements but with little if any financial input from the licensor, was going to have some difficulties complying with the integration quotas called out in the Decree.

The Peugeot is a good product. The Model 404 that IAFA was then producing was in the Decree's Category D. IKA's Renault cars at the time — the Dauphine, Gordini and R4 — were in Category C, with the Ramblers in Category E. With the Peugeot we would have been in all passenger car categories.

The IAFA plant was located in Berazategui, about 25 miles from the Federal Capital on the highway south to La Plata. It was a new modern assembly plant and IAFA was at the point where it would be faced with massive investments in engine, transmission and axle manufacturing.

The feasibility of a merger of IAFA into IKA was studied and it made a lot of sense. There were several positive aspects. With very minor engineering changes, the IKA and Transax transmissions and axles could be adapted to the Peugeot 404, eliminating the need for heavy investments for these two items. And with absolutely no deterioration in Peugeot quality or performance. The ZF transmission that IKA would shortly be manufacturing was as good as, if not better than, the standard Peugeot box and the Dana Model 30 axle was more than adequate. In fact, we in IKA thought that it would have been a major improvement over the worm gear drive differential that Peugeot used. Although the Peugeot engine would have had to stay in the lineup, IKA's broad manufacturing base would have reduced the engine production facilities' required investment to a much lesser figure than what IAFA was confronted with. In body sheetmetal, IAFA was faced with a major die build program and Press plant installation, and in both areas IKA's support would have gone a long way in ameliorating the cash requirement.

While all this made sense to the IAFA management and the Peugeot people in France that I met with, it went over like a lead balloon with Renault management.

Armed with verbal agreements with IAFA and Peugeot, in May 1964 Ordoñez and I went to Paris to meet with Michel Maison to discuss the idea. Although Renault's equity in IKA at the time was very small compared to that of Kaiser, and even though I felt confident if it came to a vote the IKA Board would approve the Peugeot plan, I just didn't think we could go ahead without Renault's unqualified support. We had received a lot of support from Renault, not only on the technical side but in vehicle financing as well, since the inception of our relationship in 1959. There also were restrictive clauses in our license agreements with American Motors and Renault that in case IKA were to build other cars under license, they could not sell at prices within 20% plus or minus the prices of any vehicle built under the AMC or Renault licenses. For example, the Gordini was the highest priced Renault product we were building at the time, and the Rambler Classic four door sedan was the lowest priced AMC product. This meant that the Peugeot would have had to sell at a price that was more than 20% higher than the Gordini and more than 20% less than the Rambler. While the Peugeot 404 fell within these limitations, one never knows what the future would bring in new models from the three licensors that would cause us to cross the boundary limitations. There was no question but that we would have to have Renault's unqualified support or we shouldn't attempt the deal with Peugeot.

Michel Maison was unequivocally opposed to IKA taking over the IAFA plant and adding the Peugeot to our product lineup. Ordoñez and I then had a meeting with Bernard Vernier-Paillez, Secretary General of La Regie Renault and second in command to Pierre Dreyfus. I'll never forget that meeting. Vernier-Paillez was shocked at our request and he stated, "under no circumstances, not even if we got the plant free," would Renault support the plan.

With the strong opposition by Renault, Ordoñez and I agreed we should abandon the plan. I met the next day in the Peugeot Paris offices with Messieurs Clamagirand and Perrin and informed them that IKA would be unable to work out the arrangements we had discussed. This was the end of the Peugeot deal insofar as IKA was concerned — mid May 1964. But this wasn't the end of the story. In April 1966, just two years later, Peugeot and Renault issued a joint press release which was headlined, "Renault and Peugeot join in France." The article related that the two firms had agreed, as outlined in a document approved by the two managements, to set as their main objective a close cooperation in everything related to future industrial developments, the rationalization of their investments to improve their production and the stability of their work forces as well as the application of common policies in the purchases of goods and equipment. These were practically the same words that we used in our discussions with IAFA and Renault management in trying to convince them to go along with our merger plan.

Over the years I have often speculated what would have taken place if we had gone ahead with the Peugeot project. While there would have been some overlap between the Peugeot and Renault models like the R18 and R21, we would have been able to handle the problem. We certainly wouldn't have been the first auto manufacturer to have model overlap. The benefits we would have derived from increasing IKA's inhouse component manufacture and tool and die fabrication, the provision of more assembly space and expanded dealer body, all outweighed any vehicle conflict that might have arisen.

Chapter XII | 1965

In March 1965 we began equipping the Rambler Ambassadors and Classics with the new Tornado overhead camshaft 6-cylinder engine that we had been developing since mid-year 1961. While June 1961 marked the official start of our joint engine development program with Kaiser Jeep in Toledo, it was long before that, during the Detroit Engine Division days, that we started thinking about the possibility of producing an OH6 version that would utilize as many components as possible from the LH6-226 we had inherited, so to speak, from Continental. The LH6 was getting old. It was the same engine, basically, that Continental Motors built for many pre-war car producers. Kaiser-Frazer began using it in 1946 and when we started IKA we knew we had an out-of-date engine but it was all we had and we had to go with it.

By the 1960s virtually all vehicle manufacturers were using overhead valve engines. The few overhead cam engines in production were installed in high-performance autos. Paul Bastien was Chief Engine Designer at the Detroit Engine Division and in previous years had worked on the famous Stutz Vertical 8 overhead camshaft engine design. He and his team developed some preliminary concepts for the conversion of the LH6 into an overhead cam version. We did enough preliminary design at the Engine Division to conclude that the production of the OHC version was feasible even though financial constraints would dictate, in large measure, the design criteria. By keeping the same cylinder bore spacing and bore diameter we could continue using most of the LH6 block machine line. This also kept our ability to produce the LH6 intact. In our early planning we only intended to use the OHC in our passenger cars — the Ramblers and the Torino — scheduled for late 1966, with the LH6 remaining in the utility vehicles — pickups and Estancieras. This policy was changed and the OHC engine soon found its way into all models except the Jeep.

We did a lot of design and prototype development of a 4-cylinder OHC but had to conclude that with the Jeep's limited volume it was anti-economical.

There were several reasons for doing the engine development work in Toledo instead of Córdoba. It could be done a lot faster since Toledo's experimental facilities were more extensive than ours and the parts unique to the new engine were more readily available. Secondly, Kaiser-Jeep owned the LH6 and IKA's royalty payments embraced not only vehicles but certain components — such as the engine — as well. Our agreement with Toledo would credit IKA's development payments to Kaiser-Jeep as a prepayment on future royalties. While Kaiser-Jeep would still own the engine, the development work wouldn't cost IKA anything. There was another good reason for Toledo's participation and that was an engineer by the name of A.C. Sanpietro, an engine designer who had a lot of experience with high performance engines and was a promoter of the OHC concept. Interestingly enough it was during the development program in Toledo that we sent young Oreste Berta there for training. Berta literally "came of age" with the Tornado's development and would later make it and the Torino famous when he was IKA's Director of Competition.

The final design was released by Toledo about September 1962 but IKA experimentally made some further improvements in the cylinder head and rocker box areas, and finally we started design of the production tooling that would be required and procurement of the additional machine tools for the parts peculiar to the OHC. IKA budgeted a little over U$S 2,000,000 to put the new engine into production, most of which was spent on imported equipment. This was a substantial investment for IKA but was a fraction of what a completely new engine would have cost us. We later brought out a 3 liter (OHC 300) version of the OHC 380 (3.8 liters) when the Torino came out, which was used primarily in taxis.

The part that required the most extensive tool-up was the cylinder head. The Tornado head had machined hemispherical combustion chambers and carried the camshaft and valve actuating mechanisms. It was a very intricate part with close tolerances and required a long series of production and inspection operations.

To digress a bit, immediately following World War II, industry really got serious in the development of automatic transfer equipment. Unlike unitized equipment designed to perform specific operations — mill, drill, bore, etc. — automatic transfer equipment performs every operation and is design-specific to the part it produces. Once a rough part is loaded on the first station by the operator, it is processed automatically through each machine or inspection station and ends up as a finished product. Compared to old style unitized machines, the savings in manpower were impressive. We decided on a transfer machine for the production of the Tornado cylinder head and ordered one in Germany where we could obtain good export credit terms. Honsberg was the firm that built the machine and did an excellent job. The Honsberg processed a part through 19 different work stations with automatic inspection devices and indicator lights that made it possible for one operator to control the entire series of operations from the main control panel while another operator patrolled the various stations, changing tools when needed. The two operators could control 19 simultaneous operations. The Honsberg was another "first" by IKA. It was the first high production automatic transfer machine to be brought into the country. The machine was 40 meters long and after try-out in Germany it was disassembled and then reassembled in Córdoba.

The original Tornados introduced with the new Ramblers that came out in early 1965 had some problems. Minor oil leaks developed, at high rpm valve bounce showed up at times and, due to the high compression ratio of 8.5:1 and inconsistent octane quality in Argentine fuels, detonation occurred intermittently. At the first sign of these problems in the field, George Harbert's engineering team went to work. Eduardo Genari was Chief Engine Engineer at the time and directed design changes that included a reduction in the compression ratio to 7.5:1, better sealing of the engine, a new carburetor — the Carter RBS —, some design changes to the cylinder head, a new camshaft, changing the engine mounts to the center of gravity of the block, better quality bearing material in the mains and con rods, the addition of a second oil filter to guarantee absolute lubricant cleanliness since a high percentage of the car population used unimproved roads, and finally, redesign of the exhaust and intake manifolds for better gas flow.

As design changes came off the drawing boards, the Experimental Division under Gustavo Flinta developed test prototypes and subjected them to dynamometer and road testing. The Tornado redevelopment covered a period of about 18 months — early 1965 to late 1966 — and coincided with the final development stages of the Torino vehicle line. The road testing program for the redesigned and "Argentinized" engine covered over a million kilometers in an eight month period, practically all of which was in disguised Torino prototypes. When it was all said and done, we would have been better off to have engineered the entire Tornado development program in IKA. But hindsight is always better than foresight.

By the time the Torino came out in December 1966, the new Tornado was available in three models: the standard OHC 380 that developed 150 hp, a short stroke 3 liter version, the OHC 300, and the high performance 380 W that had three Weber double throat carburetors and an output of over 175 hp.

While the development of the production engines was progressing, Oreste Berta, assisted by Osvaldo Zurcher, was working on the future competition engine. The OHC 380 was bored out to 3.95 liters. Special valve seats and valves were substituted, the exhaust and intake partings in the block were polished, a racing cam lobe profile, light weight pistons with a higher dome and many other refinements were introduced. The racing versions developed over 250 hp at 5400 rpm. This was taking a lot out of a four main bearing block that was originally developed by Continental to produce less than 100 hp. We were concerned about bearing overload, and the forge shop in collaboration with Genari produced a new crankshaft forging that improved balance considerably. Sometime later we began an intensive block redesign that incorporated seven main bearings and other strengthening features — without changing bore spacing — and this was no simple job. The seven main bearing OHC engine gave the crankshaft the support needed and enabled higher rpm potential. The new block and crankshaft were put into production by Renault after it assumed the management of the company.

When the Torino vehicle line was phased out in 1982, production of the Tornado was discontinued also since Renault was by then only producing its own line of vehicles. But the Tornado engine's racing victories enabled it to leave its mark in the history of Argentina road racing.

Operation Di Tella began at the end of March 1965, when SIAM Di Tella Limitada and IKA jointly announced agreement on two mergers: the SIAM foundry, SIAF, would be merged into Metalúrgica Tandil, and IKA's Tool and Die Division (DPM) would be merged with SIAM's tool-making subsidiary, Perdriel, S.A. Our objectives were to strengthen our foundry and tool-making operations by providing each with productive capacities more or less double what they were individually and making them more competitive through reduced administrative and marketing costs.

The planning for this joint operation started with a two day in-depth meeting in mid-November 1964 in Punta del Este, Uruguay. Representing the SIAM interests at the meeting were Guy Clutterbuck, President of SIAM Di Tella, Ltda., Guido Di Tella, Executive Director, and Torcuato Sozio, Guido's uncle and a principal in all Di Tella operations. Manuel Ordoñez accompanied me. It had become apparent, after three years of working under the Frondizi decree, that consolidation within the industry was inevitable. The most vulnerable were the Argentine-owned companies that operated with license agreements and with no direct financial support from the licensors. In SIAM's case, British Motors Corporation had a very small equity in SIAM Automotores and it was exceedingly doubtful that it would come to Automotores' rescue in times of need. In IKA's case, while Kaiser did have substantial equity — about 35% at the time — other than the credit it extended on royalty payments, technical assistance billings and other inter-company accounts during cash-short period — and at times these outstandings got into the seven figures — there was no way that Kaiser would stopgap IKA if it started losing substantially. The same applied to Renault and American Motors. With the wholly owned subsidiaries — Fiat, General Motors, Ford, Mercedes and, to a degree, Chrysler — it was a different situation.

They had no local stockholders to answer to and in the corporate books were treated as divisions.

Clutterbuck was well aware of IKA's progress as a major supplier to the industry and believed that participation in this market represented an insurance policy should the glut of vehicle models the Decree had spawned compel one to abandon car manufacturing. I had some personal reservations relative to the Clutterbuck hypothesis, particularly with respect to IKA's ability to remain a force in car production, but I had to admit that he had a good argument and I was willing to explore the concept of jointly exploiting our manufacturing strengths in certain areas.

We convened in Torcuato Sozio's summer home in Punta del Este on Saturday, November 14, 1964. We did not have a preset agenda but on the first page of the notes that I took at the meetings I wrote, "Considerations relative to mutual future problems." During the two days of meetings we ranged far and wide: how could new sources of retail financing be developed; what joint supplier company potential did we have, i.e., foundry, forge, tools, brakes, instruments and electrical components; engine standardization possibilities. I don't think there was a single facet of our various operations that wasn't analyzed in the context of the joint benefits that could be derived.

Immediate benefits appeared most evident in the foundry and tool and die operations. When we returned to Buenos Aires I asked Santiago Selvetti to study the SIAF foundry from the point of view of combining it with his Tandil operation and I asked Dick McGrath to do the same with Perdriel and DPM. In addition to its grey iron foundry, SIAF had a good aluminum die casting operation which was important because the industry was still importing a lot of major die castings. Selvetti and the engineers and procurement people we had studying the idea were in agreement that the foundry merger made sense. The Perdriel plant was dedicated in the main to tool build rather than the three-dimensional die making that we had in DPM, and putting the two units together would create a well balanced entity with a total tool and die build capacity equal to some of the major shops in the U.S. and Europe. We were just finishing the construction of a new plant for DPM located near ILASA which would house all the equipment that we could dedicate to new tool and die building — leaving only enough at the main plant to handle die maintenance. In addition to the equipment we transferred from the main plant to DPM, IKA invested heavily in new three-dimensional copy mills that we imported, principally from Germany, with Hermes export credit facilities. When we merged the Buenos Aires and DPM operations, we retained the Perdriel name for the new corporation and at the time it was the largest tool shop in Latin America.

At its inception, Perdriel had a tool build capacity in excess of 150,000 manhours monthly. The normal invoicing practice in the tool and die industry is to charge on a time and materials basis. The hourly rate was the measure of the firm's competitiveness — providing that it reflected balanced machine time as well. The number of hours one could produce determined the sales volume. But the catch is that it is a business that is asset intensive. The fixed asset investment per manhour of output is substantially greater than, for example, an assembly plant. As a result we had to be absolutely certain that our billing rates adequately covered our machine amortization cost in dollars, and not in pesos that were constantly devaluing. But, with all things considered, Perdriel was still more than competitive with either Europe or the U.S. There wasn't a single auto made in Argentina that didn't have some part that was tooled up by Perdriel. While the tool and die maker's hourly rate in Argentina was lower than that of his contemporaries in Europe and the U.S., he was every bit as productive.

Later, Perdriel would do a lot of exporting of tools and dies. While skilled tool and die makers are not in plentiful supply anywhere, and Argentina was no exception, IKA's in-plant training programs and the IKA Technical Institute were invaluable sources of manpower. Dick McGrath was appointed Vice President and General Manager of Perdriel. Dick was a graduate of the University of Illinois and started with Kaiser-Frazer in its Tool Engineering Division in 1948. He was in the first contingent of expatriates that came to Argentina in 1955 and had occupied several key positions in IKA — Press Plant Manager, Chief Tool Engineer and Manager Material Supply. Dick was not only a competent administrator but had also acclimated well to Argentina. His Spanish was good and he was respected by everyone. McGrath moved right into the Perdriel picture, coordinated the work load in the two plants, started a business development campaign and in short order had a backlog established and a functioning organization. Later in the year when we took over the SIAM Automotores operation, Dick became V.P. and General Manager and was replaced in Perdriel by Walter Clayton. Under Clayton, Perdriel continued to expand and when Renault took over in 1967 Clayton was one of the few Kaiser expatriates who stayed on with the French, managing Perdriel until his retirement some years later. By then Perdriel was a major supplier to the industry as well as an important producer of export earnings.

Unlike Perdriel, the Metalúrgica Tandil-SIAF union fell far short of the expectations that Selvetti and I had for it. In my usual exuberance I overestimated the foundry market, or to be more exact, its timing. Between Tandil and Acinfer, the other major foundry in the country, the market was pretty well divided and SIAF's principal business was that which SIAM gave it from Automotores and other subsidiaries. Another problem, and probably the worst one, was labor. Monte Chingolo, the location of both SIAM Automotores and SIAF, always seemed to have a labor problem of some sort and it sure didn't seem to be a failure of Di Tella management because I didn't sense this situation in other Di Tella operations.

Di Tella, the real industrial pioneer of Argentina, had several major entities — Electrodoméstica, a manufacturer of stoves, refrigerators, etc., Electromecánica, a Westinghouse licensee and manufacturer of switchgear and other items for the electrical utilities industry, a pipe mill — none of which seemed, on the surface at least, to have the labor strife that flared up from time to time in Chingolo. I remember during one of the disturbances that Guy Clutterbuck was shot by an agitator as he sat at his desk. By a stroke of luck he wasn't killed. I was sensitive to the labor situation in Monte Chingolo and in trying to better understand what solutions might be suggested, I met with Augusto Vandor, then Secretary General of the CGT (Confederación General de Trabajo).

The meeting was arranged by Vladimiro Varan, an IKA Director who knew Vandor well. Vandor assured me that labor was willing to cooperate because I'm sure he saw, perhaps much clearer than we did, the potential demise of SIAM Automotores which would take SIAF down with it.

The Metalúrgica Tandil management of SIAF was short lived. I don't think it was a year before Selvetti had to give up. The market, labor relations, labor rates compared to Tandil and Acinfer, productivity — all played a part. But the prime reason, in my opinion, for our failure to make a success of SIAF was the same one that prevented a rescue of SIAM Automotores later. We had overexpanded and had, by far, more capacity than we could competitively employ in an already saturated market place. I should have foreseen this, plus the secondary negative which was that we would never be able to get union agreement to an hourly rate scale and classification dispersal in line with the industry.

Concurrently with the foundry and tool shop mergers we continued our negotiations with Di Tella for a takeover of Automotores. The deeper we got into our analysis of the company's situation, the more apparent it became that it was in real trouble. This was when I should have called a halt to negotiations. But there was another dimension to the deal that kept encouraging us to proceed. IKA was then finalizing the planning for three new models — the Torino, the Jeep Frontal (2-ton cab over engine truck) and a new Renault vehicle that was soon to be announced in France. Adding these three models would require a large investment in plant space and press plant capacity and the Monte Chingolo plant had what we needed. The unused capacity that was available and the investment that IKA would not have to make overrode the caution I should have had, and in September 1965 IKA assumed the management of SIAM Automotores.

I should also make mention of the fact that our step-by-step negotiations with Di Tella Limitada were such that Perdriel, SIAT and Automotores were effectively "stand alone" deals and even though, as time went on, some crossover of ownership due to inter-company accounts within the SIAM group surfaced, we were, in the final analysis, able to keep each corporation separate and independent. This enabled us to salvage Perdriel in spite of the demise of the SIAT arrangement and the eventual liquidation of SIAM Automotores.

But let's get back to the subject of the IKA takeover of the management of Automotores. The agreement with Limitada provided for IKA's takeover through an exchange of shares and cash. This required that both parties had to come into agreement on the net worth of both Automotores and IKA, in order to define the share value of each company for the share swap. It was also stipulated that Limitada had to deliver at least 90% of the Automotores shares and if only 90% were delivered, the payment of shares and cash would be prorated accordingly. Since 35% of Automotores shares were in the hands of the public, we also stipulated that IKA's prior approval was required for any disclosure Limitada would make in acquiring the shares in the hands of the public. The preliminary audits of IKA and Automotores showed Automotores with a net worth of 2.5 billion pesos and IKA at 16.6 billion. The relationship Automotores/IKA was 15%. In valuing the assets of the two companies, an exchange rate of 220:1 was used, which was a negotiated number since the free market exchange rate at the time was about 280:1 and the official exchange rate was about 170:1. An exchange rate had to be agreed upon to serve as the basis for an up-to-date asset valuation. The 220:1 rate was a bit more favorable to IKA since, relatively speaking, its assets had an older average age than those of Automotores. Automotores also had some assets that we were not interested in and which were not included in the valuation. One of these was Tem-Lucas, an electrical components manufacturer operating under license to Lucas of England.

Limitada also needed cash and at the time IKA's cash position was good. I wish I could have said the same in early 1967 when we finally got out of the debacle with Automotores! On the other hand, by splitting the deal with Limitada into cash and shares we effectively reduced the dilution that the existing IKA shareholders would have experienced. The cash payments were to be stretched out over a period of nine months.

Using the preliminary net worth of Automotores of 2.5 billion pesos, and because of SIAM Limitada's need for 1.2 billion pesos in cash, Limitada would invest the remaining 1.3 billion pesos of net worth into IKA and would get an equity of approximately 7,5%. The payment terms for the cash portion called for a payment by IKA at closing of 300 million pesos and 100 million pesos per month thereafter for a period of nine months. We agreed that 300 million pesos of the total debt of 1.2 billion would carry a maintenance of value clause only if the official exchange rate exceeded 220:1 during the nine month period. Automotores had a substantial tax-loss carry forward which was not included in the tentative net worth that had been used. The Di Tella negotiating team felt that Limitada was entitled to at least 75% of the tax savings as they occurred, but we settled at 50%. Limitada agreed in the contract to support IKA management and it was specified that the September audited net worth would apply. The audits were to be made independently by our auditors, Price, Waterhouse & Co. and Deloitte, Plender, Griffith & Co., the Limitada auditors with specific instructions on the assignment of true asset values to plant and equipment and complete disclosure of all liabilities. In addition, all of the guarantees that were on the books of Automotores were to be transferred to Limitada.

In September 1965, by virtue of the preliminary agreement described above, IKA took over the management of SIAM Automotores. Until agreement was reached on the final audited net worth, share transfer could not take place and Di Tella Limitada was still the owner. Dick McGrath was appointed Vice President and General Manager. Taking on this responsibility in advance of having finalized the true net worth of Automotores was wrong, and I can only blame myself for the decision. At the time, however, it was one of those calculated risks that one takes in running a business. We knew that Automotores was in trouble and it was precisely because of its precarious situation that we acted. If we were to save it we had to get in quickly and do what was necessary or forget it. We had several ideas on how to get more work into Automotores and we finally settled on giving it the body building and final assembly of the new vehicle we planned on bringing out in late 1966 — at that time it was identified as the "Rambler Pininfarina," and later it became the Torino. The other unit we decided to give to Automotores was the Jeep cab over engine truck, the Frontal. The Frontal and the Torino were a few months away from a production start, so we had to do what we could to improve production costs and sales on the existing BMC products that were in production — the Riley and Morris cars and pickups.

We couldn't have picked a worse time for the takeover. October 1965 was a disastrous month for the industry as a whole. From September to October there was a 25% drop in factory deliveries. One of the major causes was the institution of a new government policy wherein bonds were issued for payment purposes that in turn severely restricted peso circulation and retail financing availabilities among other problems. Even though both IKA and Automotores increased their market penetration during the period, the drop in total sales volume played havoc with Automotores' cash flow and IKA had to advance funds to keep it afloat.

There were other problems caused by government intervention. The Ministry imposed controls on the quantity by model that any given company could produce each year. The Renault R4 that we had introduced in late 1963 had become very popular but the new restrictions required that we reduce our normal 85 units per day production rate to 35 — this was in October also. It would take months working with the Government bureaucracy to get approval to return to our normal production rate even though we could prove without question that the demand existed. The outlook for the future was not good either. The Ministry of Economy announced a substantial increase in sales taxes on automobiles to take effect in 1966. In addition to the new taxation that would surely depress sales, the country was experiencing a severe drought that was reducing crop output, and beef prices in Europe, Argentina's principal export market at the time, were lowering. All of these factors dampened demand.

As we moved into November the overall vehicle market deteriorated badly. But despite this we were able to bring deliveries up in Automotores. There still was a cash flow deficit, a lot of which was caused by the inefficiencies that were built into the operation. One example was the incentive pay plan in effect for the hourly production employees. Based on units produced and manhours expended per unit, which were measured against standards that labor and management had agreed to, it was possible for labor to earn up to 133% of base pay if production targets were met. Now, there is nothing wrong with a good incentive plan provided its standards have been set using valid statistical data and checked out by methods analysis and detailed time measurements. Secondly, the greatest benefit in incentive pay is usually derived from individual operations rather than a production line where the output of each work station is dependent on the production tempo of the operation feeding it. With practically all of Automotores' production operations of the sequential type, the so-called incentive plan was, in reality, more of a plant-wide bonus-sharing arrangement.

When we took over Automotores in September, we found that for the first eight months of 1965 labor had received within one peso of the 133% — or top — incentive rate in each classification, notwithstanding the fact that average production for the period was 49.2 cars per day instead of the 64 scheduled. A contradiction such as this can only be explained by poor floor management of an ill-conceived plan.

Further cost disparities existed in classification dispersal and hourly rates when we compared the Automotores hourly structure to the rest of the industry. We took the six basic hourly classifications used in the industry and compared Automotores to the industry average. The two highest skilled classifications in Automotores, Nos. 5 and 6, were paid about the same as the industry average. However, in Nos. 1 through 4, Automotores overpaid from a high of 36% in 1, to 9% in 4, and 24% and 14% in 2 and 3 respectively. And this was only part of the problem. Classification dispersal, i.e., the percentage of hourly payroll in each classification, in Automotores was definitely out of tune. The tabulation that follows points up the differences between Automotores and the average of the six companies in the study, which were Chrysler, Fiat, Ford, GM, IKA and Peugeot.

CLASSIFICATION DISPERSAL
Percentage of total hourly employees

Category	Six Co. Average	Automotores
Low skill		
1.	4.25%	0.6%
2.	17.80%	5.0%
Production		
3.	49.72%	37.6%
4.	14.39%	9.4%
High skill		
5.	8.27%	21.8%
6.	5.57%	25.6%

The result of these aberrations was that Automotores' average hourly cost was substantially higher than the rest of the industry. In the principal production classifications, 3 and 4, where the industry had about 65% of its payroll, Automotores had only 47%, and in the two highest paid classifications Automotores had 47% versus the industry average of 14%.

The combination of noncompetitive classification dispersal and an ill-conceived incentive pay plan boomeranged Automotores' labor cost per unit to a point where, in a direct comparison with IKA, Automotores was about 40% higher per vehicle produced. Getting all the facts assimilated took some time, and we were well into 1966 before we were in a position to negotiate with the union to try to alleviate the onerous situation we found ourselves in. In April, after intense negotiations over a two-month period — including a strike — we were able to agree on some reclassifications and rates of pay. Although the agreement ameliorated the situation to a degree, we were never able to get Automotores competitive with the industry.

Meanwhile, our auditors Price, Waterhouse and SIAM's Deloitte, Plender and Griffith independently worked on auditing the books of Automotores as of September 30, 1965. In January 1966, both auditors submitted their findings. The Deloitte audit showed a loss close to 700 million pesos and a net worth that had declined to 1.67 billion pesos. While this number was substantially below the 2.5 billion net worth on which we had based the agreement in principal, the Price Waterhouse audit disclosed that reserves for tax provisions, inventory losses and possible penalties under the Automotive Decree had not been adequately established, in its opinion, and would pull the net worth down another 1.4 billion pesos, which left practically no net worth whatsoever. We asked Deloitte to give its reasons for not having included these reserves in its report, but the question was never satisfactorily answered.

Audit firms certify the financial statements of their clients, but sometimes these certifications are meaningless. For example, note the differences in the certification made by Deloitte to the Automotores financial statement and that made by Price Waterhouse to the IKA statement. Deloitte's certification to the September 30, 1965 accounts of Automotores stated, "According to our opinion the accounts have been prepared in a technically correct manner and with the same procedures used in the preparation of the accounts for the fiscal year and in them have been considered *all facts brought to our attention.*" (Italics by author)

Compare this one with the Price Waterhouse audit certification of IKA's Annual Statement: "The balance sheet presents fairly the financial position of Industrias Kaiser and the results of its operations for the year in conformity with generally accepted accounting principles ... Our examination of these statements was made in accordance with generally accepted accounting standards and accordingly included such tests of the accounting records and such other auditing procedures as considered necessary in the circumstances."

At this juncture while IKA had the management responsibility, it was not in possession of the Limitada shares and could not represent Automotores in any matters involving the Buenos Aires Stock Exchange. Under our agreement with Limitada we were responsible for the management of Automotores, but until the payment terms had been complied with its Board of Directors was controlled by Limitada. We named the General Manager, the Controller and two Board Members. With the concurrence of Deloitte, the President of Automotores, Guy Clutterbuck, who disagreed with the Price Waterhouse audit and the reserves that were recommended, instructed the IKA appointed Controller to make certain reverses in the books to agree with the results as certified by Deloitte. At the Automotores board meeting called to approve the September results, the two IKA appointed Directors disagreed and their objections were entered into the minute book. IKA then served official notice on Limitada that it was suspending any further payments due under contract to Limitada and, further, would not advance any funds to Automotores.

This move brought things to a head with Limitada. We recognized we had a contract and would have to respect it, but if their auditors could not come into agreement with ours on the net worth of the company, we would have to nullify the contract. IKA had also become a major creditor, more than likely the largest, and it was evident that a financial reorganization of the company would be necessary.

Under Argentine law, when a corporation has lost 50% or more of its capital it is placed in *convocatoria,* or Chapter 11, as reorganization is termed in the U.S. Despite the vehement objections of Limitada, the Automotores Board in early February notified the Buenos Aires Stock Exchange that the company had lost over 50% of its capital. This represented a difference of more than 900 million pesos in net worth as reported by previous management and certified by Deloitte. Price Waterhouse corroborated the Board's representations and submitted a letter to the stock Exchange stating, " ... a complete audit of the company's books is in process and enough of the audit has been completed to confirm the over 900 million peso loss as reported by management." This was the first official rebuttal by Price Waterhouse of Deloitte's audit.

We immediately began working with all the major creditors, including IKA, to reorganize the outstanding debt, and in July 1966 we were able to get approval to remove the company from the *Convocatoria de Acreedores.* In its financial report for the fiscal year ending June 1966, IKA set up a reserve of one billion pesos for eventual losses in debt remission as well as the potential devaluation of Automotores' equity. IKA forgave 320 million pesos which was our contribution to the debt reorganization that allowed

Automotores to emerge from *convocatoria*. For the time being, at least, we had Automotores on a financial footing that we hoped would see it through its crisis.

We still had a contract, though, and even if the bases on which it had been negotiated had changed drastically, we had to come to terms with Di Tella Limitada. In addition to the initial payment we had made of 300 million pesos under the original contract terms based on the misrepresented 2.5 billion pesos of net worth, we still owed 900 million pesos plus approximately 7,5% of IKA equity in shares to be issued. We concluded the renegotiation of the contract with IKA paying an additional 300 million pesos to Limitada for cancellation of the contract. Limitada obligated itself to deliver to IKA its shares in Perdriel and Automotores, along with some presses and dies that were part of the original deal, and it assumed any liabilities that Automotores had as a result of guarantees it had given third parties to back up certain Limitada debts.

In my opinion the 300 million peso closing payment was justified. It suited IKA to end the affair as expeditiously as possible. IKA's top executives were being distracted from their real job — that of running IKA and putting Automotores back on its feet. Secondly, if we kept the contract alive, the end might have been years ahead, involving a lot of wasted tie and legal and accounting fees, and if Limitada went bankrupt in the interim, an official liquidator could have caused IKA serious problems by insisting on compliance with the original contract terms. And getting full ownership of Perdriel was very advantageous. We had initially booked its value at about 250 million pesos but its real worth was much greater, possibly as high as 400 million. Lastly, the cancellation of the contract also eliminated any Limitada participation in tax loss carry-forward if profits ever started up again in Automotores. For the remainder of 1966 we did everything we could to revitalize the company, but the British Motors vehicles it was building were steadily losing market share in a declining market. The total passenger and light utility market dropped about 10% in 1966 versus 1965 with Automotores' market penetration dropping from 6.7% to 5.3% in the same period causing it severe losses. We had managed to get the Torino body work and the Frontal into production in Chingolo but this additional work was too late to stem the tide.

In March 1967, notification of suspension was given all personnel and the company was again placed in *convocatoria*. A trustee was appointed by the courts and, with the Board of Directors of Automotores unable to submit a plan for reorganization, liquidation occurred. I had hoped that BMC would enter the picture. At liquidation prices, it could have maintained its presence with a small investment. In the mop-up that followed the shut down, what income Automotores still had coming in was managed very carefully to assure that any indemnity payments owed to labor were complied with. We had some public relations to do since IKA was so visible in the affair and Jacques Graviere, IKA's Treasurer, made a call on all the financial institutions we dealt with in the U.S. and gave each a report on IKA's financial status and withdrawal of its support to Automotores. Julio Nuñez did the same in Europe.

This was a serious blow to IKA but it was not the death knell that some of the media reported it to be. While it was a blow financially, it was a keen disappointment to my colleagues and me that we were unable to salvage the company and enable it to continue as a productive entity. It was indeed a bitter lesson but we survived. In the IKA annual report for the fiscal year ending June 1967, IKA set up a reserve of 1.4 billion pesos (approximately U\$S 4,250,000) to offset the losses expected. This reserve covered the advances that had been given Automotores, the debt remission granted during the reorganization proceedings in 1966 and the loss in the value of Automotores equity that IKA owned.

Since I've had to get ahead of my story somewhat to be able to relate the complete history of our Automotores involvement, let's go back to the year 1965 and get some good news.

1965 was IKA's best year to date and it would also be, in terms of profitability and production, the best year it would have during the years of Kaiser management. For its fiscal year ending in June 1965, IKA delivered some 54,000 vehicles and earned a net profit after taxes of over 10 million dollars. For the 1965 calendar year, we delivered 56,000 units, capturing a market share of 30%

against ten competing producers. IKA continued expanding during the period, investing over 15 million dollars in land, buildings and equipment, and expanding capacities in forge, foundry, press plant, tool-making and new model introductions.

Chapter XIII | 1966

In April we celebrated the tenth anniversary of the first Jeep coming off the line at the Santa Isabel plant. In the intervening ten years IKA produced 325,000 vehicles. By 1966, IKA had become more than just a car company. The following synopsis of the annual statements of IKA and its affiliated and subsidiary companies for 1966 is illustrative of its growth during the period.

Company and activity	Total Assets	Total Sales	Total Employment
MILLIONS OF PESOS			
TRANSAX, S.A.	2,469	3,612	858
ILASA	340	291	274
SIAM AUTOMOTORES	9,461	8,637	3,642
PERDRIEL, S.A.	541	444	413
METALURGICA TANDIL	3,018	3,414	2,351
ICKSA	1,150	1,557	513
Sub-total	16,979	17,995	8,051
IKA	42,280	43,003	11,362
Total	59,259	60,958	19,413
Less investments, sales and billings between companies	(2,971)	(4,405)	
CONSOLIDATED ASSETS AND SALES	56,288	56,553	

Non-manufacturing entities — Permanente, S.A. (financing), AISA (insurance) and Nucleo (advertising) — not included.

Even with Automotores leaving the list in 1967, the IKA Group gainfully employed some 16,000 people. Another point that should be borne in mind is relative to the asset values shown above. Due to the ongoing peso devaluation throughout IKA's history, the value of fixed assets is grossly understated. In 1967, it was estimated that the true value was about three times that which was stated. IKA's net profit after taxes for the fiscal year 1966 was 8 million dollars and amounted to 3.7% of sales revenue on some 52,000 vehicles sold during the fiscal year. The net profit quoted above does not include that of the wholly owned subsidiaries or affiliated companies. Transax alone threw off a profit of about one million dollars on sales to third parties. With the exception of Automotores, all of the companies were profitable.

The big event for IKA in 1966 was the launching of the Torino, which took place late in the year but was preceded by four years of planning, design and pre-production. Since the introduction in 1962 of the Rambler Classic and Ambassador, the line had done well in market penetration against its prime competition — the Falcon, Chevrolet and Valiant. The IKA dealers had an advantage in being able to offer two models, the Classic and Ambassador, and also two body styles, the sedan and station wagon. The Rambler line accounted for about 30% of the sales in Category E, which was good considering that the competition was the "Big Three." The Ramblers were somewhat larger, though, and a lot of us would have preferred a car that was sized closer to the competition due to the cost disadvantage. This was the prime reason we tried to put together the arrangement with Peugeot and when this fell through we redoubled our efforts to develop vehicle X that we had under study at the time. We had arrived at the conclusion that to get the car we wanted we would have to develop it in-house.

In 1961 when we finalized our agreement with American Motors, there was unanimous opinion that we should build the Classic and Ambassador rather than the smaller Rambler American. The Classic Ambassador model was relatively new and even though the American's size was ideal and it had the added advantage of a coupe version, its styling was outmoded and the car was to be discontinued.

After the launching of the Classic and Ambassadors in 1962 and the discontinuance of the Bergantin, Engineering decided to have another look at the Rambler American. George Harbert had a sedan and a coupe sent to Córdoba where they were completely stripped. Power train components, suspension, windows, instrument panel, seats and skin sheetmetal were removed leaving the bare monocoque body framing structure. If we could develop the car we had in mind using this as its foundation, we would save a large investment in dies and assembly fixtures.

The driving force in the creation of the Torino was George Harbert. His first line team consisted of Durward Leeper, Assistant Chief Engineer; Eduardo Genari, power train; Miroslav Mayer, suspension; Jorge Jovicich, body; Hector Cabrera, electrical; Jorge Giovanonni, trim. Jorge Malbran, one of the most knowledgeable men on cars I have ever met, worked with the team as the production liaison. In short order most of the engineering and experimental divisions' personnel were working on Vehicle X.

Early on in the design phase it became evident to all of us that the styling should be done by a recognized name. Styling is more than a skill — it is an art. It would have been simpler for us to work with Dick Teague, Chief of the Styling Division at AMC, or Howard Darrin, who had produced most of the styling at Kaiser-Frazer. But all of us leaned toward a European influence as being more in keeping with Argentine tastes.

Pininfarina was the overwhelming choice to do the styling. It wasn't easy to get the firm to accept the assignment, but with Juan Manuel Fangio's help and personal friendship with Gian Battista Pininfarina we worked out an agreement. And, no doubt, the project itself was an interesting assignment. The scope of work assigned to Pininfarina included restyling the exterior body panels on both the sedan and coupe, the design of the seating and interior trim, instrument panel, bumpers, grille and exterior trim. This gave the firm a little problem because it would not have complete freedom of expression, since it would be confined to using the two existing monocoque body structures, although before we completed the job, some alterations did have to be made to the structure in the engine area.

The contract with Pininfarina was concluded in late 1963 and we immediately shipped a coupe and sedan to Torino. Jorge

Jovicich, IKA's Chief Body Engineer, was the main liaison with the firm and spent a lot of time there. At some point in the process the clay models were finished but I don't recall a specific occasion when we all may have gathered in Torino and gave final approval to the styling. I think we all had decided to take whatever Pininfarina came up with. With Jovicich there and periodic visits by Harbert and his team, potential interference problems were solved during the course of the work. In particular the Tornado engine size was such that it required a slightly higher hood than what Pininfarina would have liked. The styling was finished early in the first quarter of 1964 and die build in Córdoba started at around the same time.

I vividly remember a trip I made to Torino with Juan Manuel Fangio in January 1964. We left Buenos Aires on a beautiful summer day bound for Milano. From there we would drive to Torino. A beautiful summer day in the southern hemisphere is the dead of winter in Northern Italy and we landed in Milano with snow and ice on the ground. Waiting to greet Fangio at the airport were friends of his from the Maserati plant who had brought a beautiful Maserati coupe for his use while in Italy. The respect accorded Fangio wherever we went was fantastic.

The *autopista* (freeway) from Milano to Torino is about 125 kilometers and driving it in the dead of winter with ice on the road and Juan Manuel Fangio at the wheel of a Maserati doing about 200 kilometers an hour is an experience not to be forgotten. I had never driven a Maserati and Juan gave me the wheel but soon took it back. The lightness in Fangio's touch on the wheel was something else. He told me once that he could always judge the quality of a driver by looking at his hands. One who had calloused hands was not for him. He wanted hands that were soft and could feel the wheel.

We were met at the Pininfarina plant by Gian Battista's son, who gave us a tour of the operations. The engineering and styling were done in a building separated from the body and assembly plant. In the styling section they not only had the American coupe and sedan but other bodies were being worked on that were covered. When the covers were removed from the Rambler bodies

I was really surprised. The transformation that the Pininfarina stylists had brought about on our cars was nothing short of a miracle. What had been a staid, boxy automobile now was a modern and attractive vehicle. The newly designed body, bumpers, grille, lamps, instrument panel, seats and trim all combined to give the car a distinctive sports car appeal. Juan Manuel was also delighted.

Back in Córdoba engineering proceeded on the many changes we were making to the Tornado engine, its adaptation to the car, suspension, electrical and other areas. Malbran, an ex-Jaguar team driver, fought for the attainment of an exact 50-50 weight distribution front to rear. This required changing the firewall design to be able to move the engine aft to get the weight shift necessary. The rear suspension configuration required a lot of work and testing. Miroslav Mayer tried several combinations of shock absorber, helicoidal spring and link bar applications on the rigid axle. The final solution was a four link bar rigging that Durward Leeper came up with and one that he had experimented with in his General Motors days. It was much simpler than the other alternates and proved very effective. The final front suspension design incorporated anti-roll bars which were an innovation. The front and rear suspension that finally emerged, together with excellent weight distribution, combined to produce a car, that, according to Malbran, drove and felt like a "Grand Routier" — a Hotchkiss, Delage, Delahaye — but far better because of the monocoque body rigidity and lower weight.

The car's road-hugging ability was one of the prime reasons for the Torino 380W's racing successes. The front wheels were fitted with disc brakes with self-centering drum brakes in the rear. A servo assist unit was designed into the system to boost the braking pressure. The only place the servo could go was in the engine compartment and to ease up on room there the battery was moved back to the trunk and helped to get as close to the 50-50 dictate as possible. A bit unorthodox, but it worked out just fine. In later years the battery was moved back to the engine compartment.

The Torinos were powerful cars and good brakes were essential. Driving at night on Argentine country roads is a risky proposition. Cattle, sheep and horses wander onto roads at times, so good braking and visibility are doubly important. In addition to the conventional high-low sealed beams, auxiliary quartz-iodine lamps were designed into the grille and were operated by a separate switch. The quartz lamps could illuminate a much greater distance and were switched on when there was no oncoming traffic.

Ever the perfectionist, Malbran wasn't satisfied with the exhaust tone. He borrowed the silencer from "Bebe" Lacroze's Hotchkiss, "Madame Sport," which was copied and adapted to the Torino, giving it a typical "Grand Routier" sound.

Vehicle X needed a name and someone, more than likely Ordoñez, proposed the name Torino, and it stuck. The prancing bull which is the city's logo was designed into the front grille. The name Torino had already been trademarked in the Argentine patent office but it was for a non-automotive product and we were able to arrange for its use. The Ford Motor Co. produced a Torino model in the Ford line-up in the U.S. a few years later, but we had no conflict since this model was never produced in Argentina.

The transmission selection was an event in itself. Carl Olson wanted to use the Borg Warner 3 speed box we were then manufacturing but everyone else involved in the design criteria formulation wanted a 4 speed. Malbran tells the story that in one of the meetings Olson asked the design team, "Does everyone in this country want to be a race driver?" Fifteen voices said "yes" and that was the burial of the 3 speed. We considered the Borg Warner 4 speed but we had some misgivings because of its association with truck use which didn't fit the profile of a high performance automobile. In one of our periodic review meetings, I asked Harbert if he had a choice of any transmission in the world which would he use. Without hesitation George responded, "ZF." He then educated me a bit by explaining that the initials ZF were an abbreviation of Zahnradfabrik, the German transmission and axle manufacturing company located in Friedrichshafen. Ordoñez was in the meeting and I looked at him and said, "It looks like George has given us a job." The ZF was a fully synchronized quality transmission used in several top European cars and if we wanted the best, this was it.

Direct contact with Zahnradfabrik revealed that Oerlikon, the Swiss armament and machinery manufacturer, had an exclusive license to produce its products in Argentina. Oerlikon had established a gear-making plant called Fábrica Argentina de Engranajes in the suburbs of Buenos Aires. FAE was fairly small and was not producing transmissions but only gears for the spares market. In fact, I had known the manager of FAE, Lucien Favre, for some time but had never connected him up to either Oerlikon or ZF. Discussions with Favre and Werner Roesch, Oerlikon's Latin American representative, concluded that a sub-license from Oerlikon to IKA was possible but would require ZF management approval.

In May 1964, Ordoñez and I flew to Europe and met with Roesch and other Oerlikon executives in Zurich, then drove to Lake Constance and took the car ferry across the lake to Friedrichshafen. Zahnradfabrik (Zahn = gear, rad = shaft or axle, fabrik = factory) [sic] was founded by Count Ferdinand von Zeppelin, the inventor of the rigid airship, in 1900, and in 1908 he established the Zeppelin Foundation for the manufacture of airships (dirigibles) and the development of air navigation. Most of the Zeppelin works and much of the town were destroyed during World War II by air raids. The story I heard was that when Count von Zeppelin died in 1917, the Zeppelin Foundation, which included Zahnradfabrik, was bequeathed to the municipality of Friedrichshafen, and the mayor of the city at any given time automatically became the president of the Foundation. We met the mayor, had lunch with him and he approved our sub-license with Oerlikon. We were given a plant tour and after seeing the quality that was produced, the testing and inspection procedures in use and the attention to detail throughout the plant, it was easier to understand why George had chosen ZF.

With licensing approval in hand we returned to Argentina where tool engineering began for the production of the ZF transmission. Practically all of the gear-making equipment that we had dedicated to the Borg Warner was applicable. The transmission case, which was aluminum and somewhat more complicated than the BW cast iron box, had to be tooled up from scratch.

The total development time for the Torino was a little over three years. It is the only mass-produced automobile designed and integrally developed in Argentina. More than likely, all of Latin America, at least I don't know of any other car developed there. The four Torino models that we produced included the 300 four door sedan that had a short stroke version of the Tornado engine and a shift lever on the steering column. It was the bottom of the line in price and was built mainly for taxi use. The other three models, the 380 coupe and sedan and the 380W coupe, all had stick shifts in a floor console.

On November 28, 1966 we brought some of the first Torinos produced to the Buenos Aires Municipal Autodrome and invited the press and IKA dealers to road test the car. We had drivers take the guests around the track and Juan Manuel Fangio was also on hand to lend support. The Torino was well received and acclaimed by the press. In its April 25, 1967 issue, after the car had been on the streets four months, *Primera Plana* featured the Torino on its cover with a caption that read, "The Boom of the Torino," and there were feature articles in all of the newspapers and auto magazines.

During the pre-production phase, Oreste Berta and his team were developing the competition versions of the car. In addition to the racing modifications to the 380W engine that Berta had been working on for some time, Competition experimented with various transmission and rear axle ratios, a larger gas tank was installed, the interior trim was stripped, the wheel openings in the fenders were enlarged for the larger racing tires — the usual changes to a production car to prepare it for competition. The Torino was homologated and approved for TC racing (Turismo Carretera) in late 1966. Berta wanted to enter the Gran Premio, which is the climax of the TC racing season and consists of five grueling stages in as many days. The collective opinion was that we had too much at stake to risk anything that could cause an adverse reaction before the car's formal release to the public in December.

Meanwhile Berta had organized his team of drivers and mechanics, and a van was set up as a traveling workshop complete with spares and tools. Durward Leeper, Assistant Chief Engineer, was the liaison between Engineering and the Competition Division. The competition group wasn't without experience since it was originally organized when we entered company teams in the Dauphine Gordini class. The original organization was begun by Horacio Stevens who ran things from Buenos Aires with Berta supporting from Córdoba. The Gordini had some great victories with Gaston Perkins and Eduardo Copello driving. It became apparent that the team should be administered from Córdoba and when the Torino was ready this was the way we organized. Horacio did a good job in getting IKA started in racing and he later moved over to Ford and ran its competition division.

The driver selection for the Torino company team was entirely in Berta's hands. He later related that he locked himself in a room with all the current racing magazines and TC statistics and drew up an initial list of 200 potential drivers. In the first cut he reduced the list to 50, then to 20, before finally selecting the three — Eduardo Copello, Hector Gradassi and Jorge Ternengo, the official factory team that made its debut in San Pedro, February 26, 1967. Copello and Gradassi had fine records in smaller car categories — Copello in Gordini and Gradassi in Auto Union. Ternengo, who had grown up in Rafaela with Berta, was the least known and had begun racing motorcycles, graduating to cars in 1964 with the sponsorship of the Rafaela Auto Association that furnished him a Chevrolet. Berta offered Copello and Gradassi six trial races and Ternengo two.

Most of the TC races were held on public roads that are closed off for the occasion and form a closed circuit. A few are run on closed race tracks such as the Rafaela oval and the Buenos Aires Municipal Autodrome. The big difference lies in road conditions and lap length. San Pedro consisted of 10 laps of 56.2 kilometers each, of which 34 were dirt road and 22 were paved. Gradassi averaged 167.257 km/hr to win the race, with Copello a close second. Ternengo was among the leaders until the last few laps when he spun out of a curve and overturned. Fortunately he was not injured. A couple of months later in the Rafaela oval, which has a lap length of 4.6 kilometers and is paved, Copello won with an average of 192.7 km/hr. Of the 31 TC races in 1967, the Torino placed first 19 times. Ford had nine wins and Chevrolet three.

On March 12, just a few days after San Pedro, George Harbert was killed in a tragic automobile accident. George was a leader in the development of the Torino and at least he lived long enough to see the confidence he placed in his organization's ability to develop a world class Argentine auto vindicated. It was a pleasure to work with George, he knew what he needed and everyone did all they could to get him the elements he wanted to get the job done.

The Torino revolutionized Argentina's Turismo Carretera and its success was all the more significant because of its Argentine origins. Many drivers with private sponsorships switched to the Torino. Torino racing versions were prepared by Berta at the factory and sold direct to the drivers or their sponsoring organization. Jose Mangano, Gaston Perkins, Luis di Palma, Oscar Franco, Cesar Malnatti, "Larry" Rodriguez Larreta were all TC winners in Torinos. In the five racing seasons — 1967 to 1971 — the Torino won the national championship four times. Under TC regulations certain alterations could be made to the basic vehicle without disqualification. The Liebre (Rabbit) models that had body changes designed by Heriberto Pronello were produced in several variations — Liebres I, I 1/2, II and III — and had front and rear profile changes for better aerodynamics. The engines were moved slightly for better balance and benefited from Berta's continual engine improvements. But the cornerstone of any of these models was the basic Torino platform.

Juan Manuel Fangio was convinced the Torino would do well in some of the European races. Yvon Lavaud, President of IKA-Renault as the company was then named, together with Fangio, laid plans to enter the 84-hour Marathon Race at Nurburgring, Germany, scheduled for August 1969. Support from all quarters flowed in and the "Mission Argentina" was organized. Fangio was Director, Tibor Teleki handled public relations, Oreste Berta directed operations and Carlos Lobbosco was the general coordinator. Three Torinos were entered. The logistics and expense of sending the cars, the supporting personnel and equipment to Germany were substantial and various entities, government and private responded: The *Clarín* and *El Gráfico* newspapers, Aerolíneas Argentinas, the Buenos Aires Municipal Bank, several of IKA's suppliers — Bardahl, Bosch, Fric-Rot, Hoesch, Ruedas Argentinas, Transax, Waldron and YPF. The Argentine state shipping line, ELMA, transported the cars and equipment. Mission Argentina was supported from President Ongania on down the line.

Ten outstanding drivers were selected by Fangio and Berta. Each of the three cars would have three drivers assigned who would alternate during the 84-hour race. The drivers were assigned as follows: Car #1 — Di Palma, Fangio Jr., Galbato; Car #2 — Perkins, Canedo, Cupeiro; Car #3 — Copello, Rodriguez Larreta, Franco. García Veiga was the reserve driver. The mechanics who made up the balance of the team were: Andreu, Batelli, Casarin, Comari, Cordero, Diez, Giacone, Huerta, Macagno, Sainz, San Felini, Zadaglia and Zurita. The team of mechanics was so good that Fangio said he'd take them to any race in the world.

There were 71 cars entered in the 1969 Nurburgring 84-hour marathon. The Torinos were the largest cars both in size and engine displacement. But size isn't the determining factor in this race — it is durability, speed and maneuverability. The competition cars included BMW, Porsche, Mercedes, Volvo, Lancia, Alfa Romeo, Renault, Peugeot, Opel, Ford Morris, Triumph — all the best European nameplates plus a few Japanese. Less than one third of the cars that started finished the grueling race. And that ratio held true for the Torinos. The Torino that finished, Car #3, was the fastest car in the marathon. It turned more laps than any other car during the 84 hours but had several laps taken away when it had to make a pit stop to change an exhaust pipe and muffler and used too much time. I think you were only allowed two or three minutes per pit stop and for each minute in excess a lap was taken away. But whatever it was, the Torino #3 had 334 actual laps and was credited with 315 versus the winner, a Lancia which did 332 laps with credit for 322.

La Prensa in its edition of August 24, 1969 carried an article by Stanley Parker datelined August 23, Nurburgring, which I quote: "The crowd burst out in enthusiastic applause when Oscar Mauricio Franco entered the straightaway leading in to the seating area and the finish line with the 4 liter Torino entered by the Escuderia Argentina, culminating its brilliant performance in the marathon. It was the warmest and loudest ovation received by any of the competitors and was set apart for the biggest car entered in the race. In the Argentine team's box, mechanics, drivers and the reporters that had accompanied the team jumped and danced with joy." Mission Argentina was a success.

The production of the Torino, which began in December 1966, ended at year-end 1981. In the fifteen year period, 100,000 units were built in Santa Isabel. The Pininfarina styling was never touched although there were some minor changes such as a modified instrument panel and console to allow for air conditioning, a slightly modified grille, tail lamps, etc. The Torino was a gamble but it turned out to be a good one.

Chapter XIV | 1967
Renault buys Kaiser Equity

In 1967, the year that Henry J. Kaiser passed away in Hawaii at the age of 85, Kaiser Industries Corporation was a major conglomerate. It controlled a vast number of corporations, either wholly or partially owned. Kaiser Industries had management responsibility and varying ownership percentages in the three principal affiliated companies, owning some 35% each of the common stock of Kaiser Cement & Gypsum Corp. and Kaiser Aluminum and Chemical Corp., and 55% of Kaiser Steel Corp. Its principal wholly owned subsidiaries were Kaiser Engineers, which performed engineering and construction throughout the world; Kaiser Sand & Gravel, a major producer of crushed rock, ready mix concrete and asphaltic concrete; Kaiser Aerospace & Electronics, a manufacturer of electronics for aircraft and solid fuel rocket motor nozzles; Kaiser Broadcasting Corp., a pioneer in UHF television broadcasting; the nonprofit Kaiser Foundation Medical Care Plan, by far the largest Health Maintenance Organization in the United States; and, finally, Kaiser Jeep Corporation.

Of all the products produced by the Kaiser conglomerate, the only ones that were consumer oriented were the vehicles produced by Kaiser Jeep and its two main affiliates, Willys Overland do Brasil and IKA. Steel, aluminum, cement, chemicals, gypsum and aggregates were raw materials sold for construction or industrial products producers. Kaiser Aerospace's output was very specialized and, in the main, was produced under direct contract for airframe manufacturers.

The production and marketing of vehicles was an aberration in Kaiser's stable of products. When Willys Overland was acquired by Kaiser-Frazer in 1953, one of the principal reasons for its acquisition was the fact that it would substantially improve its earnings through the absorption of the heavy tax loss credits generated by Kaiser-Frazer. And Willys Overland, later becoming Kaiser Jeep, continued down through the years as a profitable company. It didn't compete in the passenger car market, but indirectly it was tied into passenger car production through its affiliates in South America. This fact, together with Kaiser Jeep's vulnerability as a small — at least in industry terms — independent utility vehicle manufacturer, caused a lot of people in Kaiser Industries to consider seriously what might happen if large infusions of cash became necessary to see Kaiser Jeep through an adverse market cycle. No one could forget that Kaiser-Frazer had one major stock offering fail and suffered tremendous losses before it finally gave up.

Even though Kaiser Jeep's vehicles were unique and it was profitable, there was nothing to prevent any or all of the Big Three from developing competitive vehicles — as eventually General Motors, Ford and the Japanese did. The fact that the Jeep line survived was, in my opinion, due to its acquisition first by American Motors, and finally by Chrysler. I do not believe that Kaiser Jeep could have continued down through the years as an independent. Operating as a division within one of the majors it would benefit through corporate wide marketing, engineering, styling and distribution by a dealer body much larger than it could assemble alone.

George Woods, president of First Boston Corporation, who had also served as president of the World Bank, had been the principal financial advisor to the Kaiser group for years and had developed close personal bonds with Edgar Kaiser and Gene Trefethen. It was a well known fact that Mr. Woods had been recommending for some time that Kaiser Industries divest its automotive holdings — the wholly owned Kaiser Jeep Corp. and the equities in IKA and WOB. Woods strongly recommended that Kaiser Industries concentrate all its energies — managerial, technical and financial — on its main businesses of raw materials production, engineering and construction, all of which were synergistic. He argued, and with good reason, that to maintain its position in the automotive industry could, and most likely would, at some point require massive capital infusions for new product development or weathering the low sales cycles that occur from time to time.

The Kaiser management, with its background and expertise in raw materials production and heavy construction, was not consumer product oriented, and being responsible for Kaiser Jeep would divert resources and management time from its basic businesses. There were a lot of us who didn't like the Woods hypothesis but we had to agree that he was right. And even though Kaiser Jeep was doing very well at the time, looking back at the changes that have taken place in the industry over the last 25 years we see further confirmation of George Woods' position. The sale of the two South American equities had even more justification. Both were oriented primarily to the passenger car market and would fare better as subsidiaries of major automotive producers.

Late in 1966, Edgar Kaiser told me of the decision that had been taken to sell the Argentine and Brazilian equities first and to follow this action with a divestment of Kaiser Jeep. Steve Girard, then President of Kaiser Jeep, was handed the divestment assignment which, under the most favorable of circumstances, would be a difficult one. It should be noted that the divestment decision insofar as IKA was concerned had nothing whatsoever to do with the SIAM Automotores problem that IKA was experiencing at the time. The acquisition and subsequent demise of SIAM Automotores was a heavy financial blow to IKA but we would have survived. Several automotive and financial reporters at the time laid the reason for Kaiser Industries' withdrawal from IKA to the SIAM fiasco but Kaiser's decision was taken for the reasons stated. IKA was just one element of the whole divestment scheme.

With Girard released to carry out his assignment, it wasn't long before we received expressions of interest. Ford Motor Company was the first; I was informed of its position on a visit to Oakland in January 1967. Ford was the most likely candidate to take over the WOB equity. It needed new facilities and by eliminating its principal competitor would greatly enhance the marketability of its own products. I could not understand the Ford interest in IKA, however. Ford had constructed new facilities in the suburbs of Buenos

Aires to meet the requirements of the Frondizi Automotive Decree and as far as I could ascertain had all the capacity it would be requiring in the foreseeable future. Nevertheless the Ford interest seemed real and we spent a lot of time with the Ford team headed by Ed Molina, Ford's Vice President for Latin America, showing them all our facilities, including the IKA subsidiaries, and preparing special reports, machinery lists, financial forecasts and the like for the team to analyze and study.

It wasn't long, however, before Ford changed its position and Renault entered the picture, and a three-way negotiation began which concentrated Ford on the WOB equity and Renault on IKA. But there was an important Ford stipulation: IKA would have to sell Transax to Ford for a price in the 10 million dollar range. I have never been able to understand why Renault was not more aggressive and why it didn't pursue the acquisition of the WOB equity as well. It certainly had the financial resources to handle both acquisitions, and with Ford taking over WOB it certainly wouldn't be producing Renaults. This would ultimately mean the death knell of Renault in Brazil, where it had a much greater market potential than it had in Argentina. It also meant that Renault would not be able to participate in the bilateral treaty that was being discussed, which, if approved, would permit the duty-free exchange of automotive components manufactured in the two countries. With a plant in each country and the treaty in force, the tool-up cost for new models would, in effect, be cut in half, the production volume for a given part would at least double and the only facilities that would have to be duplicated in each country were those for vehicle assembly. Renault didn't assign any importance to this possibility nor to the Brazilian market, unless it had a plan that I was unaware of.

The other part of the deal that I couldn't comprehend was Renault's acquiescence to the sale of Transax. It is true that IKA was going through a rough period financially. It was strapped for cash because of the SIAM Automotores losses and an overall automotive market decline due to economic conditions that hit the industry in the second half of 1966 and continued for most of 1967. At the same time we were trying to digest a plant expansion program that involved investments in the new ZF transmission facilities, the Torino tool-up and the receivables and inventory build-up that would be required to support a 4000-vehicle-per-month schedule that we foresaw once the Torino reached full production. No question but that IKA was starving for cash and the infusion that would come from a sale of Transax would help tremendously in getting our past-due payments to vendors under control. But the Transax sale should have been viewed as a last resort, plus the fact that the negotiated price of 10 million dollars was far too low. Transax had an earnings potential of three million dollars a year, which would give Ford a payback period of less than four years.

At the same time that Girard was negotiating with Molina of Ford and Michele Maison of Renault, I was working on a major die build order with Howard Vange, General Manager of General Motors Argentina. We concluded a contract which provided for IKA's Tool and Die Division (DPM) to furnish well over a million hours of die build and tryout time for a new model passenger car that GM planned to introduce in Argentina. The contract called for a five million dollar advance payment from GM which alleviated IKA's cash problem at the time.

In the early stages of these negotiations Vange became aware of Kaiser Industries' decision to withdraw from IKA and, after consultation with Detroit, officially informed me that GM would be interested in talking about a possible arrangement. Brick Stone, GM's Vice President for Latin America, asked me for my recommendation on how GM should proceed and for my thoughts on IKA's future. This request was reiterated by Fred Donner, Chairman and CEO of GM, to Edgar Kaiser in the United States. In response, I developed a position paper on IKA which in abbreviated form I quote:

**POSITION PAPER FOR GENERAL MOTORS
CONSIDERATION**

Background

In the 12 years since IKA's incorporation, it has become the largest and most integrated vehicle manufacturer in Argentina, and in addition has developed a group of subsidiary parts manufacturing companies that collectively is the largest single supplier to the Argentine automotive industry.

From a long-range standpoint, IKA should not reduce its parts producing potential. Instead, IKA's directional planning should tend to enhance, diversify and gradually concentrate its activities entirely in the parts producing area, retiring from licensed vehicle manufacturing, for the following reasons:

- Lack of sufficient capital resources to maintain new model continuity and cover the sectors of the market it competes in at the present.
- Questionable future status of new product design availability in the American Motors Compact Car and utility vehicle area.
- Insufficient engineering and financial strength to create, prototype, test and produce vehicles of its own design with the assurance of presenting to the customer a product that would meet the competition in all respects.
- Lack of fund sources to provide capital at interest rates available to the competition for wholesale and retail financing.

To retire from vehicle production is not a simple matter. The problems attendant to inventory liquidation, labor and public image require rational planning and time. It is in this context that a program that would encompass a two to three year transition period is suggested.

Plan of Action

Assuming that GM long-range planning for the Argentine market requires additional facilities with emphasis on stampings, component parts manufacture, body building, paint, trim and assembly capacities; that the plan envisioned contemplates the introduction of new GM models in other market sectors, assuring the market penetration GM should attain in Argentina; the steps set forth below offer a solution to these objectives:

1. IKA would form a new corporation, Santa Isabel, Sociedad Anónima (SISA).

2. IKA would invest in SISA certain assets, wholly owned, transferring these assets at their present peso book value.

3. The final definition of these assets would depend on GM's ultimate requirement — but at the outset it would appear that certain facilities would be mandatory, i.e.,

   a. Main Santa Isabel plant and such acreage of surrounding property as thought necessary for future requirements.

   b. All general purpose machinery and equipment, all utilities, assembly lines, paint systems, office equipment and IBM installations — in short, everything excepting special tools, die jigs and fixtures peculiar to existing IKA products.

   c. Other facilities, materials and equipment that might be desired at the outset or during the transition period such as certain raw materials, various existing warehouses and sales buildings in Córdoba and Buenos Aires.

   d. IKA would not invest in SISA; Transax Forge and Chrome plate plants ILASA Transmission producing facilities Metalúrgica Tandil foundry Tool and Die plants (Perdriel and DPM).

4. The value of the capital stock of SISA would be based on present day replacement values of the items invested, including their respective installation costs, less wear and tear due to use.

5. GM would buy the capital stock of SISA on an input rate commensurate with the period of transition from current product to final product. The stock purchase agreement would grant full option rights at a predetermined price to all stock in SISA not purchased at the outset.

   During the transition period of model replacement, it is imperative that the IKA image doesn't suffer. The entry of GM into the SISA corporate structure on a minority basis would help maintain the public image of IKA as a licensee. SISA would contract from IKA to build out such product lines as would be obsolete and from GM it would contract to produce its products. The public image of IKA today — which is of licensee of Kaiser Jeep, Renault and AMC — would be perpetuated as long as it would be necessary to work out the product rationalization plan. During this period GM could gradually increase its ownership and management of SISA by exercising its option.

6. If Kaiser Industries approved the SISA plan, it is practically a foregone conclusion that other stockholder approvals would be secured. However, the position of Kaiser Industries has to be analyzed very carefully. It is both a stockholder and a licensor. Kaiser Industries wants to sell its holdings and the SISA plan does not accomplish this objective. This problem could be wholly or partially overcome through a combination of the following solutions:

    a. IKA would pass a substantial cash dividend to stockholders at time of sale of holdings in SISA.

    b. If future plans could include the production of the Jeep 101 series within the GM product line, a paid-up license agreement with Kaiser could be negotiated.

    c. Kaiser Industries would remain with 30% of the stock in IKA, a company whose concentration in parts production should provide good revenues, and whose financial position should be excellent as result of the sale of SISA and the liquidation of parts inventories. The Kaiser Industries holdings in IKA might be sold then to one or several interested parties who are present or future licensors to the parts group.

        The future of the IKA parts companies will require technical assistance and knowhow for any of the new products it is contemplating. Starters and generators — the entire electrical package — an automatic transmission, brakes shocks and radiators could all be GM products. It is possible to consider that Delco, Harrison and other GM divisions would grant license agreements and at the same time take an ownership position in IKA through the gradual acquisition of the Kaiser holdings.

7. Renault is in the position of being a small stockholder in IKA, and as licensor is dependent on IKA for the perpetuation of its product line in Argentina. The license agreement with Renault extends to 1974 and precludes IKA from entering into any

agreement to build another product that would sell within 20% of any of the Renault products in IKA current production. Renault, neither as a stockholder nor as licensor, could block the SISA plan. However, an amicable solution might be worked out along the following lines:

a. The Renault-Peugeot alliance announced some time ago in France would seem to offer an excellent basis for a solution in Argentina

b. IKA would sell to Renault all the machinery, tools, dies and fixtures plus inventories associated with its products. Renault could install its assembly at the Peugeot plant and gradually move into manufacturing operations with IKA and SISA continuing to supply components during the transition period.

c. IKA would turn over to Renault the 80 single line Renault dealers that could also dual with Peugeot and conversely, the existing Peugeot dealer body would dual with Renault.

d. At a later date, IKA could cause one of its subsidiaries to buy the Renault block of IKA stock, offering to pay a price based on Renault original cost. These funds would help Renault defray the cost of the move to Peugeot.

e. The plan would be very advantageous to Peugeot as well, since its present volume might just barely be breaking even — more likely it is running at an operating loss.

8. The AMC position has to be dealt with on a different basis than Renault. IKA cannot finance the new model continuity to maintain the present Rambler line penetration in the market, and since AMC cannot afford to finance it nor open up its own facilities, AMC can only look forward to a gradual phaseout in the Argentine market and this would no doubt take place well before the license agreement terminal date of 1974.

The plan of action for AMC could conceivably be as follows:

a. The AMC ownership in IKA could be sold to an IKA subsidiary at a price equal to its original investment cost.

b. IKA could allow AMC to retire the funds it has operating in the retail financing portfolio.

   c. A fully paid-up license would be negotiated between IKA and AMC that would cover the final build-out of the Rambler and Torino lines.

     In essence, it is felt that because of AMC's situation a cash settlement would be the most expeditious means of removing it.

9. The management changeover at SISA could be a gradual process as well. However, at the outset all operating data, facts and figures, and selection of facilities and equipment would be a matter of joint accord. Further, should a more rapid management changeover be desired, there would be no problem in achieving this as well.

10. In summary, we believe the following to be the basic advantages to GM:

   a. Gradual assimilation of productive capacities that could be scheduled to meet the timing of new model introduction.

   b. The incorporation of a dealer network that would be blended into the production scheme to market the greater production volume.

   c. A scheduled investment program at an input rate commensurate with the gradual productive capacity increase, rather than an immediate outgo of cash resources to provide capacities in advance of their full employment.

   d. GM would be performing a commendatory service, since it would not be duplicating existing production capacities nor displacing labor.

   e. A direct association with the parts producing subsidiaries of IKA would assure GM of quality and delivery of component parts utilizing GM proven designs.

Conclusion

Notwithstanding the fact that the principles set forth in this paper would be received with approval, it will take time to arrive at a definitive contract. In the meanwhile, in order to assure IKA a firm financial position, the cash advance on dies has been suggested. Should GM desire a more rapid amortization of this advance, it could also be used to cover, in addition to dies, the other products which IKA is presently manufacturing for GM such as castings, axles, transmissions and forgings.

Brick Stone and the GM team he had assembled to analyze the IKA acquisition were greatly interested in the concepts set out in the position paper and requested a "roundhouse" estimate of the values of the SISA facilities enumerated. Stone called me in the middle of a week in May and said he needed some rough indications of value for a meeting with Chairman Donner in Detroit over the following weekend. Ernie Jones, our controller, and his organization burned some midnight oil and came up with a detailed estimate of all the facilities and equipment that the position paper had indicated would be invested in SISA. The total valuation was 52 million dollars and took into account the then present day values less the estimated wear and tear due to use. This value also included the Perdriel and DPM tool and die plants which GM had indicated it also wanted to consider. The value of these two plants was estimated at a total of 8.25 million dollars.

I have always regretted the fact that we never had a real opportunity to conduct an in-depth negotiation with General Motors. Girard was moving very fast with Ford and Renault, and there was nothing I could do — other than getting Edgar and Steve pretty upset with me — to change their direction. There was just too much momentum in the triangular deal — Ford, Renault and Kaiser — to direct any attention to what I felt would be in the best interests of the IKA organization and its shareholders. If we could have agreed on a deal with GM, Kaiser and the other IKA shareholders would have received a liquidating dividend in cash over a period of time — and in Kaiser's case probably as much as it would be receiving from Renault — and the other IKA shareholders would get an amount per share substantially greater than what IKA shares were quoted on the Stock Exchange. But the real key was that IKA would continue to exist as the most important parts manufacturer and supplier in Latin America.

The same stockholders that would have received their share of the SISA liquidating dividend would, in addition, continue to own their same respective percentages in the capital of the new IKA. I don't know if we would have made it with GM but I think we should have tried harder than we did despite the complexities involved in carrying on two major negotiations at the same time. On the other hand, one had to respect the fact that if Kaiser Industries wanted to dispose of its holdings in IKA and WOB, it owned them and was free to sell them to whomever it chose. But the inclusion of the sale of Transax to Ford as one of the stipulations in the tripartite negotiation was the one factor that I objected to most strenuously. Transax had a going value much greater than the 10 million dollars Ford paid for it but, nevertheless, on June 27, 1967, the IKA Board of Directors approved the sale.

The Transax sale was the first in the chain of events that followed, and in October 1967 Renault acquired Kaiser's equity and assumed the management responsibility for IKA.

At the annual shareholders meeting on October 30, 1967, Yvon Lavaud, the Renault nominee for President, was elected by the shareholders and the company name was changed to IKA-Renault S.A.

Exactly 13 years to the month had elapsed since the signing of the October 1954 agreement in principle between Kaiser, IAME and the Secretary of Economic Affairs in representation of the Argentine Government. In retrospect, I believe the principal reason that Kaiser was able to get an agreement in Argentina — and later in Brazil — was that his aims and those of the host countries we were dealing with were essentially the same. Kaiser sought a partnership with the nation that we were dealing with and in which we would be operating. The Kaiser goals that underlay the agreement, i.e.,

- majority ownership in the enterprise resting with the people of the country involved
- rapid domestication of parts manufacture with a resultant build-up of existing local industry
- a work force composed of almost 100% of local personnel

were complied with in all respects. By 1960, the end of the five-year term of the agreement:

- There were some 10,000 Argentine shareholders in IKA representing 41% of the stock. The Kaiser organization retained about 30%, the Argentine government through DINFIA (ex-IAME) owned 17%, and IKA's foreign partners — AMC, SIFCO and Renault — collectively about 11%.
- IKA was producing over 40,000 vehicles a year, saving the Argentine nation more than 60 million dollars a year (1960 dollars) in precious foreign exchange. When IKA opened its doors, less than 30% of each vehicle it produced was made in Argentina. Five years later no less than 90% of each Jeep and Carabela was made from parts supplied by more than 1000 Argentine companies and IKA's inhouse manufacture. In 1955 Argentina possessed only one vehicle for every 44 inhabitants; nearly three fourths of Argentina's automobiles, moreover, had seen more than 20 years of service. When we turned the reins over to Renault in 1967, the ratio was one for every 14.
- IKA and its subsidiaries (SIAM Automotores not included) employed over 15,000 people, and of this total just 35 individuals were either North American or French expatriate specialists.

In June 1962 I gave an address before the Commonwealth Club of San Francisco. The title of my dissertation was, "Argentina — An Expression in Partnership." I stated that industrialization is the only long-term answer to the required increase in living standards so direly needed to assure political stability in Latin America, despite the fact that Latin America's greatest need was to increase its agricultural productivity. But even if all of Latin America's usable land was farmed by the most modem methods, it would not provide employment for its millions of inhabitants. While modern mechanized farming would substantially improve the foreign exchange balance of payments situation of the countries themselves, it most probably would bring about further unemployment. Industrialization is the only means by which work will be provided for a sufficient number of people to earn them living wages and improve their standards. But we must also realize that Latin America is not going to achieve economic development without the help of outside investors as well as expanded long-term credit facilities from international lending agencies.

We must be careful, though, of relying too much on a global approach that depends entirely on government to government planning. We have heard people speak of the need for land and social reform in Latin America and you have heard me talk of the need for industrialization, but what is really needed is a definition of small and medium sized objectives that exist within each of the different countries, or even different states or provinces within a single country. I think that if the United States concentrates solely on a government to government type of planned economy, it will overlook one of the greatest single forces it has at its disposal. If each American subsidiary or affiliated Latin American company was encouraged to work on community responsibilities in its specific areas, in the same way that companies work on community projects in the United States, the accomplishment of small and medium sized objectives would have such a significant impact overnight that the assurance of the long-range large scale projects and their successful completion would be substantially enhanced. I believe that an American company operating abroad has an obligation to participate in the host country's local community endeavors technically, commercially and culturally.

The program of community cooperation that we had in IKA is one example of what a company can do abroad. It is not a question of improving one's image. There is no difference between Córdoba, Argentina, when coming right down to it, and Bloomington, Indiana. Wherever you are, the problems and the solutions are basically the same. The real story of IKA lies in the fact that it was an outstanding example of United States enterprise and knowhow working in cooperation with Argentine capital and labor. It is a prime example of how successful this approach can be in solving a pressing need. What is important is to do things that people can see and understand.

Index

H

About the Author

Jim [James F.] McCloud was born in West Oakland, California, on July 2, 1918. Following a year in the Civilian Conservation Corps, he graduated from St. Mary's College High School in Berkeley in 1936. He graduated from Stanford University in 1941 with a degree in mechanical engineering.

Immediately following graduation, he started work as a Junior Engineer at Kaiser's Shipyard #1 in Richmond, California. He was soon appointed Field Construction Superintendent at Richmond Shipyard #2, and upon completion of construction was transferred to Richmond Shipyard #3, where he later assumed the duties of Outfitting Superintendent.

After the completion of new ship and repair contracts, McCloud was transferred to the Kaiser-Frazer Corporation at Willow-Run, Michigan, then to the Detroit Engine Division in Detroit. After several different assignments, he became General Manager of the Division in 1953.

Upon the incorporation of Industrias Kaiser Argentina in 1955, McCloud was appointed Vice President, General Manager and Board member. He was elected President of IKA and its subsidiaries in 1959.

Following the sale of the Kaiser equity in IKA, McCloud became President of Kaiser Aluminum & Chemical Corporation's activities in Argentina. He returned to Kaiser headquarters in Oakland in 1972 as Group President and Director, Kaiser Industries Corporation. In 1974 he was appointed President of Kaiser Engineers, Inc., a position he held until his retirement in 1983.

McCloud is the recipient of an honorary Doctor of Science degree from St. Mary's College. In 1964, he was named Argentina Executive of the Year by *El Economista* magazine and traveled to Rome to receive the Papal Award of St. Gregory the Great.

McCloud was married to Geneva Kathryn Edgar in 1944. They are the parents of four sons — Kimball, Kelly, Mark and James.

Jim McCloud passed on peacefully of natural causes at age 92 on the evening of December 2, 2010 in La Verne, California.

The cover of a 1967 issue of *Primera Plana* magazine features "El Boom del Torino", McCloud and Juan Manuel Fangio.

www.ingramcontent.com/pod-product-compliance
Lightning Source LLC
Chambersburg PA
CBHW071404150726
48000CB00001B/163